DEEP WATERS

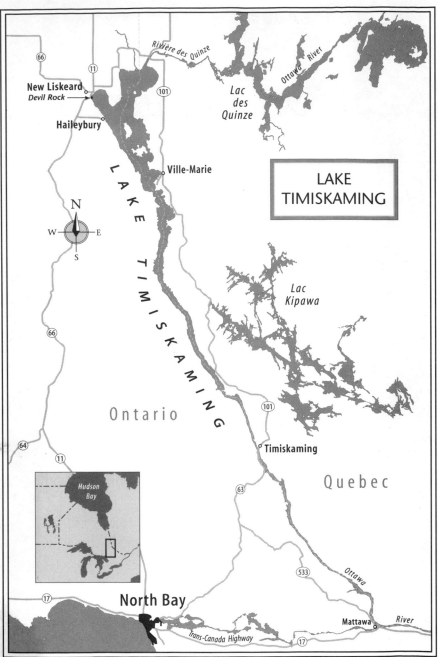

RivIère des Quinze

66

11

New Liskeard
Devil Rock →

Haileybury

101

Lac
des
Quinze

Ottawa River

LAKE
TIMISKAMING

Ville-Marie

N
W—E
S

L A K E   T I M I S K A M I N G

Lac
Kipawa

66

Ontario

101

64

11

Timiskaming

Quebec

63

Hudson
Bay

533

Ottawa

North Bay

17

Mattawa

River

Trans-Canada Highway

17

DAWN HUCK

JAMES RAFFAN

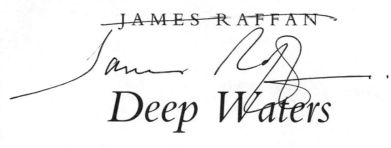

Deep Waters

Courage, Character,
and the Lake Timiskaming Canoeing Tragedy

*To the Manotick Public
Library.*

22·05·02

Harper*Flamingo*Canada
A PHYLLIS BRUCE BOOK

To Bert,
who showed the way

Canadian Cataloguing in Publication Data

Raffan, James
Deep waters : courage, character and the Lake
Timiskaming canoeing tragedy

"A Phyllis Bruce book".
Includes bibliographical references.
ISBN 0-00-200037-7

1. Canoeing accidents – Timiskaming, Lake
   (Ont. and Quebec).
2. Adventure education – Philosophy.
I. Title.

FC3095.T54R34 2002   797.122   C2002-900557-4
F1059.T56R34 2002

HC 9 8 7 6 5 4 3 2 1

Printed and bound in the United States
Set in Bembo

Character is a perfectly educated will.

NOVALIS

Contents

ACKNOWLEDGMENTS   ix

PROLOGUE   1

I   The Lake: No Place to Hide   9

II   The Boys: Molding Young Lives   18

III   The Parents: Building a School   43

IV   The Process: A Double Standard   75

V   The Boat as Teacher   97

VI   The Tragedy: In Deep Waters   139

VII   The Aftermath: Waiting for Answers   169

VIII The Legacy: Living with Tragedy   204

EPILOGUE   235

SELECT BIBLIOGRAPHY   243

Acknowledgments

This book, on some level, has been in the making for nearly twenty-four years. In that time the perceptions of those involved have faded or shifted, while some memories have intensified. Research about the reliability of eyewitness accounts shows that few agree on exactly what happened. To understand life-changing events, one strives for truth, but in doing so one must recognize that conclusions depend on whose memories, whose perceptions, and whose crystalline moments are taken into account. One book could never pretend to be the whole story about circumstances as complex as these. That is the nature of this story.

Educational adventures often involve moments of embarrassing vulnerability—fears, tears, expletives, visible apprehensions—that can stall even discussions of success. And when character-building activities go wrong, the situation is that much more sensitive. However, what these activities lack in tidiness they compensate for in sting and lasting effect. I begin these acknowledgments by recognizing the courage of those who spoke frankly about experiences that, in one way or another, have changed their lives.

I thank the survivors of Timiskaming who participated in this research, as well as the parents, siblings, classmates, teachers, and various family members of the deceased who answered my letters and calls. Some chose to communicate on the record, some off the record, and still others respectfully declined to comment. I was moved by your wisdom, courage, encouragement, and common commitment to the importance of these lessons.

My sincere gratitude as well to the dozens of St. John's staff, parents, and alumni in Ontario, Manitoba, Alberta, and elsewhere, who spoke about adventure, character, and the legacy of St. John's.

The following people also gave of their time and wisdom in advancing this research: Dr. Gerry Bristow at the University of Manitoba in Winnipeg; writer Robert Collins of Toronto; Reverend Lloyd Delaney in Midland; Peter Ditchburn at the Canadian Educational Standards Institute in Toronto; Linda Edey at the Alberta Coroner's Office in Edmonton; historian David Finch in Calgary; Don Fraser, retired employee of the Chestnut Canoe Company in Fredericton; Chief Superintendent Wayne Freschette in Orillia of the Ontario Provincial Police; Dr. Gordon Giesbrecht in the Laboratory for Exercise and Environmental Medicine at the University of Manitoba in Winnipeg; Dr. Bob Henderson at McMaster University in Hamilton; former television cameraman Gordon Henderson in Toronto; Victoria Jason in Winnipeg; canoeist and historian Fred Johnston of Kingston; civil engineer Josh Keatley at Crown Industries in Calgary; learning ecologists Ken Low and Shelly Barnec at the Action Studies Institute in Calgary; Jack Matthews in Lakefield; Liz and Dave McKenzie in Selkirk; Bill and Deb Morgan in Anola; Bill Patterson of Deep River; Stephen Riley in Winnipeg; neurologist Dr. Ranjit Singh in Guelph; Scott and Pat Sorensen at Kipawa River Lodge on Lake Timiskaming; Don Starkell in Winnipeg; Kirk Wipper in Mathers Corners; Dr. Bob Wolfe of Queen's University in Kingston; and Jim Wood in Baysville.

As always, I acknowledge the vital contributions to this project made by my editor and publisher, Phyllis Bruce, and by the assiduous staff at HarperCollins.

And finally, special appreciation to my spouse and in-house editorial confidante, Gail Simmons, as well as to our daughters, Molly and Laurel, who fill every day with joy.

Prologue

The facts of the St. John's School canoeing tragedy on Lake Timiskaming are uncomplicated and deceptively complete. On the morning of Sunday, June 11, 1978, twenty-seven boys, aged eleven to thirteen, and four leaders, set out from the public wharf at Timiskaming, Quebec, and headed north for James Bay. It was to be a tough physical and mental challenge—three weeks of privation and hard work intended to transform boys into men. The blue canoes they paddled were brand-new, twenty-two-foot "Selkirk" models made by the renowned Chestnut Canoe Company in Fredericton, New Brunswick. In each canoe were six or seven boys seated on plywood seats, their feet propped on packs and wooden food boxes. One adult steersman was in the stern of each craft. A gentle tailwind helped them make more progress than expected by lunchtime, but by dark, all four canoes were swamped and adrift in the wind, and twelve boys and one leader were in or near the water, dead from hypothermia. The remaining eighteen huddled around a smoky fire at the base of a cliff on the shore. The following day, they were rescued. Later that month, a coroner's inquest ruled the deaths accidental, and found no evidence to justify a charge of criminal responsibility against anyone.

As a teacher with a particular affection for wilderness canoeing, I have always felt indicted to a degree by association with the tragedy of Timiskaming. I was deeply affected—angered even—

by it. Because I have been on similar types of expeditions with my high school and university students over the years and encouraged them to do the same, I have always felt a need to defend the considerable benefits of educational adventuring. I have wondered if people think that what all outdoor educators do with students in canoes is somehow similar to the circumstances that led to the Timiskaming tragedy. Timiskaming has always been there. It has been a ghost that has haunted me since the day I first heard the news. This book is an attempt to face that ghost. It is a book about building character with risk. It is a book that reflects on the best and the worst in people.

My classes of budding teachers and I would agree that risk, meaning uncertainty, is part of life, especially in the rite of passage from youth to adulthood. Implicit in growing up is the need to take risks from parental influence to a life of one's own. Some people—especially adolescent males—crave risk, while others abhor it, but no matter what walk of life we choose, risk is unavoidable. We speak of war and the respect we have for veterans who put life and limb on the line for their country and become stronger as a result; of those who have faced risk and have never been the same; of the lure of the unknown, of what lies over the horizon or around the bend. Even those of us who avoid physical risk often enjoy sharing vicariously in the triumphs and disasters of others who live on the edge.

But there is another quality, besides a willingness to experience risk, that makes individuals distinct from one another. This quality—known variously as tenacity, perseverance, patience, and self-discipline—has, since Victorian times and perhaps long before that, been called simply "character," from the Greek *charasseim*, meaning "to engrave." Character is an aspect of human striving that turns volition—the will to do good—into good acts. Adventure, which has through the ages been credited with building character, can tune the adventurer's inner compass. One might think of the classical hero Ulysses, who drew much inner strength from his years on the sea. One might turn to the adage that survivors of lethal conflict can return with new courage and moral sway. From adversity comes strength: in the early years of the nineteenth century, philosopher William James was among those who took this notion to heart. He railed against "soft pedagogics," and searched to replace educational permissiveness with what he called "the moral equivalent of war" for building human potential. Educators have long sought to inculcate character in their students. In my experience, teachers or parents can demonstrate how to behave properly, or even force a child to exhibit good behavior, but they cannot force that child to have character.

My students and I would discuss risks in activities such as rock climbing, night orienteering, sailing, winter camping, canoeing, or even cemetery studies, and talk about why these might be good things for a teacher to do with a class and what benefits might accrue. We would discuss how a climber must trust the safety person on the other end of a rope when it is difficult to move forward, but even more difficult to go back (as in a career, for example). We would argue about the instructive potential of moving through wilderness terrain in the dark using only compass bearings—which, like postsecondary schooling or marriage, is often deceptively easy to start but very difficult to finish. We would talk about identifying and transferring the skills and knowledge gained from adventure and applying them to life. We would contemplate the value of those moments on a hiking trail, up a mountain side, or on the wavy surface of a big lake, when students must dig deep within themselves to find what they need to meet the challenge of the day. We would share the elation that everyone has felt at one time or another—at surviving a traumatic experience, for example—when we have triumphed over adversity. We would speak about acquiring wisdom and building character by facing risk. It is a challenge that confronts us all.

Time and again, my thoughts have returned to the human drama and tragedy of Timiskaming. There have been many other deaths on mountains, lakes, and rivers in the name of adventure and character building. People die every year on Mount Everest. In 1972, six teenage students from Ainslie Park School in Edinburgh, Scotland, died of exposure on the Cairngorm Plateau. Students and leaders have died in canoe accidents in England and Australia. Here in Canada, in the summer of 1978—in addition to the St. John's School debacle—a summer camp on a lake just west of Lake Timiskaming lost a guide on the Nahanni River and a fifteen-year-old camper on the Rupert River east of James Bay.

More recently, in 1990, fifteen-year-old Michelle Sutton died of dehydration while participating in a wilderness therapy program in Arizona. That same year, sixteen-year-old Kristin Chase collapsed and died in a similar hard-knocks, tough-love program in Utah. And in 1994, in a program fully endorsed by frustrated parents who, as a last resort, had enrolled their recalcitrant son in another Utah-based adventure program, sixteen-year-old Aaron Bacon died of acute peritonitis on a trek designed to build his character and inner strength. According to an account of that tragedy in *Outside* magazine, Bacon had gone without food, eating nothing but prickly pear cactus, and drinking pine needle tea, for eleven of his last twenty days. In a month of wilderness travel, he had lost thirty pounds. Leaders thought he was faking the bleeding ulcer that eventually killed him. The list goes on.

But Timiskaming was more grand in scale. A newspaper photograph of the upturned soles of running shoes on several small bodies lined up like cordwood under a tarp on a Lake Timiskaming dock haunts me still. What exactly were the organizers of that school trying to accomplish? Why did those boys die, and for what? And whatever happened to those who survived?

I went to that dock on Lake Timiskaming in search of answers. Here the bodies had lain, awaiting transport to the morgue in Ville-Marie. Scott Sorensen, now forty-eight, is the man who retrieved the bodies and the victims from the lake and still operates the lodge. He sparks the ignition of an outboard motor on the

same twenty-foot, tri-hulled open boat he used in 1978. The air
smells of sweet poplar and balm trees; the boat smells of old rope
and gasoline. From boat height, the ends of the cedar planks on
the dock are visible. Scott gives details about where we will be
heading. I look down the lake as he speaks, over the gray water
between sheer walls of granite and green leaves. I am not exactly
sure why I came, except to say that it seemed important to begin
looking for answers here on the lake.

It is a fine June day, the twenty-second anniversary of the accident. The wind is calm, the sun is shining, and the Ontario shore
looks invitingly close. We head south slowly along cliffs lining the
eastern shore, and then stop and drift below a lichen-encrusted,
pink granite rock face. The boat rises and falls on the water's
surface, almost imperceptibly, as if the lake is breathing.
Sorensen's voice is made full by the proximity of the rock: "I
came right down by boat, not knowing exactly what I'd find or
where to look. Right here, against this cliff, were two overturned
big blue canoes and beside them three small boys, floating in their
life jackets." He starts to falter.

With only the grumble of the motor between us and the silence
of the day, we cross the lake and slow at the base of another cliffed
section of shoreline, this time at a vertical cleft where falling rock
has made a little landing at the water's edge. Sorensen recalls his
mounting angst and despair that day when he realized that, judg-
ing by the size of the canoes, there were probably more people
somewhere on the lake, alive or dead. He recounts how his spirits
were momentarily lifted by the sight of another person in a
keyhole life jacket who was partially up on shore, only to realize
that that boy too was dead.

We reach the place where he eventually found survivors
camped at the base of another steep cliff on the Ontario shore of
the lake, and pick our way up into the trees, over moss-covered
boulders and thicket undergrowth. It is not an ideal campsite. The
air is dank and musty from lack of exposure to sun and wind.
There is barely level ground to walk, and certainly nothing that

would resemble an adequate tent site or even a place to sit or lie down. But this is where they landed, eighteen in all—fifteen boys and three leaders. According to Sorensen, one of the leaders emerged from the thicket and asked him about the missing boys. The man visibly crumpled on hearing the news and asked Sorensen not to tell the boys. Sorensen had to lie to a twin who asked about his brother.

In the underbrush near a rock overhang, the boys had a smoky fire going. Sorensen points to a mossy hollow where the leaders and the boys had tried—without success—to resuscitate three of their own who had been pulled from the water. They wrapped the three bodies in plastic, but every time the other boys wanted a drink, they had to pass by the bodies to get down to the water. I kneel at the place, wondering what it might have been like for survivors to stumble into camp, perhaps even in darkness, and see their classmates lying cold and dead. Under my knees, I notice the characteristic crinkly sound of polyethylene under fresh green ground cover. The plastic tarps are still here after two decades of exposure to the elements. The sun-aged corner that comes away in my hand even appears to have the remains of a laundry number. There is decayed gray duct tape on the plastic. I think of the young hands that placed that tape, and how frightening that moment must have been. Have any of them been back since?

That evening, after the light has ebbed from the surface of the lake, we sip hot drinks from the stove in the cabin where the survivors spent their first night after being rescued. Sorensen tells an incredible story. It is with head spinning that I say good night and head back to the dock in the darkness, to paddle a short way down the lake to Whistler's Point, a campsite my host has suggested, where I have set up a tent to spend the night. In the beam of my headlamp while approaching the sloping rock at the edge of the campsite, I fix on a craggy red pine tree on which is nailed a water-stained wooden plaque, placed there by St. John's boys some time after the accident. On a background shield is a simple wooden cross. On the horizontal arm, in carved letters on either side of a likeness of the school crest, it reads, "SJSO 13." Sorensen had told me that this memorial was placed by the school. St. John's School Ontario. Thirteen deaths. And below that, on the vertical arm it says JESUS, which tonight reads like an expletive. Before retiring, I take a flask of Scotch whisky from my pack, pour a good dram across the rock and into the lake as a gesture of appreciation and respect, then take a gulp myself.

That night as I lie in my sleeping bag and listen to rain drip through the red pines overhead, I remember wet nights in floorless canvas tents; pancakes cooked under a makeshift shelter on a fire kindled in the pouring rain; the panorama I saw from a northern fire tower after thinking that I was sure to die on the endless uphill hike to get there; bugs, blisters, suffering, self-imposed by the choice to be there; the challenges of headwinds, burnt food, long portages, and getting along with trip mates. All evoked frustration and tears, flickering resolve, encouragement, turning points, and usually a sense of profound if quiet accomplishment when all was said and done. Canoe trips were something you often hated while they were happening but yearned for from the comfort of home. And then there was St. John's, which was similar in some ways, yet so different in others. In the darkness I feel vulnerable and alone. There is fear in this place.

The following day, I paddle to the sites we visited the day before—without crossing the lake, although I am very tempted to do so. I mull over what Sorensen had said in response to my questions. If the leaders had spoken to some of the locals, for example, what would they have learned? Would they still have attempted to cross the lake? "They would have learned that there is no point in switching sides on this lake," he replied without hesitation. "On Timiskaming, as anyone who lives here knows," he said, "there is no place to hide."

By the time I am four miles south of the lodge and opposite the survivors' camp, a wind is rising from the south. I turn and head back north, conscious of the danger of heavy seas reflecting off cliffs along the shore. The waves are starting to roll, giving a strange animate presence to the water. They twist the stern of the canoe as they roll through to the bow and on down the lake, as if it is at the lake's pleasure that I am here, still upright and heading in more or less the right direction. The lake, the sun, the waves, the canoe, the following wind, take me back to that fateful day. There is so much more to this place and to this story than I had ever imagined.

Returning home, continuing to seek answers, I was surprised to discover not only that the same kind of tragedy had occurred before elsewhere—big, cold lake, war canoes, deaths of several boys and a leader—but that there was a long and unsettling history behind the St. John's incident that had to do with the values and attitudes of the school. St. John's eventually closed. Those who died were not the only victims. Those who survived, including the closely knit parents of the living and the dead, were far from sanguine about the circumstances surrounding their sons' and surrogate sons' deaths, although no one ever sued. As I researched, I would find staff incapacitated by the legacy of Timiskaming, and boys, now in their mid-thirties, still struggling twenty years later to put that June day behind them. I would eventually come to the conclusion that while Timiskaming was many things to many unfortunate people, the tragedy could certainly have been prevented.

I

The Lake: No Place to Hide

Timiskaming is not big as lakes go. Seventy-three miles long and only about ten miles across at its widest point, narrowing to about 660 feet at the south end, at the present day town of the same name, Lake Timiskaming is really just a widening of the Ottawa River, an exclamation mark on the border between Ontario and Quebec. Upstream, where the lake again narrows, Timiskaming becomes the Rivière des Quinze, named after the fifteen portages that travelers had to negotiate to reach the height of land separating Arctic waters from the drainage basin of the St. Lawrence. Adding to the lake and draining a much larger area of the surrounding Laurentian Highlands are other rivers such as Blanche, Montreal, Kipawa, Matabitchuan, Wabi, and La Loutre, with seasonal flow that could fill a shallower reservoir ten times the area of Timiskaming.

Depth gives Timiskaming its essential character. A prodigious amount of water from all these thirsty tributaries fills a valley chiselled by glacial ice into the pink and gray granites of the Precambrian Shield. Hydrologists estimate that Lake Timiskaming holds enough fresh water to cover the province of Manitoba or the combined area of Minnesota and the Dakotas with a three-foot-high flood. On its sides, especially in the southern half of the lake, are cliffs and steep, rocky shores that rise about 500 feet above lake level, so that Timiskaming has often been compared topographically to the dramatic scenery of the Saguenay. But below the lake's surface, at its deepest places—also like the fjordesque Saguenay—Timiskaming drops more than 700 feet to an unseen bottom, beyond the penetration limit of sunlight, some 130 feet below sea level, like a portal to the underworld. Although the Algonquins, the first residents, had no depth-sounding equipment of any kind, they knew all about the lake's endless depths. They called it *Temikami* or *Temikaming*, meaning "deep waters."

The Algonquins, or Anissinabeg, were a group of small communities in western Quebec and adjacent Ontario, linked by language and their connection to the Ottawa River and its far-reaching tributaries. Makers of fine birch-bark canoes, the Algonquins paddled *Temikami* regularly in summer and snowshoed over it in winter to trade, visit distant family, and find new sources of food, building materials, and game. Although the large (twenty-six to thirty-nine-foot) canoes of the fur trade that eventually traveled up and down Lake Timiskaming were derivatives of Algonquin shapes and building methods, the bark craft on the lake prior to the arrival of the Europeans would have been smaller (ten to sixteen feet) and more vulnerable to big waves. No doubt there were deaths and close calls that gave First Nations peoples reason to respect the lake. What was different in precontact days on the lake was a non-commercial sense of patience and care. Back then, the weather and the water conditions—rather than a schedule's demand—dictated when parties could travel and cross by canoe.

After European contact, Timiskaming has a rich history inextricably linked to the canoe. In the seventeenth century, French traders followed Samuel de Champlain up the Ottawa River to barter with the Timiskaming First Nations, eventually establishing a fort at the mouth of the Montreal River in 1679. Valuable harvests of beaver, martin, mink, and black bear hides were exchanged for fire steel, blankets, trade cloth, traps, muskets, and kegs of well-watered brandy. The French were concerned, however, that their Timiskaming trading partners were increasingly drawn north to British trading posts on James Bay.

To rectify this situation, the governor of the Colony of Quebec, Jacques-René de Brisay, Marquis de Denonville, ordered a newly arrived officer of the Piedmont Regiment, one Chevalier Pierre de Troyes, to travel north from Lachine on the St. Lawrence River via Lake Timiskaming to occupy the three British posts: Fort Quichichouane at the mouth of the Albany River, Fort Rupert at the mouth of the Rupert River on the opposite side of the bay, and Fort Monsoni—later Moose Factory—at the mouth of the Moose River in the southwest corner of the bay. In early April 1686, the charismatic Chevalier de Troyes set out in a small flotilla of birch-bark canoes with a drummer, an interpreter, two carpenters, a blacksmith, thirty members of the Piedmont Regiment to subdue the British, and finally seventy Canadians (voyageurs) to man the paddles, all chosen for their ability to travel, canoe, and fight.

We know little of the expedition's trip up the Ottawa River, except to say that on May 1 they were camped at the mouth of the Coulonge River, about halfway to Timiskaming, where they followed the soldier's tradition of planting a tree and firing a salvo of musket shots in front of their commanding officer's bug-infested cotton sailcloth tent. It must have been a relief for de Troyes's canoemen to pull their canoes up the final rapid and into the deep valley and even deeper waters of Lake Timiskaming. Here, while there was still current (and possibly wind) with which to contend, at least they could paddle for seventy-three miles without having to disembark for anything other than sleep. Because of the sheer sides of the lake for much of this distance, they may not even have camped until they reached the original Fort Timiskaming at the mouth of the Montreal River, or even farther north, depending on which way and how strongly the winds were blowing that June. Had wind impeded their progress farther down the lake, they would have had to huddle at the base of the Timiskaming cliffs and just make the best of it, because there is almost nowhere to camp.

The story of de Troyes's assault on the English at James Bay is grand and swashbuckling, just the sort of tale to delight young schoolboys. They came, they conquered. They attacked at night and took Fort Rupert, including a ship at anchor offshore, without any real resistance. They loaded the ship with pilfered furniture, valuables, and their canoes, and burned the fort. Then they sailed the ship across to Fort Quichichouane at the mouth of the Albany River, captured that with ease, and, in quick succession, sailed south, neutralized the enemy's cannons, and took Fort Monsoni from the flummoxed British garrison in half an hour— or so the story goes.

By August 10, his mission accomplished, de Troyes left Fort Monsoni in the hands of a lieutenant and a company of men, loaded up his bark canoes, and made his way back up the Abitibi River to Lake Abitibi and thence to Duparquet Lake via the Duparquet River, up the Kanasuta River to Lac Dasserat, over the height of land into Lac Opasatia, and then down to Lake Timiskaming via the Wendigo and Blanche rivers. It was likely September by the time he returned to the lake. The sun would have set noticeably earlier, the paddling day would have been shorter, and the steep western walls of Timiskaming would have been shadowed by evening sun highlighting a Compagnie du Nord flag fluttering on de Troyes's bark stern and accentuating the golds of deciduous leaves against a field of boreal evergreens on the eastern shore.

By 1720, the French had moved their Timiskaming post across and up the lake to a better location on clay belt soil (as opposed to the Precambrian rock at the Montreal River) at a narrows not far from the current location of the town of Ville-Marie. The growth of the fur trade required more people, more goods, and more storage. A modicum of agriculture was possible at the new site, which would help sustain the overwinterers and their families. Freight demands rose with increased trade as well, and an enterprise that had begun in the very early days with small two- and three-person bark canoes slowly evolved into one that required much larger craft. Historians describe Fort Timiskaming as a miniature Fort William in the sense that thirty-five-foot *canots du maître*, paddled by crews of ten and carrying one hundred "pieces" (four to five tons), could navigate the waters from Timiskaming downriver to Montreal, but beyond that, between Timiskaming and James Bay, smaller twenty-three- to twenty-six-foot *canots du nord*, which could carry only thirty-five pieces (one to one-and-a-half tons) were used.

The commerce of Lake Timiskaming had all the color and boisterousness of voyageur life. There were the songs of departure and arrival, the former sung like a dirge in anticipation of the difficult journey ahead, and the latter with lilt and lift to increase paddle stroke and speed the men to merriment at the end of the line. There were friendships made on the trail; rivalries between canoes; and stories of toughness and loyalty, told and retold, boasts mixed with trail wisdom that passed knowledge from old hands to new.

From 1720 onward, and even after 1763 when the Treaty of Paris ended the Seven Years' War and English and Scots traders replaced the French at Fort Timiskaming, the lake's deep waters were alive with brigades of big bark canoes. As soon as the Ottawa River cleared of ice in April or May, one or two *canots du maître* would be dispatched from Lachine with extra spring trade goods to restock up-country stores whose supplies had dwindled over the winter. The principal brigades that took provisions up and furs down the river began in June with much celebration as *engagées* (or "goers and comers") with their *canots du maître* on the Lachine runs would hand over their loads to *hommes du nord* (or "winterers"), who would continue on to James Bay in smaller canoes.

Romance aside, the lake was not something to be trifled with. Because of its high rocky walls, especially in the lower half of the lake, winds from almost any direction would be funneled north or south, as if in a tube or a rifle barrel. Waves would build over long, straight stretches of open water. Because of the relatively small size of the lake compared to Lake Superior or James Bay, waves would be steep-sided and close together so that when they struck the shore, they reflected back into open water at an oblique angle, making navigation difficult near the shore or, because of the narrowness of the lower channel, all the way across the lake. This situation was always intensified when winds funneled up from the south because the north-to-south current in the lake would go against the wind, making the waves even steeper and choppier. Voyageurs quickly learned from stories and experience that Timiskaming was unforgiving.

At several places along Timiskaming's shores, brigades would stop, and prayers would be said and offerings made in an effort to ensure safe passage over deep waters. One such place whose significance persists to modern times is Manidoo-Wabikong (Sacred Rock), an impressive vertical crag on the west shore of the lake not far from the present town of New Liskeard. In an obscure account of a trade canoe journey from Fort Matachewan, on the Montreal River, to Fort Timiskaming, written in 1879 under the pseudonym Sha-Ka-Nash (Algonquin for *White Man*), the need to appease the lake at these sacred sites is mentioned:

> So we put off and sailed down the big Lake Témiscamingue. When we came down to the big steep rocks on the west side the Indian crews had a great talk in their own language, and everyone who used tobacco, put a little in the water in front of the steep rocks, the writer adding his quota with the rest. I never learned the real significance of the performance, but anyone who passed on the lake with a loaded canoe in front of those rocks will know that such practice was very advisable to court the favor of the water sprite.

For canoe brigades, the lake offered few places to take shelter from the wind. Although it was thought that freight canoes were propelled primarily with paddles, it was in fact established practice on large lakes, especially with *canots du maître*, to sail the big canoes when conditions allowed. Sha-Ka-Nash includes a description of how his canoe was rigged for sailing:

Take two of the rapid poles [for pushing upstream] of the same length, one of the canoe coverings. Take one end of the covering, tying each of the corners to one of the poles. One of the crew takes off his beef-skin shoes, and put[s] a shoe under the iron-shod end of the poles to prevent damage to the canoe. The poles are then raised, one on each side of the canoe behind and against the second bar from the head, where it is tied to the bar and to the gunwale of the canoe, the covering being tied to the head of the pole with one of the portage straps, the other ends are brought aft for stays.

Sailing on Timiskaming was particularly dangerous because there was nowhere appropriate to step-down the masts in the event of trouble. In fact, so many pieces of freight and personnel (likely in that order) were lost in canoes on Timiskaming that, for a period in the nineteenth century, to avoid further losses, the factor at Fort Timiskaming prohibited sailing of freight canoes on the unpredictable lake. Winds could come up quickly, creating steep, choppy waves that would buffet the loaded canoes. With the power of the wind on a sail, canoes would surge forward, driving bows into troughs and causing icy water to rush in behind the bowsman's rest. Voyageurs, mostly non-swimmers, would quickly drown, and those who found respite in a floating blanket pack would soon succumb to cold. Foundering canoes spilled metal trade items that might float for an instant in their wrapping of cotton canvas bales, but eventually fall quietly through a column of black water, from lake level to sea level, and on to the depths below.

From the bottom of the lake, in a geological fault line running the length of the Ottawa River, came regular seismic rumblings that also gave voyageurs cause for worry. It was not that these quakes might cause tidal waves that would upset canoes, but they added a certain mystery to the already numinous and at times forbidding character of the lake. Details of these tremors were not recorded in traders' logs, but they were mentioned from time to time as a feature of life on the lake. Documentation of a 1935 quake reports that 80 percent of chimneys in the town of

Timiskaming were damaged, indicating a maximum intensity of VII on the Modified Mercalli Scale (which is based on surface effects of earthquakes and predates the logarithmic Richter Scale). This quake was felt west to Fort William, east to the Bay of Fundy, and south to Long Island and Chesapeake Bay.

There are also stories of mysterious bumpings on the bottom of canoes during the hourly "pipes," when voyageurs would rest on Lake Timiskaming. Some thought these might have been hermetic drum fish that would congregate in the shadows of the canoes, following them surreptitiously from south to north and back again, piscine agents of the mysterious lake sprites. Others ascribed more sinister origins to the sounds. There was no telling what an already superstitious workforce might imagine was lurking in those depths. Occasional earthquakes in the region only worsened such fears. In sum, these uncertainties proffered plenty of reasons to part with a little tobacco to pay the lake, if this respectful act would help ensure safe passage.

A 1929 visit to Manidoo-Wabikong by British occultist Aleister Crowley, further fueled the belief in mysterious power in Lake Timiskaming. Crowley, born in 1875 and variably described as an alpinist, occultist, pornographer, and guidebook author, created a spiritual pursuit known as Thelema, which centered on ideas of freedom and personal growth. On a search of northern Ontario while looking for Indian pictographs, which he believed marked places with underworld power, Crowley learned about Manidoo-Wabikong on the west shore of Lake Timiskaming, the place the miners in Cobalt, Haileybury, and New Liskeard called simply "Devil Rock." Located twelve miles south of New Liskeard and rising 490 feet straight out of the water, this imposing gray-green, lichen-encrusted granite bluff is one of the most impressive features of Lake Timiskaming. According to a modern rock climber's guide, "Crowley was attracted to the walls of Devil Rock, and appears to have attempted a climb called the 'Finger of God' via a route now known as Samson, where one of his chockstones was later found." Of all the places in the world that a heretic like Aleister Crowley might have attempted in the 1920s to commune with the netherworld, he found himself at Lake Timiskaming. Of Devil Rock in *The Book of Thoth* he writes:

> The Devil rejoices in the rugged, the rough and the barren no less than in the smooth and the fertile. All things equally exalt him. He prepresents the finding of ecstasy in all phenomenon, however naturally repugnant. . . . Essential to this symbolism are the surroundings— barren places, especially high places . . . in every symbol [of] the Devil there is the allusion of the highest things, and the most remote.

Organizers of the St. John's School Timiskaming trip may not have been familiar with Meister Crowley, but they had read the journal of Chevalier Pierre de Troyes and his merry exploits from Lachine, outside Montreal, to James Bay, and it was their intention, in the best sentimental and barbarous tradition of the Canadian voyageur, to follow his route and meet the wilderness head-on, as had their storybook hero. Had they delved deeper in their research, had they read the historical accounts, talked to people living there at the time, they might have learned that Timiskaming is no ordinary lake. It is deep, cold, and can be capricious. In his essay "Exhaustion and Fulfillment: The Ascetic in a Canoe," (written about a trip from Montreal to James Bay via Lake Timiskaming) a young Pierre Trudeau asks, "How can you describe the feeling which wells up in the heart and stomach as the canoe finally rides up on the shore of the campsite after a long day of plunging your paddle into rain-swept waters?" This is a question the boys of the 1978 Junior Trip from St. John's School of Ontario cannot answer, because on the first day of their trip on Lake Timiskaming the strong ones swam ashore, while others died of cold in those deep waters.

II

The Boys: Molding Young Lives

Ian Harling has always maintained that the fire in the portable classroom was misunderstood. At least there was nothing malicious about it. It was the spring of 1976. He was twelve years old and technically in Grade 5 at John Ross Robertson Public School in North Toronto. Uncertainty about his grade level was something that had plagued him since kindergarten because school had never really engaged his imagination long enough to give him any sense of success, so much so that his progress from year to year and from classroom to classroom had been more a matter of habit than promotion. Teachers shoved him up one grade for the sole purpose of getting him out of their hair. And the accidental fire in the portable did nothing to enhance his reputation at John Ross Robertson.

Ian's principle problem was restlessness, what the school psychologist called hyperkinesis (also known as attention-deficit hyperactivity disorder, or A D H D). He was not a mean child, but he certainly had trouble concentrating. He was reckless and impulsive and had, according to his mother, a nurse, the telltale signs in school of "lack of persistence in activities requiring cognitive involvement." It did not help matters, according to Ian's mother, that many schools at the time, including John Ross Robertson, were experimenting with new freedoms for students: "They didn't believe in desks, or times tables, or discipline. They didn't believe in most of the things a hyperkinetic would need to learn."

Sports, however, had the structure and discipline that school lacked, and here Ian Harling thrived. Skills he learned in organized hockey in Toronto's minor leagues were practised on arena ice as schedules allowed, and Ian, from the time he was six, organized games of street hockey with boys who were several years his senior. He loved to play hockey and, in the right circumstances, he had an aptitude for leadership. His mother laughs as she recalls going to their pediatrician's office. She would hear the doctor say to his staff, "Batten down the hatches, the Harlings are here." Mrs. Harling remembers the doctor saying, while writing a prescription for Ritalin to keep Ian focused at school, "You know, Joanne, he's either going to run the Don Jail [as an inmate] or he's going to be the C E O of a top company some day."

Ritalin was not the answer for Ian. It had a calming effect, but the drug did not improve his success at school without quieting him to the degree that his enjoyment of sports, hockey in particular, was adversely affected, so Ritalin was an on-again, off-again part of life for Ian in his primary school years. What seemed to affect his success in school as much as the drug were his teachers' strategies to keep children like Ian focused on tasks. Grade 3 was a particularly bad year, his mother recalls. Grade 4 was better because that teacher could apply structure and consequences to Ian's learning curve. But in Grade 5, it was either bad chemistry between teacher and student, lack of structure, leniency, boredom, or some combination of factors that put Ian Harling in a downward spiral at John Ross Robertson.

According to medical literature, A D H D is associated with a set of related abnormalities: Hyperkinetic children are often reckless and impulsive, prone to accidents, and find themselves in disciplinary trouble because of unthinking (rather than deliberately defiant) breaches of rules. Their relationships with adults are often socially disinhibited, with a lack of normal caution and reserve. Unfortunately, in the spring of 1976, someone left a can of gasoline near the school. The portable classroom was there in the school yard. Ian and some of his classmates threw a little gas on the frame building, lit it, and the fire ensued. They claimed at the time that they were just fooling around, and had no idea how quickly the whole portable would burn. This was certainly not their intent, but burn it did—books, chalkboard, chalk, carpets, and the teacher's desk—ashes to ashes, adding another memorable item to Ian's growing list of misdemeanors.

Ian changed schools the following year, moving several blocks from John Ross Robertson to Blythwood Public School, where an old-fashioned teacher called Mrs. Crestman took Ian under her wing. Everyone agreed that Grade 5 at John Ross Robertson had been a disaster—Ian's reading and mathematics skills were particularly uninspiring—so instead of moving automatically into Grade 6, he repeated Grade 5 at Blythwood. He played hockey and continued to enjoy his other sports activities that fall. Mrs. Crestman pushed Ian with his math and reading at a speed he could tolerate, and restrained him within a strict, old-school code of expectations for good behavior. But school, even with a little more structure and discipline, remained a struggle through the autumn of 1976.

Across the city at Tumpane Public School that year, a similar scenario was playing itself out in the life of David Cunningham. Although not formally diagnosed with ADHD until much later in life, David, like Ian Harling, was hyperkinetic and mischievous beyond the normal inclinations of a Grade 5 adolescent. As the only biological child among the four children of David and Thelma Cunningham of Downsview, and the youngest of the brood by ten years, David was spoiled, something he would freely admit in later years. He rebelled against school rules almost from day one in kindergarten. By Grade 3 he was a child every teacher knew, if not personally, then by reputation for goading his classmates into a frenzy at a moment's notice (and usually slipping out of the fray just before everyone else started getting into trouble). He was a handful, a hellion, but had a devil-may-care charm about him that made teachers laugh, just after they had disciplined him for the umpteenth time.

Rules, it seemed to David, were for other people. If they were for him, they were to be poked, prodded, and stretched. Other children would shoot a single paper clip across the classroom powered by an elastic band stretched across two fingers. David would slip into the teachers' storeroom, steal two or three boxes of paper clips and elastic bands, and turn the classroom into a war zone. It was a wonder that he did not get into trouble more often than he did, but sometimes it was those he incited to offend who were caught and punished for pranks that he had initiated. When he got bored with projectiles, another favorite game was to badger the older boys in the school yard until they got into trouble for threatening to pummel him. By Grade 5, he was out of control, having a great time, but failing in almost every subject, and not caring. He had already seen therapists about his behavior and had a session once a week with the school psychologist, who hoped to offer insights to David's teachers about how to handle him.

One of David's best friends from church, Chris Suttaby, was having similar troubles at school, but while young Cunningham acted out his frustrations with school, Suttaby withdrew into himself. At eleven, Chris was already experimenting with cigarettes and alcohol and, unbeknownst to his parents, was building up a pattern of truancy at school. Jack and Sheena Suttaby compared notes with David and Thelma Cunningham on Sundays and laughed guardedly about what their young sons had been up to. Occasionally, they would also run into Don and Winifred Bourchier, whose adopted twins, Frazer and Chris, were not having behavioral problems like David and Chris, but who were definitely not thriving at school either.

Up the road in Markham, a village on the northern fringe of Metropolitan Toronto, Robbie Kerr was doing just fine at school, maybe a bit too fine. His parents were starting to be concerned that their son was taking school too seriously. He had A's in everything, but seemed more inclined to read the newspaper or do homework than get involved in the neighborhood rough and tumble.

His neighbor, Tom Kenny, was having a different kind of problem at Reesor Park Public School in Markham. He was the youngest and smallest child in his class. He knew what it felt like to be bullied on the school grounds, tussled, or deposited upside down in the lunch litter bin. At home he read voraciously, but at school he consistently failed reading. His parents, Ron and Marion, were at their wits' end trying to understand why their handsome young son was not doing well, especially with his reading. And the same was true in math, although he seemed not to have a natural aptitude for this. The multiplication tables and math drills that Ron and Marion had experienced in public school had been replaced by a more lenient way of teaching—children would learn at their own speed and on their own time. Tom's teacher insisted on putting an alarm clock on his desk when he was doing his math as a way of reminding him that he was slow and that the school's mission was to make him faster. None of this was working. By the fall of 1976, like so many of the other boys who would eventually enroll in St. John's part-time school, Tom Kenny and his parents were very dissatisfied with the public school system and began searching for alternatives.

The same was true for another Markham boy, Barry Nelson, the only son of Leslie and Barry Nelson, whose marks had slipped and who seemed to be losing interest in school. More discipline and adventure in his school life would be a godsend, his parents thought.

In the village of Angus, farther north still, in the household of Oz and Joan Mansfield, trouble was brewing in another boy's life. Their son, Michael, had had cancer when he was three and had lost a kidney. Like David Cunningham, who had been protected as the baby of his family, Mike Mansfield was coddled and spoiled from the time of his illness as a toddler. "There was no doubt about it," says his mother, Joan. "I spoiled the heck out of Mike and protected him, maybe more than I should have." Because of his single kidney, Mike was not allowed to play any of the contact sports that might have provided an outlet for the energy of young boys his age—soccer, hockey, baseball, and the like. Swimming was an activity he enjoyed and in which he developed early proficiency. However, Mike's father, a pilot for Air Canada, was away for long periods of time, leaving Joan to raise the children more or less on her own. Recalled Joan, "Oz was gone. He was flying to Russia with a three-day layover. He'd be home for two days in time to change his clothes, have a good sleep, and he'd be gone again. I was the one who was home with Michael. The responsibility for discipline was left to me and I wasn't as strict as I should have been. Mike got away with a lot of things that he shouldn't have. I'd rather play with the kids than discipline them." And just as he chafed at any suggestion of discipline from his mother, Mike Mansfield rejected his teachers' efforts to guide him. He did not do well in school as he progressed from middle childhood to his early teenage years. At work, Oz Mansfield sometimes compared notes with his pilot colleague Norm Bindon, whose boys, Dean and Scott, were also not thriving academically and who, from time to time, were amply testing their mother's patience.

Paul Nyberg, of Pharmacy Avenue in Scarborough, had had a serious car accident as a child and was not developing in school the physical and mental toughness that he would need to survive. His parents too wanted more from the public school system.

And so it was for other boys who would start on the Timiskaming trip. Simon Croft, from Pickering, was, according to his mother, Jean, "wasting away in the public school system." Andy Hermann, of Toronto, was, according to his father, William, "a lazy bum in school." The Black twins, Owen and Kevin, needed a change as well. For James Doak, James Gibson, David Greaney, Robin Jensen, David Parker, and Jody O'Gorman, life was good and school was okay, but that was about it.

Aside from the problems of modest to moderate learning disabilities in some of the boys who would attend the school, St. John's students were a mix of regular adolescents whose parents thought they might benefit from more structure in their schooling and more personal attention from their teachers. They were not thriving or realizing their full potential in the public school system, a situation due in part to the nature of the boys themselves and also to the nature of the public school system at the time.

In 1968, following the publication of a comprehensive review of the Ontario school system entitled *The Report of the Provincial Committee on Aims and Objectives of Education in the Schools of Ontario*, the so-called Hall-Dennis Report, progressive education hit Ontario classrooms. The Provincial Committee had heard about inflexible programs, outdated curricula, unrealistic regulations, regimented organizations, and what many witnesses felt were mistaken aims of education. The tone of the committee's response was caught in an introduction to the report entitled "The truth shall set you free." It read as follows: "The underlying aim of education is to further man's unending search for truth. Once he possesses the means to truth, all else is within his grasp. Wisdom and understanding, sensitivity, compassion, and responsibility, as well as intellectual honesty and personal integrity, will be his guides in adolescence and his companions in maturity."

The Hall-Dennis Report had a profound impact on Ontario schooling. Memorization of multiplication tables by heart was replaced by "the new math." Gone were many of the strictures of discipline in favor of letting the individuality of students shine through. Gone in some cases were desks in rows and, in more extreme situations, gone were the desks themselves, and even the walls separating classrooms.

As one might expect, this shift in context allowed some children to thrive, while others—notably those who needed repetition and rote learning to keep them on track or those who needed structure to keep them from acting out—did not. Children like David Cunningham, Ian Harling, and many others did anything but thrive in the "new" school climate. More conservative parents, or those who watched their children slide in the permissive and individually oriented classrooms of the 1970s, became increasingly frustrated. Sheena Suttaby, Chris's mother, remembers going to a parent–teacher night at which the teacher related a situation involving her son Chris and another boy who were constantly fighting in class. The teacher asked, "Do you think we should separate them?" Mrs. Suttaby recalls feeling exasperated.

Joanne Harling remembers hearing tales of woe about son Ian from staff at John Ross Robertson Public School, where an "open-toed, love-bead principal" had difficulty guiding his staff of what she termed "loose teachers" (referring to their standards of discipline). Ian had not only *not* learned his multiplication tables, thereby hampering any further progress in mathematics, he had not even been offered the opportunity to learn them. She remembers working out a system of flash cards, work sheets, and monetary rewards to encourage Ian to learn math. "I paid him to learn his times tables," she said, "and it worked!"

Parents' recollection of standards in their own schools always seems to conjure tougher circumstances than those encountered by their offspring. Such was the case for the man who would cofound the first St. John's School in Winnipeg, Manitoba. Ted Byfield's parents wanted the best for him in the 1930s as he was growing up on the shores of Lake Ontario east of Toronto, so they sent him for formal education and navy discipline, based on the British public school model, to Lakefield College School near Peterborough. When Byfield and his wife, Virginia, settled in Winnipeg in the early 1950s, he too voiced dissatisfaction with the education system and found a sympathetic ear in his church colleague, Frank Wiens, who was equally convinced that school was no longer anything like it used to be when he was a boy. Public school was not measuring up, so they took things into their own hands.

This was how Ted Byfield, a newspaper reporter, and Frank Wiens, teacher and fellow parishioner at St. John's Cathedral in

Winnipeg in the 1950s, began offering extra lessons and weekend outings for their own sons and the other boys in the St. John's choir. Remembering his own days at Lakefield College School, in which rowing big heavy navy cutters on the Kawartha Lakes had been a pivotal challenge, Byfield convinced Wiens that they should fix up an old navy cutter and use that to toughen up their boys. So successful was this enterprise that Wiens and Byfield soon found a decaying residential school facility on the banks of the Red River, between Selkirk, Manitoba, and Lake Winnipeg in which to establish a full-time school for their sons as an alternative to the public school system. After establishing the part-time St. John's Cathedral School (not affiliated with St. John's Ravenscourt School in Winnipeg) in 1958 and the full-time school in 1962, they went on to create St. John's School of Alberta in 1968 and St. John's School of Ontario in 1976.

The initial driving force in this initiative—discontent with the public school system and a fear that their boys were not getting the education they needed or deserved—was similar to the concern that the British had had at the end of the Boer War in 1902, when they realized that it had taken 400,000 bandy-legged Tommies to subdue 40,000 Afrikaners. In his search for an effective remedy for the weak spines and general physical and moral decay of the British youth coming home from service in South Africa, returning British officer Lord Robert Baden-Powell created a set of standards and challenges for them in the context of service in adventure—a combination of Ernest Thompson Seton's notion of Woodcrafter Indians and a Crimean youth corps that Baden-Powell called the Boy Scouts.

Twenty years later, at the conclusion of the First World War, the Germans had very similar concerns about their youth—particularly the young men—who were lacking in drive and direction. As in the United Kingdom, the remedy for building strong minds and bodies was a program of organized service and adventure for young people. Locally based youth development initiatives throughout Germany, both in school and out, eventually coalesced into the

Hitler-Jugend, which, of course, had a larger agenda than strictly personal development of youth. However, another initiative for youth organized in Germany by educational visionary Kurt Hahn would, like the Boy Scouts, use adventure to build character.

St. John's Cathedral School struck a chord with parents who shared Wiens's and Byfield's skepticism about the ability of the public school system to meet the needs of their growing boys. This new school used corporal punishment on the boys when they did not conform, spanking them with wooden sticks in the tradition of the best English boarding schools. Boys were expected to stand when a master entered the room and address him as "Sir." Byfield and Wiens appeared to be involved for the good of society. As members of the Company of the Cross, a lay order they had created in association with the Anglican Church, they received a dollar a day plus room and board for their efforts. Their wives and families lived on site and were all involved. The staff, which started with two couples and grew as enrollment swelled, schooled the boys with drill and repetition; they taught the students memory work, Latin, French, and German; they taught them to sing and, on weekends, they put them in navy cutters or on snowshoes to follow the routes of the voyageurs and packeteers.

Byfield's inspiration for this educational initiative was a 1947 essay that began with the following sentence: "That I, whose experience of teaching is extremely limited, should presume to discuss education is a matter, surely, that calls for no apology." This essay was "The Lost Tools of Learning" by British essayist and novelist Dorothy L. Sayers, which advocated a return to a medieval concept of education consisting of two parts—the Trivium (the process) and the Quadrivium (the content). Sayers's conservative views resonated with Byfield because they were so in tune with the British public school traditions he had encountered at Lakefield. He was particular struck by the Trivium and its three parts: Grammar, Dialectic (Logic), and Rhetoric. Grammar was about learning the facts of language or science or any of the necessary subject disciplines. Logic was about lining up those facts in a sensible argument. And Rhetoric was education that compelled students to test their arguments against each other and arrive, sooner or later, at an understanding of the limits of human potential and understanding. This no-nonsense approach to schooling was a dramatic, antiprogressive force in the shaping of the St. John's curriculum.

Of those early days at St. John's, Byfield wrote in a school yearbook: "We found that the only possible teacher–student relationship was not one of partnership, not the let's-learn-together of the modern classroom. It was a relationship of master and servant. And the master did not need the servant. The servant needed the master." Little wonder then that when the boys were in the cutters on Lake Winnipeg, swimmers and non-swimmers alike grasping the thick handles of eight-, ten-, and twelve-foot oars (depending on the size of the boy), they called their place in those character-building vessels, in the parlance of galleon slaves, the "pit."

Between weekends in the boats with the boys and instructing them with the lost tools of learning, Ted Byfield worked as the legislative reporter for the *Winnipeg Free Press*. Part of this beat involved attending the legislature regularly and listening to all presentations and debates. Byfield would read to pass the time. In the late 1950s, while sitting through a particularly tedious part of the parliamentary process, he happened to read *The Northwest Company* by Marjorie Wilkins Campbell.

"I realized," he said, when interviewed for this book, "that we had the wrong boat!" And so as the weekend school became full-time and moved to a residential site on the Red River north of Winnipeg, Byfield and Wiens—who had no experience with canoes whatsoever—special-ordered brigade-size canoes from the Chestnut Canoe Company in New Brunswick and headed for Lake Winnipeg and beyond on the old voyageur routes.

In June 1964, at the end of the second year of full-time operation with the canoes, Byfield wrote a report in which he described the kind of hero they were trying to emulate:

. . . we did not like the image of today's hired athletic hero, who wears a particular type of shirt, who combs his hair with a particular type of lotion, and who implies a particular set of values that are not particularly selfless. We wanted to return to a masculine hero—hairy, sweaty, muddy, perhaps even a little coarse. But direct, honest, generous, fearless, neither afraid to work nor afraid to sing.

We found our man in the midst of our history. He emerges from the lands of the lakes and rivers, from the roar of the rapids, from the glow of a fire beside some still lake, from the shriek of the prairie blizzard. He is the figure of the Canadian voyageur. He is boisterous, he is tough, he is loyal, he can work 20 hours a day, and he is, incidentally, bi-cultural. He has physical strength that staggers the imagination—(considerably more, one would think, than his dissolute American cousin, the cowboy, who did not live in Canada until the advertising men brought him here)—and finally, in his own sentimental and barbarous way, he is also Christian.

Stated as a mission for St. John's School, these aspirations distilled down to three purposes: (1) to teach boys to think for themselves so that they can develop their own convictions; (2) to develop in boys a spirit of adventure that will induce them to put their convictions into action; and (3) to raise the level of religious education so that Christian doctrine can be made more relevant to modern life. In short, what they were trying to do was build *character*.

Among the first students enrolled at St. John's Cathedral part-time school was thirteen-year-old Mike Maunder, who arrived in the autumn of 1960 in a black leather jacket, slicked-back hair, and with a large chip on his shoulder. His journalist father, a friend of Ted Byfield's, had died suddenly two years before and Mike had had considerable difficulty coming to terms with that. Looking back years later, he says: "I was out of control . . . [and] giving my mother a really hard time. I had an older brother, but the dynamic of a family when a father dies is pretty profound. Nobody in the education system seemed to acknowledge that. I was taken into the superintendent's office and they said that I was misbehaving because my father had died. But St. John's seemed to understand what I was feeling. I really felt I found a place where I belonged."

On his first weekend at the part-time school, Mike Maunder received ten swats on the bottom with a wooden paddle for talking out of turn. He also remembers going to Ted Byfield early on, and complaining that the study hall was too noisy for him to do his work. Byfield just looked at him and said, "Your old man had to work in newsrooms that were a hell of a lot noisier than this." With that, says Maunder, "my allegiance to St. John's was sealed."

Boys came and went from St. John's Cathedral School. It was not for everyone. One or two in every ten would drop out midyear. Others would stay only one year, or maybe two. Others, like Maunder, stayed on. Those who stayed contributed to the spartan life set out by Wiens, Byfield, and other members of the Company of the Cross. The boys, wearing simple uniforms, cooked, cleaned, painted, and fed the animals on the school farm. They raised chickens, ran an abattoir and packing house, and sold the frozen processed birds door to door to raise money. They snowshoed, canoed, and squabbled. They worked together, sang together, and prayed together daily. The masters set the tone and the agenda. The boys deferred to their elders and toed the line as proper young boys should. On weekends they went into downtown Winnipeg to the head office of the Great West Life Insurance Company and manned the phones to sell chickens, to raise money, or, when Ted Byfield got a small press going at the school, to sell tracts (often written by Byfield himself) to generate funds to keep the school operating.

Six years after the formation of the first full-time St. John's School in Manitoba, boys were coming east from conservative homes in Alberta to attend the school, so the Company of the Cross established a second institution west of Edmonton in the valley of the North Saskatchewan River. One of the people who would eventually end up teaching at the Alberta school was Mike

Maunder, who first went to university, then into journalism before returning to St. John's where he found a sense of belonging that he felt nowhere else.

With two institutions under the Company of the Cross banner, the reputation of St. John's began to spread. Parents in other parts of the country made inquiries about sending their sons for the spartan, back-to-basics education that St. John's offered.

From the beginning, there were accidents that should have raised alarm bells about the lack of safety awareness in the school. In an interschool snowshoe race in 1971, a boy from Nova Scotia dropped in his tracks, but the school moved on. Parents seemed not to be overly concerned about the level of risk their sons were encountering in the St. John's curriculum. The core assumption of St. John's—that out of adversity comes strength—was never publicly challenged. As a rallying cry, the Alberta school adopted a passage from the Saxon epic poem *The Battle of Maldon*, commemorating a bloody fight against Viking invaders in the year 991: "Courage must be harder, heart the stouter, spirit the sterner, as our strength weakens. / Here lies our Lord, cut to pieces, our best man in the dust. / If any man thinks of leaving this battle, he can howl forever." And to this was often added a biblical passage from the Book of Romans (5:4–5): "Suffering produces persever-ance; perseverance character; and character, hope. And hope does not disappoint us, because God has poured out His love into our hearts by the Holy Spirit, whom He has given us."

In 1976, while out with peers on a winter day, sixteen-year-old Edward Milligan collapsed from cold on his snowshoes outside Selkirk. In the emergency ward of the Selkirk hospital, his pupils fixed and dilated, his body core temperature at 77°F (98.6°F is normal), and showing no signs of a heartbeat for more than two hours, the boy was clinically dead. But "miraculously"—as his recovery would later be described—an astute anesthetist, Dr. Gerry Bristow, rewarmed the boy with hot water bottles, blankets, and pre-heated oxygen, and eventually restarted his heart. The next day his parents, who flew out from Toronto fearing the worst, were talking to their son who, except for no memory of anything immediately preceding the accident, had suffered frostbite but apparently no permanent ill effects from the outing. And still St. John's tough regimen continued. The Milligan boy returned to the school. Parents continued to support the idea of giving their sons real challenges to assist the rite of passage to manhood. When asked by a reporter from the *Selkirk Enterprise*, immediately following the accident, whether her son would be returning to St. John's after his brush with death, Mrs. Milligan replied in the affirmative, adding, "The school is tailor-made for him."

As Edward Milligan recovered from his snowshoe accident, the Company of the Cross expanded again, this time east to Ontario. Mike Maunder, and Frank Felletti, another alumnus of the Manitoba school now teaching at the Alberta school, were asked if they would go east that fall to franchise the St. John's ideal one step further. Felletti, a vivacious student in the original part-time school from 1959 to 1962, had finished high school and gone on to study at the University of Manitoba. Unlike Maunder, who had dropped out of postsecondary schooling, Felletti graduated from U of M in 1970 and had taken a job teaching science at St. John's. As happened repeatedly throughout the history of St. John's School, a student fell in love with one of his teachers' daughters. Patricia Doolan and Felletti were married by Father Sargeant at the rustic Chapel of St. John the Divine on the grounds of the Alberta school on September 11, 1975.

Frank Felletti and Mike Maunder were an impressive team. Both in their twenties and completely familiar with the St. John's way, they had high hopes and vigor for extending Ted Byfield's and Frank Wiens's dream to another school, serving another parish of wayward boys. Although different in personality and temperament from the original founders, fiery Felletti was more like Byfield in his passion and determination, and the more reserved Maunder was more like Wiens in his steadfastness and ability to operationalize his headmaster's dreams. Neither man had found anything better or more stimulating than the ethos of

St. John's School in which to build a meaningful life; that conviction they shared. Although they would have their difficulties as an administrative team, these two young men were in many ways ideally suited to take the idea of St. John's to Ontario.

During this time, Ted Byfield was losing interest in the schools and becoming more enthused about the magazine press he had started in Manitoba and subsequently moved to Alberta. In 1972, Byfield's press was officially separated from the schools as a subsidiary operation of the Company of the Cross. Byfield would eventually leave the Company of the Cross to become publisher of the *St. John's Edmonton Report* and subsequently the *Alberta Report*. In the meantime, out of the ranks of the St. John's alumni came a number of bright, talented, and energetic men, among them Frank Felletti and Mike Maunder, both of whom blended Wiens's deep commitment to the cause with a measure of Byfield's charisma and gift of persuasive oratory.

In the early days, the founding members of the Company of the Cross were able to convince each other to work for a dollar a day, but now persuading new people to sign on to another person's dream for little money was much more difficult. Despite various staff problems in Manitoba and Alberta, and accidents in the outdoor program, the Company of the Cross pressed on. In the fall of 1976, Mike Maunder headed to Toronto with Frank Felletti and his wife. And so the die was cast to offer Ian Harling, David Cunningham, Chris Suttaby, the Bourchier brothers, Tom Kenny, Barry Nelson, Mike Mansfield, and their classmates the opportunity to become men, the St. John's way. It would be a new option for frustrated parents.

The plan was to follow the St. John's model that had worked in Manitoba and Alberta. They would find a home church, start a part-time school, and then work toward building a full-time school in four years' time. They would give presentations to congregations and distribute a no-frills, black-and-white pamphlet entitled "Wanted: 40 Boys to Build a School" that had photos of the dirty but happy faces of tousled boys from the Manitoba school. The boys look exhausted, which was the whole idea of the pitch. The back of the pamphlet had the following text:

THE BOYS OF ST. JOHN'S

These boys are students of St. John's School in Winnipeg. They have just completed an 800 mile canoe trip as part of their regular school curriculum. Their faces show the mud and miserable conditions, the hardship and exhaustion they have endured. Their faces also show the satisfaction and confidence they have gained.

Over the next four years, St. John's is establishing a similar school in Toronto. This winter it will operate on weekends only. There are openings for 40 boys, aged 12–15, to pioneer this program. It will be hard work. It will cost approximately $50 a month. It will take all of a boy's spare time. It will stretch him to his mental and physical limits. The academic work is heavy and exacting. The canoe and snowshoe expeditions are rigorous ordeals. Boys will have to work at constructing the school's basic facilities.

It is not a program which promises fun and recreation. But for those who want it, St. John's makes the same promise it has always made—challenge and great adventure.

For further information and applications contact: St. John's School of Ontario, 437 Roncesvalles, Tel. 535-2208.

Within weeks of arriving in Ontario, the Fellettis and Mike Maunder convinced the Anglican Diocese to let them use the parish hall of St. Jude's Church, in mid-town Toronto, which had recently been taken out of weekly service by the Anglican Church. The place was in very poor repair, but the roof was more or less sound, the toilets worked, and the doors, windows, and floors would do just fine with a bit of elbow grease. Had the facilities been any more lavish, they would most certainly not have been congruent with the spartan message and tone of the "Wanted: 40 Boys" pamphlet.

"Wanted: 40 Boys" was blunt: Standard punishment for laziness and misbehavior was a spanking with a paddle; parents were expected to help; mastery of academics could be achieved only through drill and exercise; snowshoeing and canoeing were designed to confront boys with hardship and adversity. Once the snowshoeing was done, the boys and parents would sell fifteen tons of honey donated by the western schools door to door to raise money. And, in reference to what would be required to make St. Jude's livable, the brochure says this: "St. Jude's parish hall is old and musty. Some of the floorboards are rotten. Hot water has never been installed. Since the school has no bunks, the boys will start the year sleeping on the floor in sleeping bags. . . . St. John's believes that good programs will spring out of much less comfortable conditions. It is true that the showers leak. It is also true that, come January, some boys will learn how to fix leaky showers. They will learn to install hot water plumbing. And fix rotten floorboards. And clean musty rooms."

With regard to the outdoor program: "In all boys there is a desire to be tested, an instinct to be heroic and to conquer hardships. This need is met at St. John's in the snowshoeing and canoeing programs. In confronting the hardships of this program a boy's appetite for real challenge and adventure is satisfied. Good qualities of character are developed."

Maunder and Felletti made the rounds of Toronto's Anglican community. The pitch worked. At a relatively new parish in Downsview, called St. Stephen's, they interviewed half a dozen boys who wanted to enroll in the school. The part-time school began at St. Jude's as planned on December 31, 1976. They did not have forty boys—more like twenty-five—but it was a start, and interest appeared to be growing. On New Year's Day 1977, they took the first trip with the new crew on snowshoes—fifteen miles. Some of the boys' feet were bleeding, and some said they were never coming back, but Maunder and Felletti had heard it all before. Prior to the snowshoe run, they had told the boys and their parents that their children were going to hate the experience. They were right.

35

Word spread. Eight weeks after that first snowshoe outing, on February 26, the first official snowshoe race of St. John's School was convened in the Peterborough area. The next week there was a feature article in the *Toronto Star* with a photo of happy twelve-year-old Robin Jensen, of Oakville, tightening an old-fashioned lampwick binding on his mukluks. He looks as if he knows exactly what he is doing. The headline reads, "Tough new school tests boys to the limit." Mike Maunder's message in the article is loud and clear: "Character is being able to face hardship," he is quoted as saying. "The function of the outdoors program is to make sure they don't fall in the trap of making a decision on the basis of how comfortable the alternatives are. Usually, doing the right thing involves great hardship."

While the first St. John's School of Ontario snowshoe program was beginning, the Manitoba program continued. In January 1977, sixteen-year-old Stuart Simpson, of Toronto, badly froze his feet on one of the day-long warm-up snowshoe runs around Selkirk, left his brigade and walked back to the school, alone. (This story was not reported until after the Timiskaming accident, when the newspapers were starting to put two and two together.) But even those parents who knew or who had heard rumors about mishaps at the other two schools in previous years were still inclined to listen to the enthusiastic Maunder and Felletti, to notice the positive changes in their sons, and either agree that accidents were a necessary part of the process—no pain, no gain— or believe that such accidents could not possibly happen at St. John's School of Ontario.

What the Ontario parents certainly could not have known was the extent of the staffing problems. Recruiting and keeping staff at a dollar a day was a trial for the Company of the Cross. A friend of the schools, Tam Deachman, who worked with the advertising firm of Gordon Rowntree in Vancouver, suggested that St. John's had qualities similar to historic polar expeditions and, as such, should emulate a recruiting pitch for a South Pole expedition that ran in the papers in London, England, in 1906. The ad had read:

"Men wanted for a hazardous journey. Small wages, bitter cold, long months of complete darkness, constant danger, safe return doubtful. Honour and recognition in the case of success—Sir Ernest Shackleton."

Under the heading "8 hearty men wanted to lead expansion of renowned boys' school," the St. John's recruiting advertisement read as follows:

> You may have read about St. John's in *Weekend*, or seen C B C's pene-
> trating documentary about this unique Winnipeg school [a program
> in the *This Land* series], where encouragement to think comes first;
> where students (and teachers) learn to snowshoe up to 50 miles or
> paddle canoes up to 16 hours a day, retracing routes of the early
> explorers; where building men of character is the motivating chal-
> lenge of a hearty staff. Now a second St. John's has been established
> in Edmonton, and others will be opened across Canada to meet
> continent-wide applications for admission. To do this we need men
> of immense vision and courage. They should have at least one year of
> university, and be prepared to complete their degrees under
> Company direction, they should be prepared to work up to 80 hours
> per week, sometimes more, for a salary of $1 a day plus food, cloth-
> ing, shelter and necessities for themselves and their families; they
> should like people, be able to think logically, use the English
> language effectively, laugh easily. They need not be Anglicans, but
> should be prepared to examine the Christian faith and teach honest
> conclusions.

Much to the surprise of all concerned, 150 men from diverse backgrounds replied. Personal interviews reduced this number to twenty-two, who were invited to the Manitoba school to teach one class, snowshoe up to eighteen miles, and discuss with Company members their reasons for joining. Out of these, they invited twenty-one people—seven couples and seven single men—to join the Company. Those selected ranged from a twenty-one-year-old single university dropout who worked as a gardener in British Columbia to a thirty-nine-year-old industrial chemist from Haileybury, Ontario, whose wife had been active in the International Order of the Daughters of the Empire.

Since the inception of the school, the central assumption about St. John's staffing was that men would learn on the job, and that to teach boys to think and to have character required a certain faith and tenacity of spirit, and an ability to conform to the Company's Rule of Life with its spiritual, social, and economic strictures. Beyond that, they would simply follow the lead of the old hands, eventually develop a style of their own as a master, and move on. But, of course, individual reasons for joining the Company of the Cross were as different as the varied souls who vowed to carry out the Company's Rule of Life. It was one thing to create the Rule and then commit to it, as had Ted Byfield, Frank Wiens, and their spouses in the early days in Manitoba; it was quite another to join the established community, and commit to what amounted to other people's rules. History has shown that boys' schools, including St. John's, have attracted all manner of people, some with the highest moral codes and the best characters and intentions, as well as others with flawed characters and other agendas. At St. John's, almost from the beginning, recruiting, retaining, and training good staff was a challenge.

From the boys' point of view and that of their parents, who were even further removed from the day-to-day events of the school, there was too much to do to develop a coherent sense of the whole. Looking back in later years, Mike Mansfield would say, "I have no idea what the hell they were trying to do at St. John's. It seemed to change from day to day. Half . . . the time, it seemed like their main goal was selling honey. [Those of] us down in the trenches didn't get a good feel for the big picture. Things always appeared fairly scattered, but our job was definitely not to question why. You did what you were told, and that was that."

As the Shackletonesque ad published in the fall of 1970 indicated, the plan was to franchise the operation beyond Alberta. Even as the Nova Scotia boy collapsed on an Alberta snowshoe trail in 1971; as the Royal Life Saving Society published "To Save a Life," a manual about water safety that included details about dangers of and emergency remedies for cold-water immersion in 1974; as Ted Milligan "died" from cold and was miraculously resuscitated in 1976; as the need for a systematic safety system and staff planning program increased, plans advanced for opening a school in Ontario.

Unlike the Shackleton expedition, in which participants signed on willingly to accept the risks inherent in the undertaking, St. John's School was an ongoing educational adventure that put not only its staff, but also its unsuspecting boys at risk.

Armed with faith and hubris, secure in the knowledge that the model had worked in Manitoba and Alberta, Mike Maunder and Frank and Pat Felletti continued their recruiting efforts. Gradually, boys and parents signed on. With hope and prayer, with a stick and an ironclad belief that adversity was the key to building character, Maunder and the Fellettis taught classes, snowshoed, sold honey, and socialized with parents. The idea of the St. John's concept of education took hold in Toronto.

With the blend of history, adventure, and charismatic leadership that was the St. John's way, the staff of the part-time school in Ontario captured the imaginations of the new students. David Cunningham, who had never cared about schoolwork, began to stay home from regular school, with his mother and father's blessing, to do his homework for the part-time school. His best friend, Chris Suttaby, did the same. Instead of skipping school and hanging out at the mall near his home in the Jane/Finch corridor, Chris would work on his Latin declensions knowing that if he did not, one of the weekend masters would be ready to "beat his ass." With a sigh of relief, Joan Mansfield would put her son Mike on the bus at their home near Barrie. Mike would take the hour-long journey to the main bus station in Toronto and then, showing responsibility and initiative his parents had never seen, he would report at 6 p.m. sharp on Friday nights, ready for his weekend adventures to begin. Even the recalcitrant Ian Harling will admit to being beguiled by St. John's blend of fear, learning, and adventure. As the boy who "accidentally" helped to burn down a school portable, Harling began to find the kind of success at St. John's that he never had found in the public school system.

Proof of that was in Harling's report card at the end of the part-time school year. Throughout the winter term, his public school education had maintained its usual steady decline, so much so that his parents had actually pulled him out of regular school. In regular school he was reading *Are You There, God? It's Me, Margaret* and *The Hardy Boys*, while at the weekend school he was dealing with Shakespeare and C.S. Lewis. It was a long way from *The Case of the Haunted Mine* to the Narnia series, even for an eleven-year-old. No one was more surprised than Ian when he actually passed English at St. John's. There had been a question on the final exam about symbolism and, although he had no idea of what symbolism was, he persevered. In public school, he said later, he would have just given up, but on that exam, he thought it through and wrote an answer. "It was not well written, and there was certainly nothing brilliant about it, but somehow I got the right facts in the right order in the right place with the right question, and I scraped through. It was then I realized that, hey, something's working here!"

The report card itself embodies the improvisational nature and the personal touch of St. John's that parents seemed to like. On the outside of a folded piece of fancy card stock was the name and logo of the school, printed in black and blue ink, over the title REPORT. Inside, in the handwriting of the various teachers, were marks and individual comments on each subject. Although the contents of Ian Harling's report at the end of the part-time school year were not stellar by any stretch, this was the first sign of improvement. He was, for the first time in his school career, proud of his accomplishments.

In literature, Ian achieved a grade of 54 percent, but was praised by Frank Felletti, who said that he had not expected the boy to pass. In spelling, he scored a middling B grade, but was told that he needed to channel his energy more politely and slowly. Grammar he failed because of work that was sporadic and haphazard, but the grade of 43 percent was heralded as an "immense improvement." Overall, headmaster Felletti was very pleased with Ian's performance, noting that when on several occasions Ian had been the slow man on his snowshoe team, he had realized his limitations. These trials had provided good lessons in humility.

Later, Ian Harling would recall:

The part-time school was probably the roughest schooling I'd ever gone through. It was horrible; it was really rough. But deep down, I saw something . . . that I'd never seen before in my life. I absolutely despised it. I got swats day in and day out. No question, it hurt, but you get a leather butt after a while. Mr. Felletti was an incredible guy. He was the one with the corporate vision of how things would work. Mr. Maunder had vision too, but he was more down to earth; his vision was about how things should actually work. Sometimes he went overboard and it would just be pandemonium the way he designed things, because he did so many things on a whim. But 99 percent of the time his vision was so straightforward and brilliant that that's what kept the school alive.

The ultimate plan was to build a full-time school on a site west of Claremont, outside Toronto. To mark the end of the part-time school, in June 1977, thirty-seven boys in dark corduroy trousers and white turtleneck jerseys were lined up on the lawn of the new school property for a class photo. Kneeling in front were the fair-haired Bindon brothers with Jody O'Gorman on one side, Chris Suttaby on the other, and Ian Harling at the end of the line. Behind them, on one knee, were the dark-haired Bourchier twins, David Cunningham, Robin Jensen, and Tim Hopkins, whose father Bert may already have been working behind them to start building the sports field. In the back row were Mike Mansfield, Tim Pryce, and some of the older, taller boys, all looking tousled and happy. There is an openness to the faces. Like the boys on the "Wanted: 40 Boys" brochure, they faced the camera with pride, innocence, confidence, and an unsettling measure of trust. In a year this crew, with new boys to swell the ranks, would be back in exactly the same spot, having another class picture taken on Saturday, June 10, 1978, the day before a third of them would trust enough to die in deep waters.

III

The Parents: Building a School

Like many congregations, the parishioners of St. Stephen's Anglican Church were a community within a community. Even before the new church building was opened in 1954, middle-class families in North Toronto strived to do the best for their children and supported each other. In 1976, there remained a spirit of building at St. Stephen's. Originally part of the parish of St. John's in the village of Weston, north of Toronto, the new parish came into being when rapid growth in the 1950s led to a cluster of some ninety Anglican families with 122 children in the area around Jane Street and Wilson Avenue. The first meeting of the St. Stephen's congregation was held at one of the parishioners' homes. In March 1954, the Reverend Frank Fry of Wolfville, Nova Scotia, was appointed first rector of the parish. A portable church was put on a site at 2259 Jane Street in 1956, and on October 4, 1957, a new church was consecrated. The new building was simple and elegant, made of sand-colored brick and stone, with walls in both the sanctuary and the hall below made mostly of glass. Constructing a new building brought the congregation together in ways that older churches could not, and nurtured a sense of togetherness and common purpose that made Sunday a day to look forward to for parishioners like Dave and Thelma Cunningham.

Thelma had arrived in Canada from England in 1947 as a teenager with her parents, two sisters, and a brother. After the order and predictability of life in Charterhouse School, where

43

she boarded in Kent, England, Thelma was definitely not impressed with the ups and downs of life in Toronto. People she met through church and family did, however, help her to find her way. One of them was David Cunningham, a man fourteen years her senior, who worked as a tool-and-die maker for the Avro Aircraft Company near the present location of Pearson International Airport. They were married at St. Stephen's in 1949 when Thelma was nineteen and Dave was thirty-three.

Unsuccessful in conceiving a child of their own, the Cunninghams adopted a son, Robert, some years after they were married. Although mentally challenged, Robert added life and new vigor to the family. About the same time, Dave's brother and his wife, who lived in New Brunswick, also adopted two young children. But, as fate would have it, the Cunninghams' sister-in-law was killed in a car accident in February 1960 and David's brother, who was trying to raise these two youngsters on his own, died in July of that same year. Struggling to come to terms with this tragedy, Thelma and David automatically welcomed their adopted niece and nephew—Cathy, five, and James, seven—into their North Toronto home. In the spring of 1964, Thelma unexpectedly became pregnant. To everyone's delight, a son, David, was born in January 1965, a miracle child for thirty-five-year-old Thelma, and David, who was nearly fifty. With a ten-year gap between him and his adopted siblings, young David was "everybody's baby," coddled by family and friends.

When David was born, siblings Robert and Cathy took his arrival in stride, but brother James was just entering his teens and becoming difficult to handle. Losing his adopted parents and moving to Toronto had been difficult for James. With a new little brother becoming the center of attention, James felt left out and began to misbehave. Knowing what the routines of boarding school had done for her, Thelma convinced her husband that Rothesay, an Anglican private school in New Brunswick, established in the nineteenth century to prepare boys for entry into the Royal Military College in Kingston—Canada's West Point—was the place for James. Rothesay, with its strict code of discipline and rigorous academic standards, turned out to be good for him, a point of view with which even James later agreed. When young David began having serious problems at home and school in the mid-1970s, and counseling seemed to make little difference, it was James who suggested that a boarding school, maybe even Rothesay, would be the place to straighten out his spoiled little brother. In the fall of 1976, a chance Sunday visitor at St. Stephen's put those wheels in motion.

It was November and Sunday service had just finished. David, Sr., had left to attend a men's breakfast meeting. Thelma was working in the church kitchen with other volunteers to count and roll the day's collection, and to prepare the weekly bank deposit. And David, Jr., now twelve and very much at home on his own in the corridors of St. Stephen's, had found his way into the church auditorium where a vivacious man in his twenties was presenting a slide show about St. John's schools in Manitoba and Alberta in a pitch to find prospective students for an Ontario school.

The St. John's team had received the blessing of Reverend Garnsworthy, the Bishop of Toronto, to set up a weekend school in the parish hall of St. Jude's Church on Roncesvalles Avenue. And now, to publicize the idea, Frank Felletti was making the rounds of Toronto's Anglican churches to give presentations, speak about the strict Christian values and discipline of St. John's, and show photographs that highlighted all aspects of the St. John's way, especially the outdoor programs involving snowshoes on the prairie, dogsleds in the Rocky Mountains, and canoes on wilderness rivers. Thelma Cunningham clearly remembers having her money counting interrupted that day by a breathless young David, who burst in with stories about what he had just seen and heard— about dogs, snowshoes, and canoes. He told her about the dark-haired man and the school he was starting in Toronto, pleading, "Mummy, Mummy, Mummy, can I go?"

Others heard about St. John's in similar ways. Also members of the St. Stephen's parish in Downsview were Don and Winifred

Bourchier and their four children, two girls and adopted identical twin boys, dark-haired Frazer and Chris, who, like David Cunningham, would be enthusiastic about this new rugged weekend school with its rigorous outdoor program and eventually attend St. John's. Don Bourchier was a teacher in Toronto and, although he and his wife felt that the schooling their boys were getting in the public education system was adequate, he thought the added discipline and adventure of St. John's might be more beneficial.

Jack and Sheena Suttaby were also members of St. Stephen's Anglican Church. In fact, their oldest son, Christopher, was a friend of David Cunningham. After the presentation by Frank Felletti, the boys were excited about snowshoeing, dog sledding, and canoeing, and the parents were relieved that someone finally offered a disciplined alternative to the laissez-faire schooling their boys were getting in the public system. The sheer force of David Cunningham's enthusiasm for what he had seen in the slides was enough to get his friend Chris fired up about the idea as well.

Sheena Suttaby had grown up in Scotland, where she knew the difference that disciplined schooling could make. Her husband, Jack, was equally unhappy with the public school experience their two sons were getting in the Ontario educational system. And so as word spread about this new back-to-basics weekend school in Toronto, the Suttabys arranged an admission interview for Chris at St. Jude's Church. The cost of $12.50 per weekend was manageable, especially when they knew—they hoped—that this might rescue their boy's education from the public school system.

As the recruiting pamphlet "Wanted: 40 Boys to Build a School" filtered out from 437 Roncesvalles Avenue into the Anglican Diocese of Toronto, into St. Stephen's and beyond, it caught the attention of other like-minded parents. Air Canada pilot Norman Bindon and his wife, Ruth, had been watching their two sons, Dean and Scott, spiral into indifference at Queenston Drive School in Mississauga. In 1976, with a young daughter to attend to, two boys entering their teens, and a husband whose work kept him away for long periods, it was a struggle for Ruth Bindon to manage the household and keep the boys on track with their schoolwork. Scott had a learning disability. Dean was losing interest and was starting to skip school from time to time. Both boys were lagging behind their classmates and struggling with some of their teachers. The school described in the pamphlet sounded as if it might make a difference. The Bindons' sons were close; in fact, Scott idolized his older brother, Dean, who protected him at school and occasionally helped him with his reading, but who was starting to lead him into mischief too. The weekend school might be just what the boys needed to help get them back on track scholastically.

In the village of Angus, to the north near Barrie, Norman Bindon's colleague, Oz Mansfield, and his wife, Joan, were having similar struggles with their son Michael, who was approaching puberty, getting bigger and stronger, and starting to throw his weight around. Recalling those unhappy days, especially the summer of 1976 when Mike was out of school and more or less at loose ends, Joan Mansfield sighs: "Mike was a big guy. That summer I can recall saying that I loved him, but I didn't like him very much." News of St. John's School offered the Mansfields some hope for their son.

And so the story went. The Crofts, of Pickering, were watching their son, Simon, "wasting away in the public school system." Like the Mansfields, Peter, a filmmaker and television producer, and his wife, Jean, were struggling with a prickly adolescent son who had failed Grade 7 and was headed for trouble outside school. Major Gordon Black, a logistics officer in the Canadian Armed Forces based in Downsview, and his wife, Janice, parents of nine children, had sent an older son to one of the western schools and had seen the transformation that St. John's could make in a teenage boy. When they heard that St. John's was expanding to Ontario, they wanted to send their twins, Owen and Kevin, as they too were entering their teens, for a similar dose of no-nonsense schooling. Don and Kathleen Nyberg, of Scarborough, hoped their son, Paul, whose left side had been permanently injured in a car accident when he was six, would rise to the challenges of St. John's and develop the mental and physical strength he would need to take him into the adult world. The parents of Jody O'Gorman, his best friend, had similar hopes for their boy. In togetherness at St. John's would be strength.

The expectation of parental involvement was built into the St. John's way as it had evolved in Manitoba and Alberta. And again in Ontario, as Mike Maunder and Frank and Pat Felletti went on the rounds of Anglican churches in the greater Toronto area, they made personal connections and usually highly positive impressions on the parents of the boys who became the first class of St. John's School of Ontario. The "Wanted: 40 Boys" pamphlet was quite specific about parental involvement: "Fees have been set as low as possible, because it is expected that parents will help out. All parents will be called on to help as the program progresses. There is much to do: cooking, driving, carpentry."

For the Cunninghams and the Suttabys, who knew about the power of building an institution from the ground up as a result of their affiliation with St. Stephen's Church, the idea of participating in their sons' schooling by creating a parental support network of cooks, drivers, and carpenters for the fledgling school was highly appealing. They would be helping their recalcitrant boys become responsible men of character and, at the same time, they would be building a school that, presumably, would live on long after David and Christopher had moved on. It seems clear, looking back, that the lengthy recruitment interviews with individual boys and parents at St. Jude's Church were designed not only to size up boys for enrollment but to begin a personal relationship with their parents, to bring them "on side," as it were, and to establish the expectation—commitment even—that they were an integral part of the building process. Parental involvement, from the very beginning, would turn out to be a major force in quelling anger in response to the accident when it occurred at the end of the first year of the school's full-time operation.

As the weekend school began on December 31, 1976, some parents of the twenty boys enrolled simply dropped off their sons on Friday night and picked them up again on Sunday. Others acted as drivers for eight weeks of snowshoe practice in the fields and woods north of Toronto and over in the Kawartha Lakes, near the village of Lakefield, in preparation for a thirty-seven-mile race on February 26, 1977. The Michells, whose son, Todd, went to St. John's, offered their farm near Stouffville as a checkpoint for snowshoe practices in the area, a place for a "juice break" from what were, by design, formidable challenges for the unsuspecting first students of St. John's School. Involving the parents as drivers and supporters of these snowshoe runs introduced them to the harsh realities of activities that were designed, according to school documents, "not as a recreational program" but "to confront boys with hardship and adversity and to show them how to pull through." A supplement to the "Wanted: 40 Boys" brochure pulled no punches: "Whether weak or strong, all boys will find they need fortitude and an inner determination to finish the race. The snowshoe program is designed to develop these qualities, often under crisis conditions."

Crises on snowshoe runs were often small and intensely personal. As soon as brigades of boys were down the trail and out of earshot of masters and parent supervisors, boy rule prevailed, as it did in the survival-of-the-strongest atmosphere of the school dorms. Boys would tire at different rates and the group would have to find ways to bring the slow members along, more often with brute force and verbal harangue than with encouragement or compassion. But with distances that ranged from fifteen to thirty-five miles and through varying winter weather conditions, invariably the stronger, faster boys would outpace the slower boys, often leaving them at the back of the line alone with their insecurities, raw feet, and flagging limbs.

At the Michell farm, boys would struggle in, one or two in each team hauled by others using the long scarves that students were issued. These scarves, reminiscent of the voyageur sash or *ceinture fleché*, were a nod to historical authenticity and originally intended to secure the waists of windproof parkas, but they were quickly adapted as towlines for tired and trail-crippled snowshoers. Thelma Cunningham remembers bathing boys' feet, rubbing salve into open blisters and wrapping them, while thinking that it seemed terribly macho, in her estimation, to continue on these snowshoe runs "no matter what."

The masters would often look exhausted as well during the snowshoeing, but according to the St. John's way, there would be no giving in. When it worked according to plan, as with all well-tempered challenges, boys would rise through the physical adversity of snowshoeing, hopefully accessing higher levels of mental discipline that would bring out positive qualities, and build character—fortitude, perseverance, stamina, and, in the end, humility before each other and before God.

When David Cunningham arrived home exhausted from one of his first snowshoe runs, his mother and father quizzed him about what it was like. He told a tale of hardship and eventual triumph. As an afterthought, he added: "If you think it's hard running in snowshoes, you should trying getting down on your knees and praying in those suckers!" The image of praying on snowshoes would stay with David and his family for years to come. They still laugh about it.

Oz and Joan Mansfield had a camper van that was often used to transport boys on these early snowshoe runs around Lakefield. Like most parents, they knew only as much about St. John's as they had learned from school literature, the interview process, and the occasional encounters with school personnel when they dropped off their boys on Fridays and picked them up on Sundays. But actually joining in on the snowshoe runs allowed them to see changes in their son, Mike, which were largely positive. Thinking back, Joan says: "We really had no idea what they were doing, but after the first snowshoe run, he came home and we noticed a change."

The changes the Mansfields noticed in their son had to do with learning about teamwork on these snowshoe runs. Once you were part of that team, you lived or died for the group, she remembers. Joan, a teacher, was impressed with what Mike was learning. "He was a lot more considerate and started to see where other people were coming from. . . . The snowshoeing was the beginning of a gradual but pretty dramatic turnaround. You didn't necessarily get along with everybody, but one of the character-building things I saw was having to be part of these snowshoe teams. That was something new to Mike, and it made a difference."

For the big race on February 26, 1977, the Mansfields accompanied the boys to Lakefield. Oz and Joan slept in their camper. The boys stayed curled up on the floor of an Anglican parish hall in the village. The race was circular, crossing exactly the same terrain Ted Byfield had traversed as a student at Lakefield College thirty years earlier. Recalls Mrs. Mansfield: "There was a big map on the wall. They all had compasses, so many degrees out and then back. They started out in the dark and came home in the dark. I remember it was damn cold. But these guys were teachers. We trusted them."

As difficult as it might have been to bathe feet, dress blisters, and watch the boys deal with the challenge of snowshoeing, the parents were protected from the worst of what really occurred on these early snowshoe treks. The positive changes they saw in their boys at home gave them reason to carry on. As unspeakably difficult as the snowshoeing was for many of the boys, it built confidence and character. Their boys would be dehydrated and exhausted; their feet might be bleeding; they might have frostbite on their noses or ears, but they would bounce back. In the way of St. John's, survival bestowed on the boys the right to be proud of accomplishment, and maybe even to swagger a little, but always to remember the obligation to thank God for the strength to rise to the next challenge. Pain was a necessary part of the process, or so it seemed, though many of the boys realized at one level or another that there was something riskier going on.

For example, Mike Mansfield's snowshoeing team included

Paul Nyberg, who, as a result of his car accident, walked with a limp. Mike recalls:

> It was accepted that [James] Gibson and I would drag him along with our scarves. On narrow trails one would pull and one would push. And when this happens you carry on hour after hour and your imagination goes away with you. You just learn to set aside what you're doing, and to [go] somewhere [else] in your mind. So you're physically out with four or five guys doing something, but in your head you're somewhere else—walking to the Pole or you're lost in an imaginary world somewhere.

That was when things on the snowshoe trail were relatively easy. When it started to get dark and scary, Mansfield remembers, they experienced different emotions that were very much in tune with the real risks they were being asked to accept.

Snowshoeing at its worst, according to Mike Mansfield, was like Russian roulette with no empty chambers in the revolver:

> Spin the chamber, give it a squeeze, and see what happens. If someone had broken [a] leg on any of our trips, I don't know what would have happened. Nyberg was a really nice guy, but he had a really bad leg. So we're doing this snowshoe thing, he falls down again and again, and I'm wondering what happens if he breaks his leg. Or what happens if I fall down and break my leg? . . . You have to wait for whoever's coming in the car to get you. And then it's a toss-up if those parents are going to run down the trail in their street shoes or go for help. As far as I know, there were no flashlights. If shit happens, you sit there until 10:00 at night when they *might* come and look for you.

In truth, the boys were perhaps not as alone in the field as they might have thought. The staff of the weekend school, led by Mike Maunder and Frank Felletti, always accompanied one group or another on the snowshoe treks and were often assisted by volunteers—St. John's alumni and (later) willing parents, who very quickly learned that if they were to do this on a regular basis, they needed to train during the week to keep up with the boys and to avoid becoming temporarily crippled by the exertion.

In the classroom, the master's voice was law. As dictated in the early days by Wiens and Byfield, boys were to stand when a master entered a room and to address him as "Sir." On the trail, the masters would march right along with the boys, asking nothing more of students than they did of themselves, but perhaps overlooking the fact that the boys were eleven to thirteen years old and still developing physically, while the masters and volunteers were adults.

Among the volunteers on St. John's snowshoe runs were parents like Norm Bindon, who freely admits taking his turn on the scarves to haul flagging boys down a winter trail, often feeling in need of a tow himself late in the day. He articulated his beliefs in the name of character-building experience to boys he was helping along the trail. He recalls: "The snowshoe runs were set up to ensure that they came in pretty damn tired, but not in such a way [that] there was a risk factor. But when I was on the trail, I saw them struggling through it I'd attach a kid to a scarf to help him get up a hill, saying, 'It's not that it's easier for you, it's harder for me!' That was the team concept, all pulling together to meet the goal." Norm Bindon accepted the challenges of the outdoor program—even after Timiskaming—and continued to be a supporter of St. John's, eventually becoming chairman of its board of directors for a time.

Also among those who volunteered to help at the weekend school and on snowshoe runs were alumni from the western schools, including Richard Bird and Mark Denny, who left their respective posts as professor and first-year student at Queen's University in Kingston to drive to Lakefield or Toronto to give back to their alma mater. St. John's alumni remember Bird as the volunteer master with the Porsche, pizzazz, and the pretty girl-friend. He had been one of the boys at the Manitoba school in the 1960s, giving his time freely to the Ontario school, and working hard right alongside the boys. Denny was young, fit, and, as a relatively recent graduate of St. John's Cathedral School in Manitoba, not beyond some gentle cruelty on the snowshoe trail. One older boy remembers following Denny's tracks down the middle of a frozen lake near Lakefield and coming across little messages written with a bare finger into the surface of freshly fallen snow. "Aren't you really, really thirsty? Wouldn't a Coke go good now? Aren't you dying for a Coke?" As diversion on the never-ending hike, the notes were funny for a while, but when the boys sighted in the distance a glistening red Coke can propped up in the snow beside the trail, only to find that it was empty, the humor quickly went out of the gag.

Boys like Mike Mansfield might have had an inkling about the real risks in what they were undertaking on snowshoes, but their parents, unaware of the reality on the trail, did not know just how close these treks were taking the boys to the line between character building and disaster. The parents also did not know that earlier snowshoe treks in the western schools had gone terribly wrong. They did not know about Ed Milligan and his miraculous delivery from hypothermia death the year before in Winnipeg, nor were they aware of a snowshoeing tragedy that had occurred on a St. John's interschool snowshoe race in Alberta only six years previously.

Markus Windekilde Jannasch turned fifteen in the summer of 1970, and although he attended the Grammar School, one of the best schools in Halifax, he was not being challenged. His mother, Barbara, a psychotherapist, remembers him saying that he wanted more from school. He wanted responsibility. The Grammar School was not teaching him what he needed to know. "I want to become a man," he said to his parents, so they looked for other options for Markus and learned about St. John's Cathedral School in Selkirk. When the three of them went to Selkirk for an initial visit and interview, Barbara remembers Markus liking the school, especially the snowshoeing and the canoeing activities. She also remembers agreeing wholeheartedly with headmaster Frank Wiens when he said to them, during an explanation of the harsh philosophy of St. John's, "We think it is better to die in the woods than in front of a television."

To attend St. John's, however, was Markus's decision, a choice fully supported by Niels and Barbara. The school was tough, there was no doubt about that, but the academic standards were high, and the discipline of chores, physical activity, and adventure were just what Markus had been hankering for, or so they thought. That September, of his own volition, Markus packed his kit and headed west from Halifax to Winnipeg and north by bus to Selkirk to attend St. John's Cathedral School.

From the beginning, though, he was unhappy at the school. He could handle the academic curriculum and the chores, and he loved the physical activity and the adventure. However, as in most boarding schools where boy culture/boy rule exists separately from the structure and discipline of the masters, there was the systematic fagging of new boys, regardless of age, including the unsuspecting Markus. When he came home at Christmas, he told his parents that many of his classmates were bad kids, often bullies, who spent their time making life difficult for everyone else.

His parents said that he did not have to stay, that he could come home, but this was not an option for Markus. He knew that the second year would be better, when he would no longer be a new boy, and besides, the snowshoeing program was coming up after Christmas and he was really looking forward to that. So back he went to Selkirk.

Everyone participated in snowshoeing. Depending on age, the length of the culminating races varied from twenty-five to thirty-five miles or longer, and an eight-week practice schedule for each age group was worked out to build the boys' stamina and endurance. In the West, a tradition of an interschool snowshoe race evolved, pitting the best of the senior boys from the Manitoba school against the best of the senior boys from the Alberta school, alternating year to year from the flatness of the Manitoba prairie (where you can see the same steam plant for the entire fifty miles of the race course) to the rolling hills and woods of the North Saskatchewan River, west of Edmonton.

As a new boy, Markus was not eligible for the interschool racing team, but he showed great strength and aptitude for snowshoeing in the training runs, and, when one of the senior boys on the Manitoba interschool team froze his heel in training, school officials offered the fifteen-year-old from Nova Scotia an opportunity to go to Alberta to join the race. Markus was ecstatic, and wrote to his parents to tell them.

In addition to the competitive spirit one would expect from rival schools, heightened by the never-say-die philosophy of St. John's, the Manitoba school also faced the pressure of having lost the previous two races. A report on school activities in the *Selkirk Enterprise* dated February 3, 1971, just prior to the team's trip to Alberta, described the pressure that Markus and the other boys faced:

For two consecutive years the Albertans have won the race run on both occasions for 35 miles through rugged hill country to the north and west of their school. On both occasions Manitoba teams went west with the assumption that victory over the upstart Alberta school was a mere matter of course. In 1969 confidence appeared justified. The Manitobans took an early lead, built it up to a full mile, and maintained it to a point one mile from the finish line. Here one member of the team collapsed and Alberta came from behind to win.

A scant ten days later, exactly the same thing happened, only this time the boy who fell was Markus Jannasch. He collapsed the first time twenty miles into the race after pulling a failing teammate up a hill with his scarf. Team members were able to assist Markus to the next checkpoint, where he apparently rallied after drinking a cup of coffee. Knowing full well the St. John's team-work rule—that if one member drops, the race is forfeit—Markus dug deep within his resources to set out again on the trail with his Manitoba colleagues in full support. Notes in the *Edmonton Journal* indicate that he collapsed a second and final time only two-and-a-half miles farther on. Reports the paper, "His team mates tried to rouse him, shouting at him and then rubbing his face with snow. When this didn't work, the team referee, Stephen Weatherbe, a teacher at the Alberta school, said the boys slapped his face and then broke several ammonia capsules under his nose." At 9:50 that night, after being carried unconscious back to the school infir mary, Markus Jannasch died.

Two months later, an Alberta coroner's inquest determined that the cause of death was "cerebral edema and hypoxia of unde-termined origin but probably due to unusual stress and strain." The jury found no negligence on the part of the school or anyone connected with the event, but recommended that the school "consider changing the rules, on such events, so that a team is penalized but not disqualified through the inability of a single team member to complete such an event." During the inquest, coroner Dr. Max Cantor mentioned a benign lesion at the base of the boy's skull called a pituitary hamartoma that, he said, could have been a contributing factor, but was "most definitely not the major cause of death."

By the time the Jannasch death was mentioned in the 1970–1971 *Annual Report of St. John's Schools of the Prairies*, the focus of the story had shifted. Under a heading "After 13 Years, It Came" was written the following:

A dreaded ghost shadows each St. John's master in every moment of the outdoor program. It has accompanied him from the day the first St. John's boat ventured forth on the ominous expanse of Lake

Winnipeg. It has been his ever present consort through countless days and nights exposed to the ferocities of the prairie winter, along the rocky ledges of misty mountain passes, and down the tumult of a hundred swirling rapids. It is fear of the unpredictable—a sudden storm, a blizzard not forecast, a rockslide, a serious campsite accident, an illness beyond reach of help. Accumulated experience has multiplied the required precautions and thereby lengthened the odds. Yet every man has known that, with 14 canoe expeditions a year, 15 dog treks, seven snowshoe races, scores of day-long snowshoe runs, the odds would one day run out. Last year, the 12th season for St. John's, they did. But Markus Jannasch did not die on some desolate northern lake. He collapsed before crowds in the medically supervised inter-school snowshoe race, and died in the school infirmary attended by four doctors.

A coroner's jury later cleared the school of blame in the boy's death, but it did not attempt to explain it. Medical evidence introduced at the inquiry, however, gave a strong clue to the reason. The boy had a rare tumor near his pituitary gland, virtually undetectable by examination. In almost all studied cases, such a tumor was fatal before the age of twenty. Any stress could be catastrophic.

Nearly thirty years later, I sit with Niels and Barbara Jannasch in the sunny front room of their home overlooking St. Margaret's Bay on the south shore of Nova Scotia. Around us are photographs of Markus, a strong, handsome lad with dark eyes like his mother's. They speak to me of his growing up, of his love of adventure. Niels, a sailor on one of the last transcontinental commercial tall ships in the 1930s and a veteran of the German navy in the Second World War, tells some of the stories he had told Markus, including the one about a relative who was one of the original Moravian missionaries to Labrador, a man recruited in the 1840s by the British navy to accompany Captain Robert McClure on his vessel *Investigator* in search of Sir John Franklin. I hear of a boy for whom school in Halifax was tame compared to the rich life of boats and seaside trails near his home, a boy who, on learning of St. John's School in Manitoba, enthusiastically asked his parents for the opportunity to attend.

Says his mother, "Marcus wanted more. He wanted responsibility. Sitting in school didn't feel like it was getting him there, so we went out to the school to have a look. We agreed with Mr. Wiens when he said, 'We think it is better to die in the woods than in front of a television.' We fully agreed. So Markus went off to St. John's. It was difficult for me to let him go, but I knew that he was doing exactly what he wanted to do. It made all the difference for us that Markus chose to go."

Still, the aching sadness of losing their eldest son is evident as his parents reminisce. St. John's was not perfect for him, his mother recalls, but he loved the snowshoeing, and he very much looked forward to the canoe trip in the spring. He was so pleased that they let him join the interschool race, because they normally did not let new boys onto the team. "We were proud for him that he had made the team. When they called at midnight to say that he was very, very sick, it was raining very hard and Niels was out clearing drains. I remember they wouldn't talk to me, they would only talk to Niels. Two or three hours later, they called again to say that he had died. Our eldest daughter, Tina, heard the commotion and came down. She said, 'I'll make you a cup of tea. Would you like it laced?' It was a sad, sad day. Of all the emotions that surrounded us, I knew in my heart that Markus was doing what he wanted to do," says Barbara.

Getting to Alberta was a protracted process because of rain in the east and heavy snow in the West. "It's a good thing that Markus had died," Barbara says quietly, "because if he had been gravely ill while I was trying to get out there to be with him, I don't know what I would have done. I would have gone out of my mind."

When she arrived in Edmonton, a grief-stricken Barbara was met by school officials, who accompanied her to the morgue to identify her son's body after the autopsy. While arranging with a funeral director to have her son cremated, she vividly remembers, a woman quoted a price for cremation and added that there would be a discount because Markus was so young. Exhausted from the journey and struggling to absorb the shock of her sixteen-year-old's sudden end, she recalls thinking the cremation discount ludicrous, and looked up into the corner of the funeral parlor to see Markus laughing.

Because Barbara had missed the school's memorial service for Markus, Frank Wiens and the teachers from both schools spent the evening with her, talking about her son, the race, and the schools. They talked about dedicating the interschool race to his memory. She knew that Markus had been very critical of some of his teachers, but he had liked Frank Wiens, whom he felt was stern but fair. Barbara Jannasch had the impression that headmaster Wiens had a good idea of what he was doing at St. John's. She felt that she knew more about Wiens than some of the other masters, at least enough to speak candidly with him. That evening, even though she knew he would not want to hear what she had to say, she made her one complaint to Frank Wiens. "You have too much German militarism in you," she told him. Years later, she recalls: "At the Alberta school, the teachers were much softer. They didn't need the harshness that was in Wiens to do what it was they needed to do. Underneath the harshness in Wiens was the understanding, the heart, the longing, but it was sort of clamped together by this Germanness. It goes in the blood for a long time."

The emptiness in the lives of his parents left by Markus Jannasch's passing is barely filled by the memories of his short life and tragic death, leaving room for sadness. Life has gone on for Niels and Barbara Jannasch and their three other children, but, as welcoming as they seem and apparently grateful for a writer's interest in their son, gaps widen in our conversation. Niels disappears into the house and produces two pieces of Markus's artwork that were done in the year before he died. One depicts a boy walking his dog, as Markus had done. The other is a beguiling image of a boy on a rock, head down, reflected on calm water. Niels says little, yet holds them as if he can feel the touch of his son's hand. Barbara has had enough. "I must tend to my garden now," she says politely, but with clear and firm intention to exit the conversation. Reminiscing has sapped her energy. She waves from a wonderful tangle of greenery as I back out of their laneway.

The Ontario parents I interviewed knew nothing of Markus Jannasch and his death in a St. John's School snowshoe race. They recalled that once the initial snowshoeing program was finished in the winter of 1977, academic study continued in the weekend school, with the experiential part of the program shifting to door-to-door honey sales.

Honey donated by the western schools was bottled and labeled for sale as a school fund-raiser. Just as snowshoeing had engaged parents as a support network, honey selling provided opportunities for another group of parents to get involved with the school. The act of selling was also, surprisingly, a considerable challenge for the boys. According to school literature, honey selling was to yield "much more than just the $10,000 needed to purchase [permanent] facilities. It teaches the art of persuasion. It allows each boy to play an important part in the development of the school."

As a commercial pilot, Norm Bindon had time off in blocks that he could devote to volunteering with St. John's. On weekends in the early spring of 1977, he would drop off sons Dean and Scott on Friday night and then return to St. Jude's Church later to pick up a group of boys and cases of honey to sell door to door throughout various Toronto suburbs. Although Dean and Scott were rarely in his selling group, Norm realized that both boys, especially Dean, the older one who was fading in public school, were undergoing a noticeable change in attitude. Norm got into the selling as well, watching the boys run from door to door, setting challenges for them by giving each team member four jars and offering a reward for the first one back for more. Public school, it seemed to Norm Bindon, had undergone a diminution of challenge and a flattening of rewards for winning, for jobs well done. But within the ethos of St. John's his sons were actually participating in a process in which individual excellence within a team context was not only encouraged, but lauded. Snowshoeing provided one kind of challenge, honey sales another, and academics yet another. "There was always something that you'd be good at, and something you'd find difficult. A kid might have trouble snowshoeing, but maybe he could write, or sell honey." Little David Cunningham, for whom academics were unsuccessful, and for whom the snowshoeing had been a trial because of his diminutive stature, shone at honey selling. "Honey was a beautiful challenge for David," his mother recalls, beaming.

So it was that by degrees, through this process of volunteer participation in the activities of the weekend school, the parents became an integral part of St. John's evolution. They were not aware of everything that went on in their sons' lives at the school and, as in Norm Bindon's case, they might not have agreed with the corporal punishment administered when boys and masters were alone at St. Jude's, but what they saw of the St. John's way made them eager to turn the weekend school into a full-time, year-round operation.

The original plan, as outlined in "Wanted: 40 Boys to Build a School," called for the development of a full-time school at St. Jude's over a four-year period. The parish hall was old and run down, and had not been used for several years before the St. John's weekend school moved in, but it could be renovated into a full-time, year-round residential boys' school. However, as parents like Norm and Ruth Bindon saw positive and often dramatic changes in their boys, pressure began to build among the parents to shift to a full-time operation sooner rather than later.

Ian Harling's father, who was in real estate in the Toronto area, began looking for possible properties that might be more suitable for St. John's than the downtown location at St. Jude's. One property available for sale or lease was a huge, rambling house on a plot of old agricultural land near Claremont, Ontario, that had been used as a seniors' home. This, thought some of the parents, would be a perfect site for the full-time St. John's School. Driven by enthusiasm, determination, and vision, Maunder, Felletti, and various parents inspected the Claremont site and began serious negotiations to lease it. The money accumulated from honey sales and other fund-raising efforts, which was to have been put toward the purchase and renovation of permanent furnishings and facilities at St. Jude's, was now regarded as a nest egg for creating a school on its own secluded grounds just beyond the fringe of the city. Sometime late in the spring of 1977, a deal to lease the Claremont property for two years was secured. School personnel were elated.

The parents were buoyant and full of energy and goodwill. The boys had bought into the adventure model of learning and were beginning to see that however unlikely it may have seemed at the time to transform a fledgling weekend school into a full-time residential school over the course of one summer, St. John's was about rising to the challenge and doing the impossible. What the school might have lacked in money, organization, and orderly progression of a development process, it made up for with unbounded enthusiasm and naive zeal on the part of almost everyone involved in the process. Added to that was the dollar-a-day conviction that "God will provide."

Of course, the enthusiasm and commitment to build a full-time school at Claremont in large measure masked some of the underlying issues such as recruiting staff and students to fill this new school. Staffing had been a perennial problem at the western schools, but it was nevertheless assumed that just as Frank and Pat Felletti and Mike Maunder had been drawn from the western teaching ranks, so too would other core Company of the Cross members work at the Ontario school. As for recruiting new students, parents were encouraged to put out the word, and a new brochure was drafted to entice other parents and other boys to become part of the St. John's family. In a section at the back of this new twelve-page booklet, entitled "What Makes St. John's Unique?", something of the chaotic nature of St. John's is reflected in stories about snowshoeing, honey selling, cleaning, building, praying, and living the St. John's way. The brochure defends such chaos and sets out its religious philosophy:

> All of this effort often leads visitors to remark on the hive of organized and unorganized activity that surrounds them when they visit the school—the friendliness, happiness and obvious concern the boys show for one another. But it would be a mistake to observe the phenomenon and not search out its real cause. In the end, it does not come down to the boys and teachers and activities. It comes down to a Man who told us long ago—"Love one another. By this sign all men will know that you are mine, that you love one another." His love for each of us is deep and hard and unbending—as hard as a wooden cross. As long as this Love remains at the core of St. John's, it will be a unique and special place.

Built into the emerging ethos of the Ontario school were parents' assumptions that the hard-knocks, no-nonsense approach to schooling, combining a classical education and rigorous experiential adventure, had worked and worked well in the West. With so much to do, there was really no time for reflection. Mike Maunder and Frank Felletti, both having grown up at St. John's Cathedral School, believed that what they were doing was right. They had the courage of their Company of the Cross convictions and the confidence of success in Alberta and Manitoba to bolster their pitches to families in Ontario. As soon as the decision was made to move forward with the full-time school in Ontario, there was much work to be done.

That summer, boys scraped and scrubbed floors and painted, parents built simple bunk beds and cooked. A directory of Canadian corporate directors was divided up among the boys' families;

each parent wrote as many as fifty letters to request donations to help build the school. Letters were followed up with a phone campaign, also run by parent volunteers. Bert Hopkins, whose son, Tim, was one of the original boys in the part-time school, took time from his shifts as a fuel oil deliveryman to clear a ten-acre wood on the site of the new school to make a sports field. Unlike many of his classmates who were not doing well in public school, Tim, the youngest of the three Hopkins children, had asked to go to St. John's because he wanted to experience the adventure. People remember fair-haired Tim filling up a big plastic milk bottle with well water and taking it out to his dad. Bert would climb down from the tractor and relish a long, cold swallow. Tim would put his arm around him and introduce his dad to anyone who happened to join him on the water run. "This is my dad," he'd say proudly, before scurrying off to continue whatever the boys were working on.

At some point in the summer of 1977 there was a minor setback in the renovation process. Upstairs in the old house, where students were stripping paint, applying paint, or doing something near matches and solvents, a fire broke out near where eleven-year-old Chris Suttaby was working. By this time, Chris had had a whole winter of St. John's. His experience of the part-time school was quite different from the fantasy that he had imagined when he first saw the photos and heard Frank Felletti's pitch in the basement of St. Stephen's Church. Sweating it out with a paint scraper, being whacked on the backside for insubordination, addressing as "Sir" some of the weekend teachers for whom he could find little respect, praying while wearing snowshoes—all of this was a far cry from dog sledding in the pristine snows of the Rockies. "Not sure what happened," he says, thinking back. "I'm up there working, and next thing I know the place is on fire."

The fire did not gut the place, but the smoke and water damage was substantial. Crews of willing parent volunteers were quick to regroup, however, and to continue the building and renovation process. The insurance company was so impressed with the level of volunteer effort that it decided to match the value of this labor to help the school recoup losses that were not covered in the rudimentary policy written to get the school up and running. A portable dormitory from a lumber camp somewhere in northern Quebec was procured through someone's network of connections and brought to Claremont to provide accommodations while repairs were made. Work on the school continued, and the first year of the full-time Ontario school began with a canoe trip at the end of summer 1977.

Eight yellow, aging twenty-two-foot canvas-covered wooden canoes, paddles, and orange keyhole life jackets were borrowed from the Manitoba school. It was decided that the first canoe outing would be a trip in northwestern Ontario—Ear Falls, Ontario, to Selkirk, Manitoba, via the English and Winnipeg rivers, Lake Winnipeg, and up the Red River to St. John's Cathedral School at Selkirk—350 miles in two weeks or less. Without any preparation other than what some boys might have had at Boy Scouts or summer camp, the boys, staff, food, and gear were driven out to the trailhead, north of Kenora, again by willing parents, where forty-five boys and their teachers in two teams hit the river, several hours apart, one led by Frank Felletti and the other led by Mike Maunder.

To embark on a canoe trip of this length and level of difficulty with no swimming or canoe training was a calculated risk that was certainly *not* recommended by any water safety, canoeing, or camping organization at the time or since. Many camps would not take non-swimmers on overnight trips, with or without life jackets, and all institutions who were doing canoe trips would have insisted on on-the-water instruction in paddling rudiments, acceptable boat behavior, and safety procedures. But this was not the St. John's way. Learning on the fly, for staff and students, was part of the character-building experience.

In an interview prior to leaving, Mike Maunder was quoted as saying: "St. John's stresses 'old-fashioned values': honesty, perseverance, and achievement. The feeling these days is when it stops feeling good, chuck it. But you can't do that on a canoe trip. Everybody will face failure at some point. They will be helped by other people. Then it's easier to understand what other people are going through." And then, in words reminiscent of Ted Byfield in the early days of St. John's Cathedral School, Maunder continued: "People have always had to face difficult things—the war, the Depression, the non-electric era. This generation lives in luxury and that's good, except that by facing the difficult they learn fortitude, determination, and commitment. They learn you have to experience pain to develop compassion."

On Thursday, September 1, 1977, just as Ontario public school students were beginning the long weekend before starting another school year, the Toronto *Globe and Mail* published a feature article about the St. John's School canoe trip. Occupying most of the top half of a full newspaper broadsheet was a photograph of four twenty-two-foot canoes in formation. The boys are paddling more or less in unison in their keyhole life preservers, they are sitting high up off the water, in some cases their hips almost a full paddle-blade length above the sinewy, smooth surface of the Red River. The steersmen of the four canoes sit perched not on the rear seats of the craft, where the designers from the Chestnut Canoe Company expected them to roost, but on the stern decks where they appear to need paddles much longer than those of the boys to reach the water and effect a steering influence on the motion of the boats. Each of the four canoes, borrowed from the Manitoba school, is emblazoned with the name of an explorer—John West, Rob Wallace, La Vérendrye, and Isaac Jogues—beside the distinctive white cross of St. John on a red background shield. Most of the boys are looking up, anticipating the end of a 350-mile wilderness ordeal.

In the article, one thing is clear about the nature of the trip as described by the boys to writer Peggy McCallum—there was not much that they particularly enjoyed about the adventure. Under a headline "The fun was proving it could be done," the boys related all kinds of hardships of which they seemed intensely proud and satisfied. Tim Pryce said that the worst for him was when people started to fall asleep in the canoe. Andy Hermann said that falling asleep was not a problem for him; it was waiting for the wind to calm down, trying to dry a sleeping bag, and starting out at four in the morning that he found the most disagreeable. Dean Bindon thought the worst part was when one of the teachers put powdered potatoes into the tea instead of powdered milk. Others talked about sleeping on the ground with sheets of plastic instead of tents for cover, endless portages with 250-pound canoes, 30-pound backpacks, and porridge you could "cut with an ax." One boy said it had rained every single day. But even after all that—Dean Bindon admitting to Ms. McCallum that they might have been coached on what to say to the press—the boys were of one mind that the trip had been worthwhile. "After all, we made it, didn't we?"

In their recollections of the Ear Falls expedition, boys who were on the trip admit that the physical challenges—the bugs, the rain, the long days—have faded to some degree, but they recall the other risks of the outing, particularly the waves on Lake Winnipeg. Chris Suttaby is sure they were out in eight-foot waves and says he was very scared on the big lake. "You just do as you're told and paddle." Ian Harling chooses not to estimate wave height, but gesticulates with his hands, his eyes widening as he remembers, and says, "When you went down into a trough, all you saw was water, and when you came up on a crest of a wave, all you saw was land. These were twenty-two-foot war canoes. That's how big the waves were." Knowing little or nothing of details from other St. John's trips on Lake Winnipeg, this journey that ended well became a reference point, a norm for these St. John's boys. But looking back with the wisdom of years, they wonder if they should even have been out there in the first place that August in 1977.

The *Globe and Mail* article included a second large photo taken during a lunch break at Lount Lake, east of Lake Winnipeg. It shows canoes pulled up on a gently sloping whaleback rock and at least ten boys lying exhausted on the shore, sound asleep, their heads propped up on the thick keyhole life jackets, the soles of their new runners tipped up to the sun, drying on their feet while they slept.

But for all that, as any canoe trip leader knows, the difficulty of this trip was the element that gave it pedagogical potential. Everyone on the Ear Falls trip may have found individual challenges difficult or not, but they had faced this adversity together. They had shared the experience and met their goal.

Bill Patterson, leader and founder of one of the longest-running adventure programs in Ontario public schools, the Mackenzie High School Trekkers in Deep River (downstream from Lake Timiskaming on the shores of the Ottawa River), knows from experience that his students tend to remember the most difficult canoe trips. "As far as I'm concerned," he says, "there are 'M' days and 'F' days on canoe trips. Some people may think that 'M' stands for miserable and 'F' stands for fine, and in fact they do, but it turns out that miserable days are the most memorable and [the] fine days you tend to forget. Those are the times when you're dry, and there's lots of food, and . . . the bugs aren't bad, or when you're getting along with everyone. You remember the miserable times . . . when kids have to dig deep to find the resources they need to cope with what's happening. Ideally, when they dig down, they find what they need to see themselves through or, if they're coming up short, this is when their peers and the leaders can pitch in and lend a hand."

By any account, there was plenty of "misery" on the Ear Falls trip, lots of "M" days that made the trip memorable. Having been on this route before and having spoken to other leaders who had done the same, Mike Maunder and Frank Felletti knew exactly what they were getting into. With the exception of no training or pre-trip instruction, it was the perfect expedition to get things under way at the full-time school. There might have been trips like this in southern Ontario, but, being new to the area, Maunder and Felletti opted to go with a route in northwestern Ontario that they were familiar with. It might have been a long way to drive, but this too would be part of the adventure. And, to boot, they would be able to borrow St. John's Cathedral School's canoes. It was a tough trip, but not too tough, and ideally suited as a first canoe trip for the inaugural class of the St. John's School of Ontario. In addition to providing a cornucopia of individual tests for boys, hoping, as Maunder told the *Globe and Mail* writer, that "everybody will face failure at some point," the trip provided a common challenge for the class as a whole that would allow students to bond, to become one, as they began the fall term.

Looking back on the early St. John's canoe trips—with Timiskaming as an exception—Ian Harling's mother, Joanne, captured something of the sense of accomplishment the boys felt following those challenging expeditions. "Those boys came back taller than tall. They just said, 'Look what we did.' It made my heart sing to see those kids so proud. They walked proud. They could walk tall just knowing what they had done. That was the essence of St. John's."

With everyone returning more or less intact from the English River trip, even if there were precious few stories that suggested to the boys' families that the outing was in any way enjoyable, there was reason to think that the trip was difficult by design as was the St. John's way. Parents may even have recalled the school recruitment brochures that said these physical challenges were not designed as a recreational program. Canoeing and snow activities were designed to "confront boys with hardship and adversity and show them how to pull through." If nothing more, the expedition reinforced in parents' minds the understanding, established through the snowshoeing program, that boys could be exposed to substantial risk with really nothing to lose and only character traits like honesty, perseverance, achievement, fortitude, determination, and commitment to gain. How close the boys might have come to irreparable harm or how well the leaders understood the level of hardship and their role in creating it on the English River canoe trip, one can only guess. The canoes they were using were known.

The route they were traveling had been paddled by previous St. John's School brigades. Everyone came home from the trip.

Through the flurry of summer building and the hasty planning for the English River trip, Maunder and Felletti knew they needed staff for this full-time school they were creating. Desperate for staff in Canada, the Company of the Cross in the West had worked through the Anglican Church in the United Kingdom to recruit young masters. This effort had yielded modest results. Several young British men, familiar with the notion of hard-knocks public schooling, came to Canada for adventure and the dollar-a-day recompense for their labors at St. John's School. Hence, as the small staff from the weekend school took their places at the head of classes in September 1977, they were joined by Peter Cain and Neil Thompson, two of the British recruits who had moved to Ontario from the Alberta school. Cain, twenty-seven, had been in the British army for a time before coming to Canada, and Thompson, twenty-four, was idling out of school and looking for experience and adventure overseas. In addition to the regular teaching staff, there were, of course, the parent volunteers who continued in a variety of supporting roles, as well as the two alumni from St. John's Cathedral School, Richard Bird and Mark Denny, who came up from Kingston from time to time to assist on weekends when school began in September.

Almost miraculously, the transition from part-time to full-time school, which was supposed to happen over four years, happened in mere months. In September 1977, after less than a year of development, the building that was to house the full-time school was far from perfect and there was much work yet to be done, but it was adequate to start with. The sports field was not yet ready and the school had no canoes of its own, but it had students, teachers, a building, and a cadre of willing parents who had been part of the process since day one.

To combat loneliness and the possible problems of homesickness in boys who were in residential school for the first time, the students were cloistered at Claremont for the first six weeks of the fall term. They were not allowed to phone or go home for that period in the hope that they would settle into school routines and become accustomed to the unofficial norms of boy rule in the dorm. During the week, with cooking and cleaning chores on top of a heavy academic and physical fitness program, there was little time for anything other than working through the curriculum and school schedule. But weekends were another matter. It was a bit of a scramble, as it had been all along with so much going on in creating the school, to keep the boys entertained. But Mike Maunder and Frank Felletti managed to find things for the boys to do, taking all of them to the Markham fall fair, giving each of them five dollars and telling them to spend it however they wished. Some bought food and tickets for midway rides. Others bought cigarettes and settled in for a day-long smokefest. David Cunningham turned some of his money into change and talked to his friends and family on a pay phone.

In addition to the challenges of the outdoor program and academics were cooking and cleaning chores that the boys were forced to do on pain of swats, public belittling, or other consequences for bad behavior. Some fought the chores for much longer than they should have, trying to avoid work as much as possible, while others took to them with relish or resignation. This was a devious way of keeping costs down, as St. John's had known since the beginning in Selkirk, but it was also a way to build responsibility. The boys, just like the parents, were an integral part of the infrastructure that built St. John's School of Ontario. Some, like Chris Suttaby, took the responsibility and leadership they were given—in Chris's case it was leading a kitchen crew—seriously enough to allow them, or their parents, to say later that this aspect of the school had made a significant difference in shaping who they became.

And so the year progressed, norms were established, and lessons were learned by all. At one point in the year, David Cunningham came home for a weekend and, as he was getting into the bath, his mother, Thelma, noticed welts across his lower back. She had understood that punitive swats with wooden paddles were applied to the buttocks, so she was horrified to see that David had been struck and marked in the vulnerable area over his kidneys. She went directly to Frank Felletti and insisted that the offending new master be admonished.

These swats for David and other boys had become routine and, in some cases, preferable to other punishments they had endured from their teachers in public school. It was better to clear the air with six of the best on the backside than to undergo days or weeks of haranguing from teachers. And there was no doubt, even in Thelma and David Cunningham's minds, that the strict discipline of St. John's had had something to do with sorting out the "twelve-year-old monster" they had first sent to the part-time school. He was still mouthy and getting into trouble, but he was reading, writing, doing chores with his chum, Chris Suttaby, and developing new friends in his dorm. Best of all, he was excited about school. On weekends he would sometimes bring friends home from St. John's and they would go to the Ontario Science Centre where David's father was the head engineer. On a Saturday morning, young David and his pals would roam the museum prior to public opening, trying out all of the interactive exhibits and reporting to David's dad the location and nature of any malfunctions.

On May 3 of that first year of the full-time St. John's School, however, life changed for David Cunningham. They had planned to go to the Science Centre that day to sell honey for the school, but in the morning his dad was not feeling well. By mid-morning his father had been taken to hospital by ambulance, and later in the day he was dead of a ruptured aneurysm.

The family was devastated. The people of St. John's supported each other like an extended family. The parents and staff of St. John's, as well as the congregation of St. Stephen's Church, rallied around Thelma Cunningham and David and his brothers and sister. David Cunningham, Sr., was quite a bit older than the other parents, but his passing was nevertheless a shock to everyone concerned.

Most of the people who attended David Cunningham's wake and returned afterwards to the Cunningham house remember that this was the first time Richard Bird and Peter Cain started discussing where the Junior Brigade might go for their end-of-year canoe trip. It was a way of breaking the tension of the moment, especially for young David, who was unable to come to grips with his father's death. They talked about a swashbuckling French explorer called Chevalier Pierre de Troyes, who made his way up the Ottawa River in the seventeenth century and attacked the unsuspecting British on James Bay. They talked about a trip that would be even harder than the Ear Falls expedition of the previous summer, a trip that would begin on a big lake called Timiskaming.

IV

The Process: A Double Standard

Nineteen seventy-seven would be a good year. As the boys moved their belongings into brand-new plywood lockers, and tucked clean flannel sheets under new mattresses on rudimentary wooden bunks varnished by volunteers in the hot days of the summer, they did so with a sense of camaraderie lingering after the canoe trip. There were boys in the school now who had not participated in the part-time school, but they had all been on the English River canoe trip together. They had all faced the trip's various challenges, and they had prevailed. The portable dorm from the Quebec lumber camp (brought in after the fire) and living spaces inside in the refitted old nursing home outside Claremont hummed with hard-won pride and expectation. Soon enough, the masters would check this flush of enthusiasm with academic adversity. As the school year began, the character-building process was already well under way.

The St. John's way was to restrict phone use, ban radios and televisions, remove all outside influences, and establish school rules and norms in the first six weeks of term. Boys were allowed to communicate with their families, but they had to do so by letter. Getting school schedules and routines established took time, and it was a process that did not always sit well with the boys. The formal and often severe separation of masters and boys, which Mike Maunder and Frank Felletti had learned from Ted Byfield and Frank Wiens at the Manitoba school, had to be established in order for the system to work. One way or another, boys had to learn to conform. Instead of the adversity of the trail, there was now the challenge of old-school discipline. If a boy would not capitulate, the masters would apply a stick repeatedly (the number corresponding to the offense) across his buttocks. At the Manitoba school, the stick was sometimes called the "stretcher," a term coined in the old days when boys would be stretched out over the thwarts of cutters on Lake Winnipeg to receive their punishment. The name stuck. The universal diminutive for physical punishment was "swats."

Mike Mansfield roots through his mother's garage in Cochrane, Alberta, as we talk about his experience at St. John's. He pulls out a piece of wooden baseboard about eighteen inches long and proudly shows me scrimshaw, in blue and black ink, along its dusty length. It's a souvenir, he says with a grin. He tells me the story of how he and his close friend, Peter Knight, on that first day of the full-time school in Claremont, were egging each other on to see how far the masters could be pushed. "We were probably being total jerks," he continues. But as would happen time and again as the year progressed, master Peter Cain reached his limit with Mansfield and Knight that first day and asked them to find a stick that could be applied to their backsides. Knowing from experience that an implement of insufficient length or thickness would be discarded, Knight and Mansfield searched until they found an old piece of baseboard, left over from the renovations, and received their punishment from Mr. Cain. But, as was the case with this sort of punishment, when the swats were complete, all was forgiven and everyone got back to work with no lingering malice. As this was the first official swatting in the new school, everyone, including Peter Cain, signed the swat stick and Mansfield, as the instigator, received it as a memento of the occasion.

While history had shown that corporal punishment had little long-term effect on the behavior of pupils, and that correlations could be drawn between the incidence of beating at residential schools and the incidence of bullying, St. John's persisted with this somewhat arcane practice. Boys like Ian Harling and Tom Kenny, who had had trouble all along in their schooling, told their parents that they actually preferred this get-it-over-with-quickly form of retribution. However, Kenny, like most of the smaller boys in the class, suffered the anticipation of swats as much as the punishment itself. In a daily diary that Tom Kenny kept, he mentions an early "swat test" in Mr. Cain's French class, in which every boy except one received three swats on the spot for failing. This part of the disciplinary system Kenny appears to have accepted and understood, but when the punishments continued at the dinner table, he wrote: "At dinner Mr. Cain said that he won't have any conversation, if he says to do something, you do it No 'but sir.' Do it! So he has been swatting people for that a lot. He has been mean all day and I expect he will be tomorrow too."

But that was part of the St. John's way—living the rule of strict discipline around the clock. The formal curriculum for grades 7 to 10 included lessons in literature, grammar, spelling, mathematics, science, history, French, Latin, and public speaking. When the Ontario school was established, the Trivium/Quadrivium nomenclature was gone, but certainly not the conservative spirit of Dorothy L. Sayers's "Lost Tools of Learning," which was alive and well within the cloister of St. John's. In the calendar describing those first classes at the full-time school, the learning expectations are set out in the following manner:

Classes are small and a unique combination of formal and informal. Students must stand and address adults as "sir." Arguments are encouraged [the stick notwithstanding] and good logic applauded. St. John's believes that the object of education is to teach a boy to think clearly and to express himself correctly and even eloquently. To accomplish this, St. John's has returned to several old fashioned ideas. St. John's courses are structured: students pass or fail depending on regular exams and tests. For younger boys, drill and exercise is stressed to learn the basics. Older boys with good ability are pushed considerably beyond their normal limits. Homework and study are essential.

Boys are taught to make their own notes. Notebooks are regularly marked. Discipline is strict and the standard punishment for misbehaviour is a spanking with a paddle.

Throughout the day from 7 a.m. to bedtime at 10 p.m., classes, meals, study periods, sports breaks, dorm inspections, chapel services, and choir practice would be separated by cooking and cleaning chores, which were done on a rotating-crew basis. When they had a few unstructured minutes, the boys were free to roam outside on the school property, develop pictures in the darkroom, play cards or board games—do anything other than listen to the radio, read newspapers, watch television or, heaven forbid, head into town to hang out (not that there was anything like a mall in tiny Claremont). During any part of this highly compartmentalized day, masters were free to indict and swat boys for any infraction, real or imagined.

Living together in more or less the same space—the single masters lived on the third floor, Frank and Pat Felletti and their new baby lived in a house next door—there had to be some flexibility to this seemingly ironclad system of rules and rough justice. At the founders' discretion, "rowdy time" would be called and the boys and masters would engage in an all-out rumble outside or in the dorms. At rowdy time, all bets (within limits) were off with the masters. It was fair game for Mike Mansfield to use his considerable teenage bulk to tackle Mr. Cain and have little Tom Kenny or Peter Knight pile on for good measure to administer a knuckle rub on Mr. Cain's thinning blond pate or to give him a "pink belly" in the best tradition of boyhood antics. On one occasion, the howl of Mike Maunder stopped the boys in their tracks; Bindon I (Dean, the older brother) had inadvertently smashed the assistant headmaster in the nose, leaving him bloodied and smarting with pain. As often as not, though, it was the boys who ended up with various cuts and bruises, having been bounced off one of the hand-hewn bunks or dropped onto the corner of a locker after being pitched unceremoniously through the festive air. Inevitably, someone would finish the day in tears.

Ian Harling describes rowdy time this way:

> Here and there, when things were getting out of hand, they would call rowdy hour and we would go nuts and beat the crap out of each other. Instead of the school clamping down on everybody and being jerks about what was going on, they [took] us out and [ran] us ragged. And then we'd all come back to a rowdy that the teachers were all involved in! It was the one time that you *knew* you could jump a teacher and put him down, and do whatever you wanted to him, until they yelled stop.

As the boys became comfortable with dorm and school routines, the perennial game of cat and mouse began. The idea was this: If a master caught a boy in the act of breaking the rules, then he was obliged by convention to dole out the appropriate punishment. However, the game between boy and master sometimes became finding ways to make sure a confrontation never occurred. Such was the case with David Cunningham's penchant for listening to baseball games on the radio.

Having radios was forbidden, everyone knew that. Within the first weeks of school, little David had been found with a crystal transistor radio under his pillow and was beaten accordingly, but he persisted. When he was allowed to go home after the first six weeks of class, he came back with another crystal transistor set that was, in due course, found and confiscated. He was swatted as a result, but still he persisted. Eventually, the masters would wait until he had fallen asleep with the little plug tucked into his ear and simply confiscate the radio without even waking him. Thelma Cunningham remembers that by the end of that first term, Frank Felletti had about seven of David's transistors in his desk drawer.

The same rules applied to smoking. Like many teenage boys

given the opportunity to leave home and explore, even within the somewhat close confines of a boarding school like St. John's they would try cigarettes. Like listening to the radio and a host of other offenses, smoking was punishable with swats and/or extra duties, but the masters were not always on duty, and they certainly could not be everywhere on the school grounds at all times. Smelling smoke on boys' hair or clothing or on their breath was impossible for many of the masters because they themselves smoked. So the game of cat and mouse would continue over smoking as well, the boys doing their best to be discreet and the masters doing their best to be diligent but not too diligent in enforcing the rules.

Chris Suttaby fondly remembers the game of cat and mouse in the smoking area. To this day, he still has no idea how headmaster Frank Felletti found out where they were smoking, but he remembers an uncanny ability on the part of Felletti, whom they came to call "Tricky Woo," "Tricky Phil" or simply "Trick" (after the character in James Herriot's *All Things Bright and Beautiful*, remembers David Cunningham), to catch them in the act of smoking from time to time, just to keep them honest. When it was cold, the boys would slip the hooded woolen capotes they used for snowshoeing over their pajamas and escape to a dark corner among the cedars outside the dorm for a smoke. Chris remembers that they never really paid attention to who was out there. They would often just stand there in silence, smoking. On this occasion, the lads had had at least one cigarette, and were lighting a second when a hooded figure in the shadows at the corner of the little smoking area flipped back his capote and said, "Ah-ha! Gentlemen, what have we here? What have we here?" It was Trick, living up to his nickname.

By all accounts, headmaster Frank Felletti was different from either of his St. John's Cathedral School mentors, Ted Byfield or Frank Wiens. He was full of energy and enthusiasm, he had a charismatic charm, but he had been a St. John's boy, so he knew most of the antics from the inside, from the boys' perspective.

Teamed with Mike Maunder, who carried with him the program ideas and the wherewithal to see them through, Felletti was an excellent leader. The fact that the full-time school got up and running years ahead of schedule was due not only to the extensive parent support network and the cadre of boys who did the work, but also to the leadership of Maunder and Felletti. Maunder was stern and businesslike, but he had heart and was predictable in his creative approaches to teaching. Felletti, by contrast, was scattered. The boys never knew where he would be or what he would do next in moving the vision of St. John's forward. Recalls Mike Mansfield, "Getting a straight answer out of Trick was like nailing Jell-o to the wall. He was intense on just about everything [but] things weren't always what they seemed."

The system of law and order set and enforced by the masters was what one might call the visible curriculum. There was also a hidden curriculum within St. John's. As with most boarding schools, going back to the very early days of British public schools, two parallel disciplinary structures existed within St. John's. There was the system set up by the school itself and administered by the masters. Among the boys themselves there was a different and often harsher code. Quoting a ten-year-old in *The Old School Tie*, his 1978 book about the history of the British public schools, Jonathan Gathorne-Hardy makes the point that this system of parallel justice should be expected in an educational context in which corporal punishment prevails. "The bigs hit me, so I hit the smalls; that's fair" was what the boy said. And that's more or less what happened in the St. John's dorms, although size did not always determine one's place in the hierarchy.

Gathorne-Hardy contends that as long as there have been private residential schools, there have been masters who have chosen to overlook this parallel system of boy rule. "Anyone who has been at a school knows that a cruel pupil is more to be feared than a cruel master," he writes. Boy rule, out of which grew the organized process of fagging and eventually the prefect system, is a fact of residential school life for all, especially the smaller, weaker members of the dorm: "The big boys forced the smaller ones to be their slaves, beating them up if they refused or did their jobs badly." The upshot of boy rule in the St. John's dorms, often similar in intent if not in tone to the brutality described in Gathorne-Hardy's book, was that boy rule was as effective as master rule, and often more so (depending on the master), leaving some less respected masters to enlist the support of unofficial dorm rulers to exert influence on the student body as a whole. It was another version of cat and mouse.

"There were four or five of us who ran the dorm that year," says Ian Harling, looking back. "Chris Bourchier was my bunk mate and we were really close friends, and there was Dave Cunningham and Chris Suttaby. It wasn't mean or anything, but it was the one thing at St. John's that you [could] get away with. We ran the dorm. It was our dorm until someone came up and beat us for it. When something came up, we had to go first. If you were a rookie (i.e., didn't attend the part-time school) or [if] you were weak, it was a little bit tougher at the school for you because you had to do what the dorm leaders said. Rob Doak—we called him 'Mother Doak' because he was always cleaning up for us—he was one of the people who had to keep our beds neat. This way, I could sleep in until five minutes before inspection time. I'd roll out and Doak would have to neaten up my bed. That was the way it worked."

Sometimes, when the two systems of justice intersected, interesting scenarios could result. Saving face was crucial, remembers Bruce Christie of his year in St. John's Cathedral School in Manitoba. Humiliation was the name of the game, but often it would backfire. He remembers Mike Maunder as a young master publicly beating Bruce's older brother in front of a study hall for stabbing a wood tick with his math divider. "Break the will. And somehow . . . breaking the will . . . [one would find] God. I was never sure about the connection," says Christie. He recalls their science master, Frank Doolan:

He would go from being friendly, almost sappy, to getting into power struggles with some of the boys [when] he would have to save face. There was a story that he was on a canoe trip with Ted Byfield and some of the students. Late one night, those boys heard Doolan say, "Ted. Ted, would you get me a glass of water." I don't know if he said it or not. But basically the St. John's guys just wanted to crucify him for wimpishness. You've got to realize that in a school of 110 people, you hear every story several times. Storytelling was what we had. It didn't matter if *Gemini* was flying to the moon, we didn't know anything about it. No newspapers, no radio, no TV, but we did have our stories. [There was] another master, who taught us English I heard stories that he lost face too many times and had some kind of mental breakdown, at least that's how people talked about it. Not everybody lasted.

Jim McKay remembers his days in the early 1960s at the Manitoba school when some of the bigger boys were terrorizing his dorm by chasing boys around with an ax. Frank Wiens intervened and suggested that chasing people around with an ax was inappropriate, and that if they had an issue to settle, then they should go behind the barn. That they did, and in the process, McKay broke his hand on another boy's jaw. As a result, Wiens insisted that the boy with the offending jaw sit beside McKay at meals for the next few weeks, while Jim's hand was in a plaster cast, to cut his archenemy's meat. Character building though this may have been, to this day McKay thinks this punishment was heavy handed.

As he looks back on his years at the school, what Jim McKay most regrets is the application of disciplinary rule that he had learned from his masters at St. John's. He was captain of a Grade 10 snowshoeing team and took his newfound responsibility seriously. At one point in the multi-mile run out on the windswept ice of Lake Winnipeg, a member of his team became tired. He fell again and again. Encouragement to get up became verbal haranguing, which led, some would say inevitably given the disciplinary context in which they were all situated, to physical abuse.

"I got a little brutal with him," says McKay quietly. "He was lying down wanting to die, or saying he wanted to die. I don't feel good about this, but I used a stick on him . . . I regret this incident more than any other, but to this day—there were no masters on this run—I think that kid would probably have died."

St. John's was established within a quasi-Christian context wherein God empowered the masters, the masters ruled the big boys, and the big boys ruled the little boys, who, in turn, were encouraged to appeal to God for help to face the challenges of the day. The belief that people were fundamentally flawed but could be improved through discipline promoted abusive power relationships. Beating someone for misbehavior was not necessarily good, but, as a means to the end of building character, rough justice was tolerated—even expected or encouraged—inside the generous frame of the notion that what does not kill a person will make him strong.

Chris Suttaby remembers becoming chief of his kitchen crew and heaving commercial kitchen whisks at his workers to get them to wash the pots faster. He would verbally harass them or do whatever it took to get the job done, emulating the leadership strategies employed by his masters. Although the antiquated notion that masters know all and boys know nothing had been tempered by the time the Ontario school opened, St. John's School of Ontario allowed boys to reapply the behaviors of one's masters—abusive or otherwise—to one's work crew charges or snowshoe team members. When the time came to lead, Chris Suttaby's techniques of leadership might have been crude, but they were based on what he had learned from his masters and, in the end, they were effective. As a leader, he was right there with his crew—as his masters had been with him in the canoes on the Ear Falls trip—and he asked of his crew nothing that he himself was not prepared to undertake. This leadership experience on the kitchen crew would become the basis of his success as a pressman and team leader in a huge printing plant north of Toronto.

But the Christian messages were mixed. Mansfield remembers praying to the Almighty for good sales, then going door to door selling honey that year, having been told that the goal was to raise money to build a school for the future, but knowing full well (through his mother who helped in the school office) that the money raised on a weekend was often used to buy groceries on Monday. God would provide, they were told at chapel and in daily meditations. "I thought they took that whole thing a bit too far," said Mansfield. Mostly he remembers little sermons about character, courage, valor, kindness, persistence, humanity, and brotherly love, and wonders why it was that the only black boy enrolled in the school was teased mercilessly about his race out of earshot of the masters. The boy did not come back one Sunday night after a weekend at home. "There were people there who should have put a stop to it. This was completely contrary to the stated goals of Christian tolerance and churchifying. Hypocrisy. Double standards. It was accepted practice to say one thing and do another."

Some educators argue that it is the formal, visible curriculum that makes all the difference in achieving the desired ends of a pedagogical process, while others maintain that it is the context—the so-called hidden curriculum—on which ultimate outcomes depend. Which type of rule affected boys individually likely varied from boy to boy. It may have been the visible curriculum that affected the boys who ran the dorm and the hidden curriculum that affected the boys whose lives were controlled by masters and dominant classmates. But there can be little doubt that a variety of messages were conveyed to students by the St. John's School context and that there were a variety of outcomes. There may have been more to the hidden curriculum than any of the masters ever knew or imagined.

While traveling in the vicinity of the Manitoba school on the flat prairie north of Winnipeg, it dawned on me that on snow-shoe runs in this area, the scenery very likely did not change for twenty-five, thirty-five, or even fifty miles. Initially I had assumed that these long snowshoe runs were a physical challenge, which they most certainly were, but with this relentless sameness to the scenery, the mental challenge to finish must have been equally difficult. When I asked alumni about this, the answer was surprising. Rick Wiens wrote a story as part of his adult therapy called "The Secret of Lemons," in which, ironically, he talks about thirty-two-mile snowshoe runs on the flatlands around Selkirk at −20°F as "glorious release" from the "suffocating, mind-numbing, stultifying routine of classes taught by . . . dogma mongers." While out stomping on their snowshoes, Wiens and his team members would buy candy in the village of Clandeboyne and lemons in Libau, which would slowly freeze in their pockets and serve as bitter relief from the tedium of the task at hand in the final stretches of a Wednesday afternoon race. The psychological challenge of the experience is something that he has never been able to shake. Whatever character-building potential his father and the other St. John's staff hoped there might be in snowshoeing was lost on son Rick. In "The Secret of Lemons," he writes:

It is easy to freeze a lemon. You just leave it in your parka pocket and the job will be done. It is just as easy to freeze yourself. Our keepers did not believe that the fickleness of the elements should be any deterrent from the rigid program they had prescribed for us. If it was Wednesday, it was snowshoeing and that was that. If your team—we were always divided into teams so that we would learn the vital nature of cooperation and patience required in having to travel at the rate of the slowest member—had chosen a route that was full in the face of the current gale blowing, there was no changing. You must accept what God had provided. One Wednesday, the temperature was seventy-two degrees below zero Fahrenheit with windchill. Even an Eskimo would stay at home. Not us. We went out. Tom Oldham froze his ear so badly, he nearly lost it. When it first thawed out, it

swelled to the size of a grapefruit, another member of
family, no doubt with secrets of its own. I shared a dormite
him. His moans and cries of pain in the night were piteous. But
his own stupidity, according to our keepers. He just hadn't dre
properly. I must admit, after that they decided they really must have
proper dress code for these activities, but it was still poor Tom's fault.
The hypocrisy and irony never struck me until much later that in their
environment of incredibly strict rules, where almost every moment
was governed by some rule or other, it was only when something
went awry [that] it was our fault. Our keepers could never admit that
they had planned poorly or screwed up.

Rick Wiens goes on to talk about "too many lads who froze
their penises" walking against the wind, and a variety of other
untoward events on snowshoe runs in the 1960s. One of his classmates talked about regular bouts of "institutional diarrhea" and
how tending to this and keeping clean on the snowshoe trail at
−30°F was a laborious and often painful challenge. Paying attention to boys' perceptions of the challenges of snowshoeing might
have given St. John's masters clues that their snowshoe runs were
crossing the line separating constructive challenge and physical
harm to their young charges, leading to anger, resentment, and
potential for irreparable harm.

Bruce Christie, who was at school with Rick Wiens in
1965–1966, remembers very clearly Ted Byfield's espoused view
about the value of a boy's opinion. When a boy presented a point
of view or an argument contrary to the party line, Christie
remembers, Ted Byfield would bellow. "When you're older,
you'll have an opinion, but in the meantime, you don't know
anything, so shut up and listen to what I say." He adds, "That's
what it came to. Of course Mr. Byfield was charming enough to
say that with a smile on his face."

But the fact remained that what St. John's masters thought they
were doing in the early days and what was really happening to

were not always the same thing. Rick Wiens's essay, about his experiences snowshoeing in the 1960s, could ʌnsidered another sketch of his father's dogged determina-ʌ to push boys beyond their limits, another snapshot of staff ʌot fully understanding possible consequences of these enforced activities, what Barbara Jannasch would later call an excess of "German militarism."

By contrast, old boy Bruce Wardrope, who is now a successful Winnipeg interior designer, encountered another perhaps unintended—certainly unexpected—outcome of his snowshoeing experiences at St. John's Cathedral School. As an adolescent, Wardrope had been sent to St. John's in the 1960s to socialize a bit more with boys of his own age. In public school, he was a loner, and when he was not at school he spent what his parents felt were inordinate amounts of time alone in his room where he drew and exercised his designing impulses and artistic sensibilities in private. So off he went to St. John's, where it was hoped the residential experience would bring him out of his shell a bit. There was very little in the way of an arts component in the St. John's curriculum; free time was taken up with chores, church, choir, and other imperatives. The dorm was a boisterous, noisy, often violent place to be, not the ideal locale for artistic endeavors. However, on the snowshoe runs around the Selkirk school and, to a lesser extent, on big lakes on the canoe trips, boys like Bruce Wardrope could settle into a pace, ticking off mile after mile, hour after hour in an unchanging scene, and retreat totally into their imaginations. Snowshoeing, which the masters thought would be an impressive physical challenge to build endurance and mental discipline, was for some of the boys a psychological opportunity and a venue for creative thinking, once they worked through the pain. The cadence of crunching prairie snow and the sound of leather moccasins sliding on babiche harness, the squeak of varnished wood—these would be a passport to cross over into the recesses of memory and imagination. Wardrope felt that there were more

St. John's alumni than one might expect, given there was no real arts curriculum, who chose careers in the arts and culture. He, for one, thought that the snowshoeing might have had something to do with that.

Not everyone accepted the rules and values at s J s o. Parents wondered, for example, how it was that the masters could be so insistent about cleanliness in the dorms when the staff quarters on the third floor were an absolute shambles most of the time, complete with dirty laundry, drying socks, and empty beer bottles. Others railed at the sexism in the assignment of roles for the parents. The women in particular were always relegated to subservient cooking and cleaning roles, while the men, with Maunder, Felletti, and the rest of the staff, were involved in decision making. And still others wondered why boys would be swatted for being late while the masters could start things whenever they happened to be ready. This was especially galling on dark and frosty weekend mornings when parents were asked to be at the school at 7 a.m., only to wait for a couple of hours until the masters were ready to get the snowshoeing under way.

The fall term came and went. After the six-week initiation period at the start of term, the boys were permitted to go home on weekends and for Christmas and, almost a year after the opening of the part-time school in St. Jude's Church on Roncesvalles Avenue in downtown Toronto, the full-time school resumed in 1978.

Going back was difficult for little Tom Kenny. He had enjoyed the fall term, but the connection to family back in Markham was strong, and weekends with his gerbils amid the simple comforts of home always made it difficult to return to the discipline of school. In a diary entry for January 6, 1978, he wrote:

> Today was a great day. I played with the gerbs & didn't think much about school. But when the time [came] to leave home I began to cry

a little. I went into the laundry room & prayed that I would not cry & God would give me courage. It worked all right. I didn't cry again at all. When I got to school there was snacks & when the parents had left (with a notice) there were announcements. Then I went to bed happily. P.S. I am now on Infirmary crew.

For Tom Kenny, who used to hide his report card from his parents because he knew his performance was substandard, St. John's seemed to bring out the best. Reading and writing were never his forté at public school, but these were activities that became part of his daily routine at St. John's, including almost religious devotion to keeping his thoughts in a pastel-colored Hilroy 990 exercise book from Woolworth's. Tom's father fondly recalls his son explaining that there was no time in the day to make entries in his diary, so after lights-out in the evening, he would slip into a stall in the bathroom, where there was light, sit on the toilet, and write down his thoughts for the day. Entries from the diary reveal a boy's impression of the second full-time term at SJSO.

Jan 9/78 This morning I was in my term 2 lit class for the first time. I guess it was pretty good but Mr. Claydon only made me & O'Gorman do what we learned in Term I. I also snowshoed for the first time today and my snowshoe came loose once or twice, otherwise it was fun & easy. Mr. Felletti said it would be hard & I would hate it. Tonight Mr. Maunder announced that someone had placed a cigarette package and some other objects which he didn't want to mention on Knight's pillow. And we will know if the person owned up or not because we will not get any music in the morning if he doesn't own up. P.S. Other than Mr. Maunder's announcements it was a great day as usual. P.P.S. The announcements made me sweat and get very scared as I usually am due to announcements like that one. Just forgot something. Tonight Mrs. Felletti's bible study group was taken out of study for our class. We went on the third floor and said some prayers [instead of doing homework]. I am now writing this during the extra study I get because of that class.

Jan 10/78 Today was okay. I was really scared that Mr. Maunder would kill me because no one owned up to placing the cigarette box & other article on Knight's pillow. At lunch Mr. Maunder told us what the other object was & made us look at it. It was a piece of toilet paper with crap on it. Disgusting! I am afraid I will not get my homework done for tomorrow, and then . . . BANG! BANG! BANG! I prayed that I would get it done, and I have faith that God will help me to get it done. I am now in the dining room with Flint who is writing a play for fun. It is lights out now upstairs. I pray again now in my diary that God will help me get my lit done for tomorrow. Amen. P.S. Please answer . . .

Jan 12/78 Today was good. I didn't have all my homework done but no one found out so I didn't get swatted. I took out the book *Star Trek* which was really good. Then I took out *The Day of the Jackal* when I was finished *Star Trek*. I brought *Dracula* back. I think *The Day of the Jackal* is a bit too hard for me yet so I'll take it back and take out *Lassie, Come Home* instead because my dad said it was a good book. P.S. I'm looking forward to going home on Sunday, especially to see the gerbs.

14 Jan/78 Today was good. We went up to the snowshoe place but the weather was too bad. You couldent see 4 ft in front of your even from in the van. So we went back to the school and ate all our munchies on the way back. At the school we went either on a short snowshoe run or stayed at the school and shovelled snow (at least that was the rumor). I went snowshoeing & it was pretty good.

Jan 19/78 Today I got a lot of swats (4 I think) but none in the 5 beat swat test. Mr. Cain was in a better mood today. We had library period today and I was going to read *Lassie, Come Home* but I couldent find it. So I read *The Time Machine* by H.G. Wells. Tomorrow we have another test on memory work. I don't have my math or french done, but I will I hope. I understand reducing fractions but I just can't do them (probably my times tables). It was a good day except for swats. P.S. I cheated in history and copied Gibson's work. P.P.S. I found *Lassie, Come Home.* One more thing I remembered is that we had communion and I didn't go because I had been play with two other boys.

Jan 21 Today we went on the first real snowshoe run. It was pretty hard but I managed not to stay at the end of the line, except near the end when I was feeling really sick. When we finished the long run I threw up in the back of the van and also in the snow back at school. I couldent eat any dinner. I also couldent think how I got so sick but now I know it was because I ate an orange peel on the run. I won't do that again. P.S. One good thing about the snowshoe run is that we got a great breakfast. We had no lunch . . .

Jan 28/78 Today the school went snowshoeing, it was really hard and some teams didn't get back to the school until 2:15 in the morning. Mr. Felletti said it was the hardest run the school has ever done. But it was very beautiful also. Branches covered with ice and sun shining through, and the branches forming great domes and arches. P.S. Bindon I and Carmichael cleaned up the infirmary for me.

Feb 4/78 Today was easier than the last snowshoe run. I guess my muscles are building up. The master who came with us was Mr. Saunderson & and all he can say is "fuck." He even let our team captain smoke cigarettes. Our team captain fell into the water up to his waste & we had to wait one hour while he dried up in someone's house and we froze outside. P.S. Mr. Saunderson (who's really still a boy who used to go to the Man. School) said he would have brought some pot if he knew there were no masters coming. Pot makes you grow he said. I also found out that Goodwin (our team captain) got 25 swats for selling pot.

Feb 16/78 This morning I got up at 7:00 and wasn't feeling very good. A few hours before Michel had vomited on the floor. Then I barfed. When Mr. Duddy came down at 10:30 he told us to stay in bed for the day as we were sprawled all over the hall floor. During the day many more people entered the infirmary. We had to make the junior dorm quarintine and Jensen worked for me because I was sick. I was one of the worst cases. I just kept vomiting continuasly. The doctor saw me and said don't eat anything. I had a temperature of 38.

Feb 18/78 I got out of the infirmary this morning & was on duty all day. Most of the people are out now but I still got help from Bourchier II. Tonight I was being really silly & acting out stuff to entertain the boys in the inf. I also did impression of other people. They thought I was a really good actor and said this was way better seeing me act than see the movie. We were having so much fun that we mist the first 5 min. of the movie. The movies tonight were good first we saw "Laurel & Hardy" in the army, which was subperb & then we saw a hilarious movie called "No Deposit, No Return."

Sun. Feb 19/78 Today I went home and cleaned out the 2 gerbs cages. After that we went to the zoo because they were having a party. There was no parking charge, we got in for half price, and when we went in there was a big parade but we missed it. And there were people dressed in funny costumes & shaking everyones hands. . . . We went back to school after. But Daddy was talking to Mr. Skinner and he said he wanted it to be his sons choice if he stayed or not. Daddy said it was my choice but I knew it was a big decision and let Mom & Dad make it. . . .

After all of the snowshoeing practice through January and February, many of the boys were fitter than they had ever been. Hockey fanatics like Ian Harling and James Gibson, who arrived at the school in excellent physical shape, still spent any spare moments playing shinny on the frozen pond behind the school. Others just waited for the physical exertion of Saturday to arrive, as they did from week to week through the eight weeks of term.

The final team race from Port Perry Yacht Club to Lakefield was held on Saturday, February 25. Many parents were in attendance to encourage the boys. Todd Michell's father, Jim, fired his twenty-gauge shotgun to start the race and the boys were off. Like many of the parents, the Michells had been extremely pleased with the progress their son had made at St. John's. Todd, a dyslexic, had had endless problems in public school, but at St. John's he had not only developed confidence through activities like snowshoeing but also greatly improved his ability with language. When his mother asked him what had raised his marks, he replied, "Mother, it was a one-by-two-inch stick." The boy for whom reading was a chore was apparently now reading for pleasure and, unbeknownst to his parents until later, actually starting to write poetry. Like the rest of his class, Todd awoke at 4 a.m. that Saturday morning to do his utmost in the 1978 final snowshoe race of the year.

Tom Kenny picks up his version of events in his diary: "It was awful hard & the juice breaks were one of the best than you could see or want to get. I almost started crying, but I held most of it back. O'Gorman cried a lot & we had to pull him along on a scarf. Even if we came in second last we still know we tried our best. The winning team get their names engraved in the trophy."

Around Easter, Mike Maunder left quietly for the Alberta school and a master, Paul Gazin from Alberta, joined the Ontario school. No one said much about it, although some of the parents, especially in retrospect, wondered why this capable leader and cofounder of the school was transferred during the critical last few weeks of term. Who made the decision? Why was it made? Was it because Maunder and Felletti were not getting along? What could be so horribly wrong at the Alberta school that one of the two principal people, one of the cornerstones in the fledgling Ontario school, would be relocated? Did the Company of the Cross not care about the English and history courses Maunder was teaching in Claremont, or about educational continuity for the boys, or would this just be another surprise challenge, another spurious exercise of authority, another act of hubris on the part of the St. John's administration?

After snowshoeing, the challenge of honey selling continued, even without Mike Maunder to help direct it. The newfound confidence that some of the boys had developed through the winter had manifested itself in some surprising ways. The Cunninghams and the Hopkinses were called one day to meet with Frank Felletti to discuss a grave breach of the rules involving their sons, David and Tim. It seems that these two scallywags had created a game played during honey selling that had nothing to do with selling honey. The game was to use the bathroom in as many houses as possible along one's honey-selling route. And to prove that one had actually been in the house, one had to snitch a small souvenir from the vanity as evidence of entry—lipstick, hair clips, whatever was handy. Unfortunately for David and Tim, the women on that particular street all played bridge together and were chatting at their next bridge night. When one mentioned the strange disappearance of a favorite tube of lipstick, another did the same, and another, and another, until they started puzzling over what had happened and came to the conclusion that the only thing they all had in common was the arrival on their doorsteps of nice young lads from St. John's who sold them honey and asked to use the facilities. They contacted the school, which in turn invited the parents in to discuss the matter. "I remember sitting there with David, feeling like a couple of idiots," recalls Thelma Cunningham, who did her best not to laugh when young David was hauled up on the carpet to receive his swats for stealing.

The unexpected death of her husband in May 1978 had left Thelma suddenly alone. Her older children were grown and gone and her youngest—the miracle child, the baby they thought she could never have—was away at school. Having made such a contribution to the school over the months since David had first heard about St. John's, she too had become part of the St. John's community. It was only natural that members of the St. John's family would cluster around her in the wake of her husband's passing and help with the pain of grieving.

Just as parents and staff had been there for Mrs. Cunningham, the masters and boys of St. John's were there for young David as well. On his return to school after burying his dad, the boys were drawn together and David was asked to come forward. "Bend over," commanded the master. Young Cunningham knew, like the rest of his peers, that emotion was not something to be tolerated at St. John's, even if it was your father who had passed away.

Instant obedience was expected, so he bent over for swats, only to be greeted with a chorus of laughter and great guffaws. The joke was on him. This was the St. John's way of saying "Welcome back." As he straightened up, boys came forward with gifts of a soccer ball, baseball bat, and a glove. Mark Denny, whose first year at Queen's University had come to an end, presented David with a gift—the lacrosse stick that had been given to him by boys at the Manitoba school after his father had died while Mark was a student, seven or eight years before. There was security in the family of St. John's.

V

The Boat as Teacher

In Alfred Lord Tennyson's epic poem *Ulysses*, the old salt recalls a lifetime at sea and reflects on the power of these experiences to shape a man's soul. He has seen the world and survived a variety of experiences, but he has also confronted challenges that have tested his ability to persevere physically and mentally, to be brave and patient, to be bold when circumstances require tenacity of spirit, and to meet nature and human nature with humility and respect above all else. As he says, "I am a part of all that I have met; / Yet all experience is an arch wherethro' / Gleams that untravell'd world whose margin fades / Forever and forever when I move." For the aging sailor, a life at sea has taken him back and forth between the known and the unknown, over the threshold of adventure and through a rite of passage that has, in the end, proffered simple truths and enduring wisdom he feels compelled to pass on before he dies. Nowhere in human enterprise is the notion of quest—preparation, separation, tribulation, and return—better exemplified than in a sea voyage, the boat as a vessel of discovery for all who sail her. *Ulysses* is but one of many renderings of humankind's fascination with boats and their potential to build character.

While St. John's may have drawn from traditional British public schools and the inspiration of Dorothy L. Sayers for its educational practices, its belief in the value of boating and canoeing experience can be traced back, through Ted Byfield's experience at Lakefield College School, to Kurt Hahn, the German educator, who believed that it was only through service and serious adventure that young men would develop the character needed to become contributing members of society.

Born in Berlin in 1886, Hahn grew up steeped in the classics, Greek mythology, and, in particular, the writings of Plato, which eventually led him to found Salem, a school in Germany, in 1920, where the notion of building whole persons—building character—was paramount. The principles of Salem were set out in seven laws: (1) Give the children opportunities for self-discovery; (2) Make the children meet with triumph and defeat; (3) Give the children the opportunity for self-effacement in the common cause; (4) Provide periods of silence; (5) Train the imagination; (6) Make games important but not predominant; and (7) Free the sons of the wealthy and powerful from the enervating sense of privilege. In due course, these Seven Laws of Salem would have a catalytic effect on the use of boats to develop education that would go beyond academic achievement and influence students' attitudes, ambitions, and perceptions.

Salem thrived through the 1920s and early 1930s, as did other German youth movements, notably the Hitler-Jugend, which was formed in 1936. The common thrust of all these initiatives was nurturing self-effacement in the common cause, building strong minds and bodies—in short, inculcating character. But in 1933, having spoken out against Hitler's congratulation of five young soldiers who kicked to death a young communist, Hahn was arrested. After his release, he left Germany for the United Kingdom, where he established a similar school. At Gordonstoun School on the Moray Firth, near Elgin, Scotland, boat work was an integral part of the curriculum, training that would at once develop mental acuity, physical fitness, technical skills in seamanship, and compassion through sea-rescue service to the local community. Among the first students at Gordonstoun was a young prince of Germanic stock, Philip, who transferred from

Salem, and who would go on to marry Queen Elizabeth II and become the Duke of Edinburgh.

When war was declared in 1939, Gordonstoun was moved—largely because of the strategic importance of the Moray Firth for Allied shipping—to a temporary home near Aberdovey on the coast of Wales, where the idea of sea training became the central focus in the school. Hahn became increasingly concerned about what he called the "three evils facing modern youth"—the decay of care and skill, the lack of enterprise and adventure, and the loss of compassion. In the small harbor at Aberdovey, Hahn launched a series of lifeboats he brought down from Scotland, which could be rowed or sailed, and he purchased a small schooner, the *Prince Louis*. In a search for funds to help establish this relocated school, Hahn contacted Lawrence Holt, the owner of a large shipping firm called the Blue Funnel Line, who was very much taken by Hahn's idea of building character through experience on the sea.

Coincidentally, Holt made the observation that when his and other merchant ships were torpedoed by German U-boats in the North Atlantic in the early days of the war, it was invariably the younger sailors who perished in the open boats, even after surviving the initial submarine attacks. These more technically trained but less experienced younger sailors appeared not to possess the stamina or toughness of the older sailors, who had been trained by direct experience in open boats. In conversation with Hahn, Holt, himself a sailor, became convinced that, if left to their own devices in a simple boat on the sea, young men would develop not only a relationship with the wind and weather but also a reliance on their own resources. Holt helped Hahn's school at Aberdovey on the condition that Hahn would create a twenty-one-day course (the typical length of one tour at sea for merchant sailors) using his small boats to instill spiritual tenacity and the will to survive in young seamen. Using a nautical term that describes a ship leaving the safety of the harbor for the hazards of the open sea, Hahn called this new educational enterprise "Outward

Bound," a name and an idea that would become synonymous over the succeeding decades with building character through risk and adventure. Not surprisingly, Hahn turned to Tennyson for the motto of Outward Bound—"To serve, to strive, and not to yield"—a variant of the last line of *Ulysses*.

As one of the pre-eminent British-style preparatory schools for service in the navy, Lakefield College School near Peterborough, Ontario, had two ten-oar cutters very similar to those used at Aberdovey. From the boathouse on Clear Lake, members of the school's Navy Cadet Corps would row and sail these sturdy wooden craft farther and farther through the Kawartha Lakes, developing boat-handling skill, weather-reading abilities, physical fitness, discipline, and the ability to push through fatigue and exhaustion as they fought their way home, often in the dark, against the prevailing westerly winds. Among the boys affected by these experiences was, of course, a teenaged Ted Byfield, who attended Lakefield through the middle years of the war. As with every residential school, there were rivalries in the dormitories that were often played out in challenges of speed and endurance with the cutters on Clear Lake. Byfield loved the idea that the winning dorm gang could be determined by performance in the boats. The competition was spurred on by the honorary chairman of the school's board of directors, a vice admiral of the Royal Canadian Navy.

And so it was when they established their school in Winnipeg in the late 1950s that Ted Byfield and Frank Wiens sought and found a derelict navy cutter through connections with the Navy League of Canada. After renovating this twenty-five-foot wreck with new wood, oars, and oarlocks, it seemed obvious to Byfield that rowing cutters up and down the Red River and out on Lake Winnipeg would be the same for St. John's boys as it had been for him and his dorm mates at Lakefield. Through rowing in the Kawartha Lakes, he had come to the conclusion that using sea craft in inland waters was not dangerous.

Not one to do things by half, Byfield planned an ambitious first trip for this cutter, christened the *St. John*—a 300-mile journey on lower Lake Winnipeg. He sat on the stern deck of the craft as coxswain, faced the preteen boys as they pulled the oars, and goaded them into line as they rowed through wind, rain, and broiling sun. According to a report in *A St. John's Scrapbook, 1957–1982*, "the boys rapidly acquired responsibility, a concern for each other and a maturity uncharacteristic of youngsters." A headline in a Winnipeg paper on their return read, "Choir boys triumph over lake." At the time, Frank Wiens was quoted as saying, "I learned more about boys on that trip than I'd learned in eight years in the public schools." What Wiens and Byfield appear *not* to have learned from these early experiences in boats on Lake Winnipeg was that for some of the boys (Wiens's son, Rick, among them), the cutter experience was a setup for failure. As Rick Wiens noted, "Who in their right mind would send an eight-year-old on such a venture under conditions and requirements that guaranteed failure?"

Rick Wiens has spent much of his adult life coming to terms with what happened to him at the school of his father's co-creation. Writing to the *Winnipeg Free Press* on September 18, 1999, on the occasion of publicity about a St. John's School reunion, he made the following observations about the St. John's way:

> Its mould was one-size-fits all, singularly lacking in imagination or even the simple recognition that boys are different, and what is simple for one can be absolutely soul destroying for another. . . . Some boys flourished and I say good for them. Some died a little each day. . . . How many times did we hear Ted Byfield hollering: "The trouble with you guys is that you never lived through a war or a depression," as though the accident of our birth was our fault?

But it was looking back on the cutter experiences on the Red River and Lake Winnipeg that Rick Wiens remembered with most angst. It was there, as an eight-year-old, that he was pushed to his limit and beyond. He writes:

The day I reached down for something I'd been told would always be there [but it] wasn't, was the first day of a long sojourn in hell for me. . . . Our teachers' anger and rages directed at us, though, were for our benefit, "our own good" and were, in fact, righteous indignation. We would understand the difference when we were older.

What self-serving claptrap! What a convenient way to justify their beatings and abuse and make us feel guilty at our own resulting anger. And all under the careful wrapping of Christian dogma. Ridiculous as it may sound, a part of me waited for the grand day when I would see the difference. It would be an obvious milestone of adulthood. It never happened, of course, because it was a lie. That didn't stop me, though, from feeling that somehow I just hadn't made it.

I failed in one of my earliest tests at St. John's. I was a scrawny, weak, under-sized eight-year-old in a 25-foot, 2,000-pound navy cutter rowing from Grand Forks to Winnipeg down the Red River and I couldn't do the tasks assigned me. I was punched, ridiculed and sworn at by my crew mates the whole trip. I was a failure, and being a failure was always my greatest fear.

Responding to a *Free Press* article promoting the St. John's reunion written by Mike Maunder, Wiens took particular exception to Maunder's contention that joy in life was what St. John's developed more than anything:

I was only eight years old when I first thought that, perhaps, the best thing for me to do to deal with my perceived inadequacy was to end my own life. And as I was continually confronted with what, for me, were well-nigh impossible challenges, pointless or otherwise, that option eventually became a daily question. I learned to deal with it in strange ways. I was also glad when I heard the adage, "Most men lead lives of quiet desperation." I figured it must be this way for everybody, this was one of the hidden secrets of growing up, so I just had to tough it out, it was part of the program and you just never said a word! I didn't contemplate my demise all the time; I laughed, I played, I did my work, I kept my desperation quiet. But at least once a day, usually just before I went to sleep, I would mentally measure the distance between myself and my suicide. If I was more than five steps ahead, it had been a good day. I did this for 27 years.

Bruce Christie, another St. John's old boy, saw Rick Wiens's letter in the *Free Press* in 1999 and spent a sleepless night mulling over his memories of St. John's and debating whether or not he should respond in writing to the paper. In the end, he chose to respond. A few days after Wiens's letter was published in September 1999 under the headline "Anger, disgust over St. John's remain," Bruce Christie, himself a successful schoolteacher in the Winnipeg school district, mentioned recollections that included a story about his trouble with reading and Ted Byfield's response:

> I had documented troubles with reading comprehension and Ted Byfield used to assign us at least 20 pages a night of reading Winston Churchill or Thomas Costain. I repeatedly failed the quizzes and took my swats on the behind in stride. Finally, he assigned me to a reading program with Mike Maunder, as Mr. Byfield claimed he recognized my struggle. Mr. Maunder chose the rather simply written public school text as the source of remedy, and I was able to read and interpret its essential themes. Mr. Byfield decided that I had been faking it—something he announced in front of 30 other students. After class, he led me down the hall to an office where he methodically beat my bottom six painful swats. After the beating, I told him that I had read my history, to which he uttered, "Baloney!"

Wiens and Byfield moved quickly to acquire more boats. With the help of friends and volunteers from St. John's Cathedral in Winnipeg, they built a forty-foot sailing vessel, the *St. Peter*. As with many projects at St. John's that were hastily conceived and executed in a flurry, it was realized at some point in the process that the craft was too large to pass through any of the doors of the building in which it was being constructed. On the day the vessel was to be launched, a portion of the building's roof had to be removed and a crane used to lift the wooden vessel from the building to the muddy waters of the Red River. But no sooner had the *St. Peter* been commissioned than Ted Byfield had his "we're-using-the-wrong-boats" epiphany at the Manitoba legislature and in the early 1960s the school switched to canoes, when St. John's Cathedral School was moving from weekend to full-time attendance.

Not totally unaware of the physical risks of boating on Lake Winnipeg, St. John's published an essay entitled "Lake Winnipeg: Tribute to a Tiger" in the 1966–1967 *Annual Report* of the Company of the Cross. The author (likely Ted Byfield) writes about the sinking of the fish freighter *Suzanne E* and the tug *Teddy* that year on Lake Winnipeg, two separate incidents in which crews drowned. He goes on to ask what St. John's School is doing out on Lake Winnipeg, offering the reader the following in reply:

> For one, the school's canoes do not go "out" on Lake Winnipeg; they run along the shore. Here only the on-shore winds are dangerous and these would only wash an overturned canoe up on the beach. Then, too, the water is warm; the survivor of the *Suzanne E* clung to floating debris all night in October. St. John's boys must wear life jackets at all times in the boats. Finally the lake stands athwart the canoe routes from west, north and east. Expeditions from Fort William must run the last 50 miles of the southeast shoreline. Expeditions from Hudson Bay and Edmonton must cover 250 to 300 miles of the coast.

The writer goes on to celebrate the elemental and historic link between the boat and the lake, and to consider the inherent risks of canoeing. But implicit in the essay is the conviction that to confront these risks is to reap their benefits in terms of character development. And in a final passage, with brimstone zeal, the idea of death as a consequence of character development is faced:

> Into those waters in a thousand years men numbering hundreds have plunged and lost their lives—Crees and Nor'Westers, Scots and

d scores of those to whom no particular name applies.
:ome and today the little pleasure boats of Winnipeg
ore deeply into the lake's alluring north. And we at
n our life preservers, check the weather, trim the
e worst and pray that it doesn't occur. For years to
ur yellow boats may be known around the lake's
g shoreline.

die who ventures out upon Lake Winnipeg, and
o dares to set out to swim. But what of the child
l? For him, there are other deaths, more dread-
eal so silently upon the soul. They are deaths
and into which no inquests are ever called.
y they are everywhere. They occur in thou-
usands of television sets where thousands of
r want of those very charms, those very
e so bounteously stores.

de to switch to canoes in 1962, Wiens
estnut Canoe Company in Frederic-
ered three twenty-six-foot "Ogilvy"
estnut Brothers along the lines of a
y family, a venerable line of New
'Ogilvy" had proven itself to be a
ough to be carried with relative ease.
aneuverable enough to negotiate
he keel to be stable on big lakes, yet
without scraping. But for reasons
r—"It might have just been for the
field later recalled—they specified
g that an additional three inches of
des. Always pleased to meet the
dified the twenty-six-foot "Chief"
'Ogilvy" style, and in subsequent
eeboard to their twenty-two-foot
vy" style, calling this the "Selkirk"

group paddling canoe in honor of the special order from St. John'
For Wiens, the Mennonite farm boy from the prairie, and Byfiel
the Navy League cadet, who knew little of canoes, compared
cutters these craft were simply a more historically authentic ve
in which to expose their charges to the bounteous dangers of
lake. No one acknowledged that these custom craft might
dangers of their own. History would indicate that this migh
fact, have been the case—not just the dangers inherent i
canoe as a type of vessel but the risk of modifying a canoe wi
any real understanding of what adding three inches of free
might do to the performance of the boat.

Like all canoe-building companies in Canada and the
England states, Chestnut was happy to meet a customer's n
modifying their existing line of canoes. For big retail op
like Eaton's or the Hudson's Bay Company, it was commo
tice for a canoe company to make small adjustments on bi
such as installing wooden slats instead of more expensiv
on bow and stern seats or putting on fewer coats of finis
prices down. But more substantial alterations were possil
that included adding or removing wood to the forms
steamed cedar ribs were bent, in the early stages of
canoe, that would allow the finished width of craft to b
or decreased. In the case of the canoe orders from
schools, Chestnut took their original twenty-two-fo
Special," described as "so straight on the bottom and
side to side that it skims over the top of the water
through it," and increased the length of the cedar
than three inches on either end. Longer cedar batten
around a building form to meet new inwales, i
inches beyond the standard positioning, and new le
pieces were added to either end of the craft. Th
modified canoe to meet St. John's needs.

As Byfield and Wiens had done before, guided b
would show them the way and that character
St. John's went forward into its canoeing pro

research or exploration into what other programs were doing with children in big canoes. Although there were almost no schools in Canada with canoeing programs as such, summer camps across the country—including Y M C A Camp Stephens and Manitoba Pioneer Camp, both based in Winnipeg—had been canoeing for decades, and had developed along the way substantial instructional technique and technical know-how. Had St. John's personnel done more homework, instead of just forging ahead through trials and errors of their own, they would have discovered that, since the summer of 1926, camps had been intensely wary of programs involving multiperson canoes on big lakes.

In July 1926, ten boys aged fourteen to nineteen years and one leader, twenty-six, perished from drowning and hypothermia on Balsam Lake, not far from Lakefield, Ontario, where Ted Byfield would row cutters as a boy. The circumstances of this case are stark and tragic. The boys went to a leadership camp at Long Point on Balsam Lake run by an organization affiliated with the Anglican Church called the Brotherhood of St. Andrews. The two-week camp that was to have a curriculum of games, duty, and devotion was, according to a report at the time, "based upon the idea that there is an age, between the teens and later twenties, when something of this nature is needed to hold a boy's attention." The boys would live in tents, engage in campcraft and water activities, and would be instructed by various volunteers, led by camp director and veteran Arthur Robert Shea-Butcher, thirty-one, a member of the Mississauga Horse Regiment, who had been orderly to Sir Arthur Currie during the First World War. Shea-Butcher had carried the Allied colors into Mons and had been decorated three or four times for bravery in the line of duty—but he had never learned how to swim or canoe.

On the first night of the camp, July 21, Shea-Butcher and a group of boys climbed into a borrowed thirty-five-foot semi-racing war canoe made by the Peterborough Canoe Company to paddle ten miles across Balsam Lake to the town of Coboconk for supplies. As some of the crew besides Shea-Butcher were non-swimmers and unfamiliar with the canoe and the activity of paddling, they turned around and returned. But on the second fateful night of the camp, July 22, about 7:30 in the evening, Shea-Butcher, another leader, and thirteen boys loaded the big canoe and headed out into Balsam Lake. Somewhere in the middle of the lake, about two miles from shore and too far from the camp to be seen with the naked eye, the canoe upset. Whether this was from a sudden gust of wind on an otherwise calm summer evening, or from a novice paddler "catching a crab" (a paddle) on the water and shifting position, is not clear, although there was a tendency for some newspaper writers (as there would be with Timiskaming fifty years later) to concoct a violent storm to overturn the canoe. There was likely no storm. In any case, the big canoe upset. It had no air tanks, sponsons, or flotation chambers, and, as a canvas-covered wooden hull with its own buoyancy quotient, settled into the lake right side up with gunwales about a foot under the water. Even if they had rolled the canoe over in the water, catching a little air pocket underneath, the gunwales would still have been submerged and the painted outer hull would have been impossible to grip. Either way, in order to take advantage of the small amount of flotation afforded by the canoe itself, the crew would have had to remain totally immersed.

As the sun was setting, after only thirty minutes in the water, cold started to take its toll. Try as they might to swim with the canoe toward shore, the task seemed impossible. And splashing out the water seemed not to be an option either. They cried out for help, but were too far from land to alert anyone. The first to lose his grip and begin sinking was eighteen-year-old Oliver Mardall, a payroll clerk at the Wrigley chewing gum factory in Toronto. During the first few minutes in the water, as they struggled to right the canoe and move it toward safety, Mardall shouted words of encouragement. With everyone spaced out around the canoe, any one survivor could see only one or two others on either side. Those toward the ends of the canoe and on the opposite gunwale could only be heard when darkness fell.

Camp adjutant Arthur Lambden described to the *Toronto Star* that twice Mardall sank and twice those on either side were able to pull him to the surface, but when he let go a third time, he sank never to rise again. "There was no outcry, no plea to the others to save him. Completely exhausted, he sank without a word and I think that only I and Shea-Butcher saw him go. The others continued to struggle, shouting words of encouragement to one another. Happily those in front had not observed that Mardall had gone."

As adjutant Lambden went on, he described Shea-Butcher, a non-swimmer, struggling to come to terms with this desperate situation, weighing his sense of responsibility and duty as camp director against his own will to survive:

> Greater love hath no man than this, that a man should lay down his life for his friends—and this is exactly what Shea-Butcher did. He prayed to God that he might save the lads still clinging to the boat and bring them safely to shore. He said to me that he could not swim and that he knew that he was a hindrance to the others and then without another word he shoved himself off from the stern of the canoe, and vanished, never to be seen by us more, at least till the waters of Balsam Lake shall give up their dead.

The scene that ensued as the moon rose was bizarre. Most of the boys were quiet. Lights of the camp could be seen in the distance over relatively calm water. At one point Raymond Allen, of Peterborough, struck out toward the lights and was never seen again. From time to time, over the next six hours, Lambden swam around the canoe, and each time there were fewer souls still hanging on. They sang hymns to pass the time. Birch Cliff, sixteen, watched his older brother, John, disappear under the water, unable to hold on any longer because of the numbing cold. Delirium set in. Describing the effect of immersion on his friend Vernon Clark, Leonard O'Hara said, "In the last few hours he didn't seem right in the head. He kept talking about [someone named] Ham Smith. I can't believe that in the end he knew what he was saying." By the time wind and current moved the canoe to shallow waters off a large island in Balsam Lake, sometime well after midnight, Vernon Clark dropped off, so close to safety, and there were only four survivors of the original fifteen left clinging to the canoe. They hauled themselves ashore and collapsed on the beach.

At first light, the four emptied the canoe and attempted to paddle back to the mainland, only to turn back to the island after another struggle with wind and water. This time, they slept again, but with three of them more or less naked by this point after removing their shoes and most of their clothes as a survival measure, they suffered severe sunburn. The only survivor who had clothes was dispatched to a farmhouse on the island for food, but did not tell the owner about the fatalities, according to the newspaper, because "his comrades did not wish to be seen, without their clothing." Eventually, the survivors paddled the big canoe back to the mainland and struggled back to camp, where their story was told and the search for bodies began.

As news of the accident spread and reporters and photographers raced to the scene, it took many days to locate and recover all of the bodies. The story was on the front page for nearly two weeks and the tragedy of Balsam Lake was the topic of conversation across the country. The lake was dragged again and again. A bi-winged, single-engined flying boat, the *Buzzard*, was lent for the search effort by Premier Ferguson and the Province of Ontario to help locate bodies. The accident was recreated by members of a local canoe club, and there was much speculation about how and why the canoe had tipped. What was first reported as a squall became "a savage flush on the face of Balsam Lake" in a column by Greg Clark. Shea-Butcher was hailed as a hero.

As the news expanded to fill page after page on the second and third day following the accident, the minister of one of the churches involved made an attempt to control the damage: "While those concerned appreciate the public discussion over the tragedy," he was quoted as saying, "it would be perhaps in the best interests of the church as a whole if the matter were discussed privately by Anglican representatives. It is needless to reiterate that the deepest sorrow is felt by all."

Following the funerals, one of which saw five of the victims buried side by side at St. James's Cemetery in Toronto, public shock, admiration of heroism—real and imagined—and condemnation continued to reverberate in the papers. A letter to the editor suggested that there should be straps on the outside of all canoes. An editorialist wrote in response: "As to war canoes, the use of them as utility craft . . . has been ill-advised. Nor are they suitable for extended canoe trips away from camp. . . . The practice of using war canoes for other purposes than racing, which led to the Balsam Lake tragedy, should never be revived."

During a memorial service held in Wesley United Church in Toronto, Reverend J.D. Fitzpatrick told the congregation, "They have not died in vain. Their faith, their courage, their Christian heroism in the face of death will be an inspiration to the boys' and girls' camps of Ontario for a generation to come." Another memorial service was convened in St. Paul's Cathedral on Bloor Street where Reverend Canon Cody preached, "God uses pain as one of his sharpest chisels to model human character."

On July 28, the *Toronto Star* reported that the Ontario Attorney-General's Department had instructed the Crown prosecutor in Lindsay to conduct the fullest investigation possible into the tragedy, reflecting broad public determination to see that such an accident would never happen again. Said the *Star*:

The object in view is for the future protection of all summer camps, and for that reason it has been deemed advisable to go beyond the usual coroner's inquest which concerns itself with the cause of the death under consideration. The inquest will, therefore, consider the whole question of the safety of such boats for use by summer camps and residents.

Even before the inquest had convened, the Boy Scouts of Canada had put an absolute ban on the use of canoes for their programs: "[Balsam Lake] should be sufficient reason for us all to utterly taboo for all time the inclusion of a canoe as a part of scout camp equipment." The Girl Guides of Canada pointed out that they already had a rule that all leaders and guides must be able to swim in order to go in a canoe; they saw no reason to do anything other than continue to vigorously enforce this rule. They would continue to canoe.

The inquest lasted two days. Survivors and canoe experts testified. By now everyone had an opinion about what went wrong. Testimony centered on the notion that the canoe in question was top-heavy, that it was for racing, that it required special expertise to be paddled properly, expertise that the Brotherhood of St. Andrews crew clearly lacked. The jury deliberated for an hour. The next day, under the banner headline "JURY URGES LEGIS-LATION TO BANISH WAR CANOES FROM ALL BOYS' CAMPS—Finds craft responsible for Balsam Lake tragedy was unfit and unsafe for cruising—HIGH AND TOP-HEAVY; NOT USED FOR YEARS," the following recommendations were published: "From the evidence submitted to us we are convinced that a war canoe should have no place in boys' or girls' camps and therefore recommend that war or racing canoes should be prohibited by law for use in such camps." And then, countering the swell of emotion and the need to find Arthur Robert Shea-Butcher a hero, the jury continued: "We further find that the canoe used on this occasion was a war or racing canoe built for the express purpose of racing, and was absolutely unfit and unsafe for cruising. And while we recognize fully the heroism displayed in this tragedy, we cannot but feel that there was great lack of judgment shown in the use of this canoe as a utility boat."

Some camps burned their big canoes, while others simply set them aside and never used them again. And while the province did not see fit to follow the jury's recommendation and ban the use of big canoes, people in the camping community were now

ac
of
aj
d
tl
d
t
r
s

, not only of big canoes but also
he term "hypothermia" never
of the reportage about the acci-
by drowning was the impression
onsciousness, but the idea that this
y the cold was very much part of
vhat eclipsed by the death of so
columnist Greg Clark, already a
wrote quietly in the *Star*: "The
dies as if it flowed. The air was
p into the friendly air. They grew
ey lost the power of gripping."
ion in cold water, though known
understood only since the early
a physiologist at the University of
fe's work to understand the body's
, explains that there are several
, there is a respiratory response: A
—make a short sharp inhalation—
t gasp happens under water," says
s." He adds that in his controlled
ects immersed in ice water in his
riments in which he himself has
es), he has seen the gasp response
—rapid breathing—that, in one
faint. With no other means to keep
erson in real conditions who faints
as well. Similarly, as muscle move-
aired by cold, a person in the water
hang onto a canoe or to the edge of
e water, and drown in that instance

y common way to die in cold water
sbrecht. He points out that most of
r diving into cold water and never

surfacing, or entering cold water and taking only four or five strokes before sinking to the bottom. The reason why the heart stops in this circumstance is not well understood. Physiologists surmise that immediate changes in blood gases and a sudden increase in blood pressure, brought about by a narrowing of peripheral blood vessels in response to the cold, could either interrupt the regular rhythm of the heart or stop it altogether, resulting in sudden death in cold water.

Ironically, says Giesbrecht, the least common way to die in cold water is from an actual lowering of core temperature—hypothermia—which, depending on the temperature of the water, what the victim is wearing, what the victim has eaten, his or her level of activity in the water, and various other factors, usually takes much longer than death by drowning. "In fact," says the physiologist, "when a person's peripheral blood vessels close down and there is much physical activity by the victim immediately on entering the water, in the first instance, body temperature can rise momentarily when a person enters cold water."

Once in the water, the body's natural response is to generate heat through shivering. In water that is less than 50°F, shivering, in combination with other factors such as the amount of body fat, can keep the core temperature of a person's body more or less constant for fifteen to thirty minutes. The surface of the body will cool, the speed of nerve conduction slows, hands get clumsy, and speech begins to slur. When the surface temperature of the body drops below 59°F, cold receptors in the skin cease to register and the initial pain of immersion ebbs. But sooner or later, with heat moving through conduction from the body to the water, the core temperature begins to drop.

Hypothermia is considered mild when body temperature drops three to five degrees Fahrenheit below normal. Generally at this temperature range, a person is still alert and capable of self-help. However, as core temperature falls into the 87.8° to 91.4°F range (so-called moderate hypothermia), shivering slows or stops altogether, muscles begin to stiffen to the point of uselessness,

confusion or apathy may begin, speech becomes vague, breathing shallow, and drowsiness or strange and erratic behavior may
be manifest. Below 87.8°F hypothermia is severe. Skin is cold
and often bluish-gray; eyes may be dilated and unfocused; there is
often little or no apparent breathing; and victims appear rigid,
unconscious, or even dead. In fact, at any time in stages of severe
hypothermia, with the person likely long past cognizance or
perception of the predicament, the heart will fibrillate (lose its
regular beating rhythm) or stop beating altogether, at which
point the victim is effectively dead from cold water immersion.

Since the late 1960s and early 1970s, when active physiological
research into the mechanisms and treatments for hypothermia
began, much has been learned both empirically and clinically
about who succumbs to and who survives hypothermia. It is
known, for example, that children and adults whose core temper-
atures dropped into the 60°F range have made full recoveries.
That recent data notwithstanding, knowledge of cold injuries
goes back to classical times. Hippocrates, Aristotle, and Galen
apparently mention various treatments for cold injuries. And,
according to literature on hypothermia published by the Search
and Rescue Society of British Columbia, "Cold has had major
impacts on military history. Hannibal lost nearly half his army of
46,000 crossing the Alps in 218 B.C. Baron Larrey, Napoleon's
chief surgeon, reported only 350 of the 12,000 men in the
Twelfth Division survived the cold. . . . The winter of 1777 took
its toll on Washington's troops. There were large losses to cold
injuries in the Crimean and both world wars. About 10% of the
United States casualties in Korea were cold related." Hypothermia was not a new problem in 1926, nor in 1978.

Even if St. John's genesis occurred some three decades after
Balsam Lake, it seems astonishing that no one remembered that
disaster sufficiently to admonish Frank Wiens and Ted Byfield as
they proposed switching from 2,000-pound navy cutters to 200-
or 300-hundred-pound canvas-covered canoes. In any case, the

prohibition of canoe use stood in the Boy Scout record, and the tragedy of Balsam Lake had clearly left its mark on the Canadian camping and water safety communities. Kirk Wipper, director of the Ontario Camp Leadership Centre at Bark Lake in the 1950s, remembers purchasing two twenty-five-foot canvas-covered Couchiching Freighter canoes, also made by the Peterborough Canoe Company. These craft had been out of use for many years for one principal reason: Balsam Lake. As a leader in the Ontario camping community, Wipper gradually started putting these so-called war canoes back into regular use for leadership development, but he did so carefully and in the context of a full program of swimming, life saving, and instruction in canoeing technique developed and regularly updated by the Canadian Camping Association and the Royal Life Saving Society, which included awareness of the lessons of Balsam Lake.

To their credit, Byfield and Wiens sought canoes that were more like the freight canoes of the fur trade and less like the war canoes one would see at regattas across the country. Craft produced by the Chestnut Canoe Company had been used by all manner of surveyors, poets, prospectors, gentleman adventurers, and latter-day explorers on watersheds across the country, including writers Robert Service, Sir Charles G.D. Roberts and Margaret Atwood, and the infamous Henry K. Wicksteed, chief of Location and Survey for the Canadian Northern Railway.

Like a racing canoe, although narrow in the beam relative to its length, the "Ogilvy Special," with its generous depth, flat bottom, modest rocker, and shoe keel, was a working canoe ideally suited to moving people and freight long distances across the country. Adding three inches of freeboard to the sides of the "Ogilvy" (changing the depth from fifteen to eighteen inches and changing the height of the bow and stern from twenty-six to thirty-one inches) as a measure of safety may have seemed at the time to be simply enhancing an already serviceable shape, a benign if not helpful modification. From the moment St. John's first put the canoes in the water, however, history seemed to indicate otherwise.

As a camper at Kirk Wipper's summer camp for boys, Camp Kandalore, through the 1960s, I spent a considerable amount of time in the twenty-five-foot Couchiching freighters, loaded and unloaded. They were used for night paddles, cookouts, overnight trips, multiday trips, portages, paddling on big lakes and small lakes, creeks, swamps, and swift-flowing rivers in the Haliburton Highlands area of Ontario southwest of Algonquin Park. I do not remember upsetting, or hearing of an upset, of one of these canoes. What to do in case of upset was always a feature of instruction on the use of these crafts, as were rules for righting the canoe and getting its occupants to safety in the event of a dump. These were standard operating procedures.

From the beginning, however, it seems the St. John's canoes were prone to upset. In 1962, the first time St. John's went from Fort William on Lake Superior to Winnipeg over the famous Grand Portage, they did so with two boats and eighteen senior students, and no incidents were reported. But in 1963, the following year, according to Ted Byfield, "we launched the boats and they all dumped one after the other . . . right at the end of the breakwater we dumped. It went over as soon as the boat turned and took the broadside sweep from the lake. She went like that."

St. John's old boy Jim McKay, who still lives near Selkirk, remembers Byfield's dump, because a Hudson's Bay Company blanket coat that the founding teacher had been given by the boys went missing. He also recalls a young Richard Bird in his Grade 9 class that year who, although he would leave the school before graduating, volunteered at the Ontario school, and eventually assumed the role of assistant leader for the Timiskaming trip. But Ted Byfield's dump was just the first of a series of mishaps on the trip. "It was quite a trip," he recalls.

> I was in the boat that went to get them. They couldn't stand because the water was too cold. I remember playing splits [a game involving knife throwing] that night and cutting my hand. The doctor told me to put my hand in the water for ten minutes. He stitched me up.

Never felt a thing. There was a guy who fell in the fire before we got off Superior. He went home. . . . Another guy broke his leg tracking the canoe. His name was James. They got him out. I think at a lodge. The saving grace was . . . a Native guy whose name was Charlie Macrae. His nickname was Tailgun Charlie. He had quite a bit of experience canoeing. Ted was just one of those guys who'd never be able to canoe. He was very cautious after that. Frank came from the farm and knew a lot about wilderness. Down the road he became a very good canoeist, but on that first trip he was learning.

The following year, inspired by a group of adult paddlers from Ottawa known as "The Voyageurs" (with whom Pierre Trudeau was affiliated), St. John's planned an autumn expedition that would begin at Grand Rapids, Manitoba, and end at York Factory, the old Hudson's Bay Company post at the mouth of the Hayes River. The September weather was typical of the season and latitude, dropping snow on the boys as they made their way north. Unfortunately, as crews were lining their loaded canoes down a rapids, one of the boats broke free, swung about, and trapped fifteen-year-old Keith Veale against a rock. It was feared the boy had broken his back, so the canoes were cached on the spot, the injured boy was removed by helicopter, and eventually the rest of the expedition had to be evacuated by air. Remembering his experience on this trip in a later C B C Manitoba television documentary, Pat Treacy said this:

> That was one of my worst memories ever. It was hell. The trip was a disaster from beginning to end. We ran out of food. It was a miserable trip. I'm really surprised that some of us didn't drown on that trip. It was just reckless. I was really angry. I was frozen. I was cold. It was [snowing]. We were sleeping in wet sleeping bags. It was late into the year. . . . I was just outraged. I thought it was absurd.

In 1968, in accord with the St. John's tradition of ambitious trips on historic routes throughout western Canada, the starting

point of the 1,400-mile Grade 10 Churchill River trip was
La Loche, Saskatchewan. The boys and their leaders would paddle
back to the school in two to three weeks. Without benefit of
canoe training other than direct experience, of which some of the
boys had a considerable amount by this time, they would take two
yellow canoes to big water rapids on the Churchill River and try
to avoid damaging their boats on rocks or swamping them in huge
standing waves at center stream. At 8 a.m. on day three, the expedition had covered some 140 miles to that point and had already
paddled for three hours that morning. One of the two canoes
upset. Writing about this event in that year's annual report, Ted
Byfield's son, Link, describes water "not much warmer than
35 degrees" that numbed members of the other crew who were in
the water. Referring to Keith McKay, who would later become
the headmaster of St. John's School of Alberta, and another grade
10 classmate, surname McDowell, Link Byfield writes:

> By now they had reached a small island and stood on the shore, hardly
> able to move. McKay couldn't get his leg over the side of the boat,
> but fell back into the water after each attempt. Someone finally
> dragged him in. McDowell kept murmuring "fire and water" over
> and over to himself. Mr Isherwood was silent, but got into the boat
> on his own. All three paddled hard and thereby warmed themselves.
> The only illness that resulted was a light cough.

The title of Link Byfield's essay about this Churchill River trip
was "Adventure in Hunger—1968," making the focus of the
piece not the cold water immersion but the fact that they lost one
of their supply boxes in the dump and soon ran out of food, forcing the crew to subsist on dehydrated potatoes, which they mixed
into a watery soup, and "pitiful portions of oatmeal" for several
days until the chief of a local Native band supplied them with fish
and flour for bannock. Years later Keith McKay still laughs guardedly about the trip. He remembers running out of food, but it is
the swim that makes him shiver. "It seemed like I was in the water

for six hours, but [it] was probably more like an hour. I know I was pretty well out of it by the time I got to the fire, and that it took hours to get warm. They stood me up on a tree by the fire and then turned me, like a rotisserie, and eventually I got warm. I do remember being very scared at the time."

School documents record another close call in the big canoes, this time on Lake Winnipeg at the end of the new boys' canoe trip on the English River back to the school in Selkirk. One of the steersmen on this trip was Mike Maunder, who had returned to St. John's as a staff member after not finding what he was looking for in the working world. Fifty miles up the east coast of Lake Winnipeg, at the mouth of the Winnipeg River, they were windbound for a time, unable to travel on the big lake because of waves, so they decided to travel the flotilla of seven canoes at night when, theoretically, the lake would be calm. In addition to low visibility, the main hazard on the first thirteen miles of this run down the Lake Winnipeg shore was a line of low sand cliffs, five to twenty feet high, with no beach at their base. In the darkness, a landing would be almost impossible. The plan was to set out with one master in the front and Ted Byfield and his crew at the rear. When the lead master, Mr. Bennett, in the canoe *Peguis* would flash a light, the bowsmen would shout the names of their boats in turn: "*Turney, Dollard, Marquette, Jogues, LeMoyne, John West.*" The names of these canoes evoked historic figures and presumably added to the quest flavor of St. John's expeditions. Peguis, for example, was the Saulteaux chief who taught settlers in the Red River region how to live off the land; Father Turney was a Cowley Brother who used his pension to help start the Manitoba school; and Jacques Marquette and Isaac Jogues were Jesuit missionaries familiar with the joy and pain of wilderness travel in North America. The 1969–1970 *Annual Report* picks up the story there:

But with the darkness on this night brought fear, well founded. With the darkness came the wind; and with the wind came waves, big waves, that growled beneath them, tossed them angrily, and yet remained dark shadows in the night. Within an hour of their departure they found themselves in a turmoil.

The Bennett light kept flashing, but it careened about wildly in a boat pitched high and low on rollers they could feel but not see. The twin dangers of separation and collision bore alternately on the minds of the steersmen. . . .

So they moved on, mile by mile, the crewmen kneeling in their positions for stability, their legs so cramped they longed to stretch. But to stretch them might mean to swim.

"Boy, my legs ache."

"Keep paddling."

"What time is it?"

"Don't know. Keep paddling."

A crash of water as a breaking wave lapped at the gunwales. "Did we take on water?"

"Not much."

"Keep paddling."

There were calculations. Speed in storm, 3½ miles an hour. Distance to the first possible landing, 13 miles. Course, varying 280 to 315 true. Departure 9:30. Ought to hit landing spot at 1 a.m. Watch for a break in the shoreline. It will mean a beach.

Another crash, this one immediately beside the boat.

"Breaker! Right over the side."

"No. 3 man bail."

His paddle comes out. He slips into the bottom of the canoe and gets to work with his mess can.

"How much have we taken?"

"Two inches by me."

"Keep stroke! Get that bailed out of there."

Although the story eventually ends well—they are able to paddle along thirteen miles of cliffs in the dark without upset— they do not make landfall without foundering in breaking waves as they approach the beach, some of the boats swamping, the boys being ordered in the dark into thigh-deep water where they "staggered like drunken men, their knees, so long cramped, defying the sudden demands made upon them."

The school literature presents this not as a story with a moral or lesson about safety, or weather prediction, or about the relative merits of paddling in waves in the dark; it is a happily-ever-after story of adventure and ultimate triumph in the hands of a benevolent God, the final paragraph in the yearbook reading as follows:

> And so it was. There and then on the beach they formed a circle, knelt and gave thanks for such a simple thing as land. In the morning they would continue along the lake, grown calm as glass. The next night they would reach St. John's, their first trip in the school a success. But for now, they lit their fire and sipped their tea, slipped deep into their [probably soaking wet] sleeping bags, watched the high poplars dance above them in the wind, and fell asleep.

The following summer, Ted Byfield was leading a crew going the other way at the north end of Lake Winnipeg, in much less hazardous conditions, but this time fate was not on his side. They decided to paddle the seven miles across Pigeon Bay, some ten miles south of the community of Berens River, instead of paddling around the shore of the bay, about twice the distance. About halfway across, three-and-a half miles from shore, the canoe commanded by master Frank Jones upset. Speculation in that year's *Annual Report* is that one of the boys in the Jones canoe fell asleep and pitched forward, irrevocably altering the balance of the canoe. Whatever the cause, it is a day that Ted Byfield remembers well. In his own words, he recounts:

> The first thing we did—there were three other boats—I got them to throw their freight in the water [and] empty their boats, except for the crews. And they sat in the bottom of the boat. Because we had so much weight in the bottom of the canoe, we were able to bring the

kids from the top of the overturned canoe into our boat. I took four of them. If I had been thinking better, I would have taken all of them, but I took four of the smallest ones—because they were the ones most likely to get hypothermia—to shore. That left Frank Jones and the two biggest kids in the water. It was a sunny day. It wasn't very rough— rough enough to put the boat over. They were able to take turns, two guys on top of the overturned canoe, while the other one stayed in the water. I got to shore, and sent two boats back out to get them. It was two hours at least. They managed all right.

And then there was a fisherman who came along—he was going out to pull his nets. He saw us, found all the gear that was in the water, and towed the canoe to shore.

The trick here was that we used other boats to save the one that had dumped. If you don't put freight in the water, as I did that day, when the kids come in from the other boat, then they're above the balance line, the boat goes over, and you have two [canoes] over. So you have to make sure that the bottom of the boat has weight in it. . . . A canoe is a very stable thing if the weight, logically, is in the bottom. The minute you put anything above the waterline—I used to demonstrate this with a table knife—if you have the knife with the weight [handle] hanging down, it's bloody near impossible to turn over, but if you have it the other way, the knife flops over. It's the same principle with canoes.

Back in the yearbook version of the tale, more so than in published accounts of the night crossing, there is at least an acknowledgment that dumping a canoe three-and-a-half miles from shore on a seven-mile open water crossing is a risky proposition. It says: "The Pigeon Bay incident was a dangerous way to acquire experience but it added a new chapter to the school's repertoire of rescue procedures."

Unfortunately, aside from the annual reports and the stories that St. John's staff told around their own campfires or over beers in the Selkirk Hotel, there was no organized way to learn from close calls, and no apparent effort was made to assess or analyze why these dumpings were occurring in the first place, to say nothing of the foolhardiness of exposing students to risks of rapids, night paddles, open water crossings, and the rest. The table knife example illustrates that at least Ted Byfield had an understanding of the center of gravity and the propensity of their canoes to upset. Conversations with dozens of St. John's alumni from all three schools indicate that dumps were commonplace on trips. A *Reader's Digest* article about the Timiskaming disaster would later report that there had been "scores of dumpings on other St. John's trips." Most of these, however, were benign in the sense that no one was permanently harmed by the events. It was assumed that the dumpings were caused by circumstances that were partly a function of how the boats were being used and partly a function of the boats themselves.

Reflecting back on his early years at St. John's, Ted Byfield vigorously defends the notion of risk, but he also admits that luck had played a part in all of the dumpings prior to Timiskaming. He said, "In order for there to be an adventure, there has to be risk. There is physical danger, yes, but obviously there is no way you can justify recklessness. Chesterton has written on this. If there is no risk, then there is no adventure. The risk has to be worth it. If all goes well, the hero wins, but you have to measure that risk very carefully. I think . . . we had an awful lot of luck—more likely it was the grace of God."

Had they analyzed more carefully the reasons for the dumpings and upsets, St. John's staff might have concluded that adding three inches of freeboard to otherwise stable "Ogilvy"-style canoes could have made the "Selkirk" paddling canoes more susceptible to upset. The modification of the St. John's canoes, the decisions to paddle in large bodies of water, the sense of urgency, the impossibly long days, and the effect that additional wind pressure would have on a five-inch higher bow and stern—all these factors may have combined to create a situation full of risk.

The boys, who were rarely privy to or part of the decision-making process, knew that their job was to sit in the "pit" and paddle. Clearly, some of them rose to the occasion and survived, knowing they had beaten the odds. Others, however, like Pat Treacy, were negatively affected by St. John's canoe trips. Another old boy, who chose not to be identified, said simply: "At St. John's we learned not how to canoe but how to sit in a boat and pull a paddle. The purpose of the trips did not extend beyond making us do something hard. The instructors did not have much experience [in] canoeing. The learning was mostly through discovery for the students, and for the masters."

But, Ted Byfield would argue, these trips were *meant* to be hard, just as they had been for the voyageurs. A recruiting manual published in the late 1960s, in a chapter entitled "Mud, Water, Canoe and Growing Pains," describes the process of trip learning with the following story:

> "Just think," said the boy called Peters, "we've gone 120 miles and we only have 420 miles left to go. We ought to make it within a week."
>
> The remark was supposed to be funny. It was directed to the huddled figure whose arms moved mechanically beside him. But the figure made no reply. It only shifted its feet in the rainwater that filled the bilge.
>
> "Why don't you guys bail some of the water out? Jonesy and I bailed the last time."
>
> "Because," said a voice from up forward, "the human socks can only absorb so much water and after that it doesn't matter any more."
>
> "It makes the boat lighter," said Peters.
>
> "Dry up," said the voice.
>
> "Bail the boat," said the teacher.
>
> He was paddling in the stern and steering. The trip—Breckenridge to Winnipeg on the Red—was a typical trip for new boys before school opens. Among the teachers it was not a coveted one. It was [a] dirty job. But it made or broke the new boys and it nearly always made them. The teacher's business was to find out what made them tick so that the academic approach to them in the fall could be more accurately planned. . . .

A long, low, distant rumble of thunder brought the soliloquy to an end and silence fell upon the boat. For five minutes it reigned and then all aboard the canoe heard what was unmistakably a sob.

The teacher, professionally, did not hear it.

"Sir," said Peters.

"Peters," said Sir.

"It's Jones. Something's wrong with him."

"You all right, Jones?" said the teacher.

No reply. More silence. Then again, a sob.

"He's crying, sir," said Peters.

With a burst of unleashed emotion, the sob became a howl. Out from the water came his paddle. He slammed it down into the centre of the boat. This broke the rhythm of the stroke. The boat lurched.

"Weigh up!" shouted the teacher, a signal to stop paddling. Behind them the [other canoe] saw the incident and hove to.

"I've had enough! I've had enough!" screamed the voice of Tommie Jones. "Get me out of here. Take me home. I can't stand this any longer. It's crazy. You're all crazy. The whole school's crazy. My mother and father are crazy. They have no business doing this to me. I won't stand it any longer. I'll quit. I'll quit. I'll quit. . . ."

The whole river valley echoed the speech and as it died to a whimper, silence returned to the thunder-struck crews of both canoes. Jones, his head huddled in his hands to hide both tears and shame, sat in a dejected heap.

At last the teacher spoke. The words came firmly but without menace.

"Jones," he said, "pick up that paddle, get to work and shut up."

Jones obeyed.

It is evident from stories of boys going AWOL on canoe trips and from dropout rates at St. John's in the twenty percent range that not all character-building episodes in the big canoes reached the desired goal in terms of toughening the boys. These were difficult trips. To average forty or fifty miles per day, even in the big canoes, which had a top speed of five to six miles per hour, still meant twelve to fifteen hours a day on the water and even longer on days when hauling loads back and forth on portages slowed progress to a crawl. An estimate in the 1966 *Annual Report* of the Company of the Cross suggested that most boys would lose between ten and twenty-five pounds on a three-week canoe trip.

Clearly, as with all canoe trips, there were moments of fun and hilarity interspersed with the hard work of paddling and portaging. Dumps and tense moments on and off the water were commonplace, or so published trip reports would lead a reader to believe, but as they traveled on these monumental expeditions on historic routes, the boys must have developed a sense of accomplishment and a feeling of camaraderie in the collective experience of surviving from one day to the next. Still, with the level of difficulty, the autocratic decision making, the deliberate introduction of circumstances in which it was hoped that, at some point, every boy would fail at something, St. John's trips were a breed apart from other canoe trips. St. John's prided itself on toughness, and it used this aspect of its programming as a hook with which to garner public attention. For example, a 1970 *Reader's Digest* article, which was included as part of the recruitment information package for parents interested in the Ontario school, calls St. John's "one of North America's toughest, most remarkable little prep schools, which prepares boys for manhood by subjecting them to the rigors of intensive study, Spartan living, manual labor, hickory-stick discipline and enough athletic demands to daunt a Decathlon champ." Tempering this statement, Frank Wiens is quoted as saying that the only way to draw forth the best from a boy is to stretch him to the limit of mind, body, and spirit. "We never demand the impossible from kids," said Wiens, then forty-two, "just one hell of a lot more than they *think* is possible."

Very few people outside St. John's ever saw what the process looked like from the inside. However, in the fall of 1973, a National Film Board film crew followed, from Ear Falls to Winnipeg, the first canoe trip for a new crop of recruits and made a film called *The New Boys*. We see the ritual public head shaving, *à la* boot camp, complete with guffaws from spectating old boys. We see the little boys lugging huge food boxes, packing paddles and life jackets on a bus, and then paddling in the big canoes. On a portage around a dam, there is bickering and a canoe is dropped. Boys appear cold and underdressed. And then, with a long camera shot near the end of the film, the brigade is caught rounding Breezy Point on Lake Winnipeg in big surf, not far from the site of the fateful night-crossing episode. The boys are exhausted, leaning over their paddles. The boats are filling up with water. As breaking waves accelerate the canoes up onto the beach, paddlers stiffened by many hours on the lake fall out of the canoe into the surf because their game legs buckle under them. It is not a pretty sight.

When asked in his Edmonton home in the spring of 2000 about how such experiences lead to the development of character, Ted Byfield spoke from his heart:

What happens with most individuals, probably with all individuals, is this: the more effort you make to have character, to live a good life, the more you become aware of the fact that you are not succeeding. You can't make that discovery unless you make a real effort, but when you make a real effort, you discover that there are things going on in your head—things in your own life, things you shouldn't do, things you should do but aren't—that make you very aware of your own sinfulness. And this is a state into which a Christian logically falls. The ideal Christian education program is framed to make the boy have that discovery. In St. John's, a boy will discover resources within himself that he didn't know he had. But what he will more probably discover is that he doesn't have resources within himself that he thought he had. Having made that discovery, as so often happened in the boats, he will make a pact within his soul or with God that says, "I haven't made it. I've failed. Lord have mercy. That's all I can say. That's my final statement." When you can say that, you have character.

The parents who enrolled their sons in the part-time and eventually the full-time St. John's School in Ontario knew about this recipe for building character. Presumably by 1976, some of them might have seen *The New Boys*. Bert and Barbara Hopkins, whose son, Tim, was enrolled in St. John's School of Ontario, in fact knew firsthand about some of what went on in the western St. John's schools because their oldest boy, Dan, was one of the new boys featured in the National Film Board film. In the fall 1973 *St. John's Bulletin*, here is how Tim's older brother's experience was described:

Dan Hopkins, aged 14 from Maple, Ontario is in Grade Ten. He found the canoe trip [a] worthwhile experience with several personal benefits.

Dan made a lot of new friends while he was paddling his way from Ear Falls to Selkirk. . . . Also he believes he has an entirely new and better appreciation for common things, home and its comforts.

The experience also helped him to find out some of his own strengths. "I didn't think I could hack it," was his comment. Now that he has "hacked it," he feels that he can hack a lot of things that require patience and will.

This adventure caused him some anxiety and misgiving, however. "When we were standing in the muck of the swamp at Old Mill Park, I wished I had never left home to come to St. John's, I just wanted to get out of there and go to sleep in a warm bed."

Dan reports further that he had some doubts about his self-discipline in the public school and that's what he wants to have more than anything when he leaves St. John's. He plans to stay only one year because he intends to take advantage of everything he does this year. If he is successful, he wants to finish public school and then study veterinary medicine.

When asked about what he missed most about being away from home, he thought that the most enjoyable thing about home was working on the fuel trucks with his father.

Dan Hopkins's new-boy trip had been challenging, but he had lived to tell the tale, his scrapes and bruises had healed, and he had stuck out his year at the Manitoba school. Three years later, his younger brother, Tim, seemed to be getting on just fine at St. John's. During the fall of 1977 and the winter of 1978, he came home on weekends, bubbling with what he was doing, what he was learning, and how much he was enjoying St. John's. Sure, there were the swats and the dorm shenanigans to deal with, but Tim, with his great sense of humor, seemed to rise above all that.

For Tim, St. John's was a superb venue for playing out his creative pranks and practical jokes—fake black spiders set out for Mrs. Felletti gave him no end of delight. Of course, Tim, like his older brother, had survived the Ear Falls–to–Winnipeg trip—it was the same new boys trip for both of them three years apart. The trip had not been easy for Tim either but, when the bug bites healed and he had had a good rest and a few good meals, the experience was behind him and was part of the new boy he was becoming.

Throughout the winter of 1978, as staff and volunteers at the Ontario school were endeavoring to pull things together, there was much to do, classes to be taught, funds to be juggled, discipline to be administered, and a school facility to be built around a functioning, living, breathing, scrapping, singing, smoking, fractious company of teenage boys and their dollar-a-day masters. With staff being transferred from the western schools—particularly Maunder and Felletti from the Alberta school—the activity in Ontario began to take its toll on the western schools. By Easter 1978, an unfortunate staff situation at the Alberta school meant that Mike Maunder, the assistant headmaster and cofounder of the Ontario school, had to go to Alberta to help out. A teacher from Alberta, Paul Gazin, was shipped summarily from Alberta to Ontario, effectively to replace Maunder, but things at the Ontario school were not the same. An order for new canoes that should have gone to the Chestnut Canoe Company was delayed. Frank

...enced trip leader, k

...rigade trip in his ow

...en the case for the Ea

...igade trip would have

...well. Instead, however,

...nior master Peter Cain,

...who had some canoe-

...ver organized and led a

...e to accomplish this the

...ry early days: He would

...e other master tentatively

...the other imported staff

...r off the boat from England,

...school for a year prior to join-

...had been on only one canoe trip in

...ing trip. Mr. Thompson told school

...oking forward to the trip, but admitted

...ce as a steersman. Cain and Thompson

...ed when they learned that Mark Denny and

...had been coming up to Claremont from

...ity to volunteer at the school, would be masters

...Brigade as well. As alumni of the Manitoba school,

...d Denny had several trips under their belts. It was not

...weekend of David Cunningham's father's funeral in May

...at the four of them began talking about where they would

...d how the trip would be organized.

The end of term was approaching. The boys had to study for final exams. They had to start thinking about the canoe trip. The older boys would be with Mr. Felletti and follow the old trade route up the Michipicoten River and down the Missinaibi River to James Bay where they would meet up with the Junior Brigade, who would come down the Albany River to Moosonee. Boys were paired up for purposes of stowing their sleeping rolls and plastic tarps for sleeping—two boys to a canoe pack. In spite of

bers were allowed t
his father if he could
his dad first showed it
knife with belt sheath
training. Until now,
he needed to take
matured during his
knife, Norm checked
oldest son as a mark of
St. John's. As Dean
urday, he did so with
on his belt. It was a
rm snapped a picture

day is the class photo
permanent marker of
at everyone but two
et. Everyone except
remembered to wear
are wearing white

of wire stacking chairs
nt row will sit cross-
rth row would stand
oodwin and Durden,
e taller boys, so they
the arrangement look
original plan for the
quiet and all arranged.
legged, are the small-
eople remember as a
but "brutal" student,
share a tent with that

said

's post
ome so
upcomi
gade, and
te on the
galvanized
the special

...rotests and the fact that one of...
arch-enemies David Cunnir...
up. They would learn to...
necessarily be assign...
to spend entire...
gear togeth...

And...
Exa...
began...
trip. Vo...
supplies fo...
Chestnut Ca...
term, there was...
they floated. They...
seats were too flimsy...
to cut and bolt plywoo...
the seats. Someone else th...
seats of the new canoes. The...
much to do. The leaders wou...
modate the boys' feet. They wou...
the seats and leave the food boxes b...
would the boys put their feet if the fo...
seats? If St. John's had taught them anyt...
Mike Maunder was back from Alberta fo...
He reminded them that resourcefulness is a...
improvise.

The night before the Saturday Open House was...
and packing to make sure that all was set because the...
leave for the trips immediately after the festivities. Th...
drive through the night, as St. John's trips had often don...
past, and start their trips in the morning, like real voyageu...
minimal sleep.

And so the final day of term dawned, Saturday, June 10, 1978...
Because events with parents were scheduled for later in the day,

occasion. As the trip's kitchen crew mem...
carry knives on the expedition, he had aske...
borrow a special knife he had coveted since...
to him. It was a standard Air Force surviva...
that his dad was issued as part of his pilo...
Dean had not had what his father reckon...
responsibility for such a tool. But Dean h...
year at St. John's. When he asked about the...
with the masters and gave the knife to his...
just how far the boy had come in his year...
tended the demonstration campfire that Sa...
his father's Air Force knife proudly displaye...
memorable moment for both of them. N...
he would treasure for years to come.

One of the most important formalities of th...
that the boys and their families will have as...
this happy moment in time. It is a miracle...
of the boys has remembered his school jac...
Robin Jensen and Chris Bourchier has also...
white turtlenecks, but at least they bot...
T-shirts that will add symmetry to the phot...
The photographer has arranged two lines...
to accommodate four rows of boys. The fr...
legged on the grass. The next group will s...
chairs. The third row will stand, and the fo...
on the second row of chairs. Mercifully, G...
who are without their jackets, are among...
will be able to bookend the top row, making...
as if those two white shirts are part of the...
photo. And so, finally, the boys are lined up,...
In the front row from the left, sitting cross...
great athlete, great swimmer, great runner...
perhaps wondering how he is ever going to...

occasion. As the trip's kitchen crew members were allowed to carry knives on the expedition, he had asked his father if he could borrow a special knife he had coveted since his dad first showed it to him. It was a standard Air Force survival knife with belt sheath that his dad was issued as part of his pilot training. Until now, Dean had not had what his father reckoned he needed to take responsibility for such a tool. But Dean had matured during his year at St. John's. When he asked about the knife, Norm checked with the masters and gave the knife to his oldest son as a mark of just how far the boy had come in his year at St. John's. As Dean tended the demonstration campfire that Saturday, he did so with his father's Air Force knife proudly displayed on his belt. It was a memorable moment for both of them. Norm snapped a picture he would treasure for years to come.

One of the most important formalities of the day is the class photo that the boys and their families will have as a permanent marker of this happy moment in time. It is a miracle that everyone but two of the boys has remembered his school jacket. Everyone except Robin Jensen and Chris Bourchier has also remembered to wear white turtlenecks, but at least they both are wearing white T-shirts that will add symmetry to the photo.

The photographer has arranged two lines of wire stacking chairs to accommodate four rows of boys. The front row will sit cross-legged on the grass. The next group will sit on the first row of chairs. The third row will stand, and the fourth row would stand on the second row of chairs. Mercifully, Goodwin and Durden, who are without their jackets, are among the taller boys, so they will be able to bookend the top row, making the arrangement look as if those two white shirts are part of the original plan for the photo. And so, finally, the boys are lined up, quiet and all arranged.

In the front row from the left, sitting cross legged, are the smallest boys: clear-eyed Barry Nelson, whom people remember as a great athlete, great swimmer, great runner but "brutal" student, perhaps wondering how he is ever going to share a tent with that there was a chance the boys might have slept in. But by now, the excitement of finishing their year, having their awards ceremony, and starting the final canoe trip all on the same day was too much to sleep through. Dress for the day was dark trousers, white turtle-necks, and, for the class photo that would be taken in the varie-gated shade of the big maples on the school lawn, they were expected to wear their crisp melton wool school jackets with white bars on the shoulders, white snaps, with white piping on sleeve and pocket on a background of rich royal blue.

For friends and families, Frank Felletti had organized a number of skits and displays in and out of the school, manned by the boys themselves, to illustrate what had happened throughout this first year of the full-time school. There were samplings of poetry and prose, artwork, math sheets, and all manner of work collected by the masters for determining a final grade for each boy. There was a liberal sprinkling of black-and-white photographs around the school, some of which were even for sale, taken and developed by the boys themselves. (Nothing in the photographic display let on that closing the door of the darkroom and flipping on the "In use" sign, from the outside, was a handy foil for slipping out along the railroad tracks to the store in Claremont for smokes and candy, as long as the photographic quotas were always met.) There were lots of little secrets in the smiles that day, but mostly there was an overwhelming sense of pride in the masters, the boys, and the parents, that this year had yielded such varied accomplishments. Sheena Suttaby, Chris's mother, said "the difference was in their eyes."

Norm Bindon saw new confidence in his son Dean's posture. Bindon I had made strides in many areas. He had even come so far as to be assigned to the food preparation crew for the upcoming trip, given responsibility for nutrition for the Junior Brigade, and, as part of that role, he manned a demonstration campsite on the grounds of the school, where he tended a sample galvanized bucket of food by a fire that he had made himself for the special protests and the fact that one of the boys had just lost his father, arch-enemies David Cunningham and Barry Nelson were paired up. They would learn to work together, or else. They would not necessarily be assigned to the same canoes, so they might not have to spend entire days together, but they would be packing their gear together and sleeping together under plastic.

And so the days ticked down through May and into June. Exams were written, final marks computed. Cain and Thompson began to organize bulk bags of pasta, oatmeal, and granola for the trip. Volunteer parents and boys made food boxes to stow supplies for the trip. When the canoes finally arrived from the Chestnut Canoe Company on the last Thursday or Friday of term, there was no time to test them on the water, even to see if they floated. They were here. Someone decided that the cane seats were too flimsy and instructed the food box–building crews to cut and bolt plywood pieces on top of the caning to reinforce the seats. Someone else thought to try the food boxes under the seats of the new canoes. They did not fit. Too late. There was too much to do. The leaders would figure out some way to accommodate the boys' feet. They would stow the bedroll packs under the seats and leave the food boxes between the seats—but where would the boys put their feet if the food boxes were between the seats? If St. John's had taught them anything, it was to make do. Mike Maunder was back from Alberta for the last day of term. He reminded them that resourcefulness is a virtue. They would improvise.

The night before the Saturday Open House was spent cleaning and packing to make sure that all was set because the plan was to leave for the trips immediately after the festivities. They would drive through the night, as St. John's trips had often done in the past, and start their trips in the morning, like real voyageurs, on minimal sleep.

And so the final day of term dawned, Saturday, June 10, 1978. Because events with parents were scheduled for later in the day,

Felletti, Ontario headmaster and experienced trip leader, kept plans for the St. John's Ontario Senior Brigade trip in his own head. Had Maunder been there, as had been the case for the Ear Falls trip, organization of the Junior Brigade trip would have fallen to him, and all would have been well. Instead, however, leadership of the Junior Brigade fell to junior master Peter Cain, fresh from England via the Alberta school, who had some canoeing experience, but who had certainly never organized and led a whole expedition before. He would have to accomplish this the same way Wiens and Byfield did in the very early days: He would have to make it up as he went along. The other master tentatively assigned to the Junior Brigade was the other imported staff member, Neil Thompson, one year off the boat from England, who had worked at the Manitoba school for a year prior to joining the Ontario staff, and who had been on only one canoe trip in his life, a Manitoba staff training trip. Mr. Thompson told school authorities that he was looking forward to the trip, but admitted that he had no experience as a steersman. Cain and Thompson must have been relieved when they learned that Mark Denny and Richard Bird, who had been coming up to Claremont from Queen's University to volunteer at the school, would be masters on the Junior Brigade as well. As alumni of the Manitoba school, both Bird and Denny had several trips under their belts. It was not until the weekend of David Cunningham's father's funeral in May 1978 that the four of them began talking about where they would go and how the trip would be organized.

The end of term was approaching. The boys had to study for final exams. They had to start thinking about the canoe trip. The older boys would be with Mr. Felletti and follow the old trade route up the Michipicoten River and down the Missinaibi River to James Bay where they would meet up with the Junior Brigade, who would come down the Albany River to Moosonee. Boys were paired up for purposes of stowing their sleeping rolls and plastic tarps for sleeping—two boys to a canoe pack. In spite of loudmouth David Cunningham for three weeks; Jody O'Gorman, who knows the trip will be even more difficult than the last one and wishing he were a better swimmer; fair-haired and bespectacled Kevin Black, one of two sets of handsome twins in the class; chubby David Parker, who is wondering whether anyone will find the ten pounds of candy and other culinary contraband in his bedroll; the diminutive Tom Kenny, with the sun shining on his shock of dark hair and long eyelashes, who is thinking about how hard it will be to be away from his family for three whole weeks, and how he is going to keep his diary dry through thick and thin; smiling Scott Bindon, who is glad his older brother has not been bumped up to the senior trip; Robbie Kerr, from Markham, in his horn-rimmed glasses; and, on the end of the first row, the dark-haired Bourchier twins, Frazer on the left, Chris on the right, together as they so often were during the year.

In the second row from the left, sitting on chairs: Andrew Skinner, who decided to stay; Tim Hopkins, ready to show his brother Dan and his family that he is up to the final challenge of the year; James Gibson, who is thinking that the portaging and paddling may be good for his hockey career; Chris Suttaby, who will turn thirteen on the third day of the trip; Peter Knight, who is holding a secret he cannot tell; Todd Michell, looking tentative; David Cunningham, who is looking out at all the parents taking pictures of the class and wishing his dad were among them; Robin Jensen, the one they called "Can-I-Have-Some," hoping there would be more fulsome rations on this trip than there were on the Ear Falls outing the year before; Paul Nyberg, who is glad that Gibson and Mansfield, the two who had helped him and his bad leg so often in snowshoeing, will be there on the trip to lend him a hand; and Ian Harling, smiling so smugly, knowing that there is enough candy in his sleeping roll to keep everyone happy for the whole trip, tucked into the second row, third from the end where he always liked to be in his hockey pictures—he was a bit superstitious about that. Beside Harling are Paul Lockie, smiling, and Simon Croft, looking tentative and a bit small for the chair, but who has been given the honor of being altar boy for the last official church service before the end of term.

In the third row, standing, are Gallagher, Patterson (to whose sister Mr. Cain has just proposed), and Doughty, all of whom will be on the senior trip. Then lanky David Greaney, who had gone to Runnymede Public School with his friend Andy Hermann and who, on the strength of this connection, decided at the last minute to attend St. John's and was squeezed into the 1977 year. Beside Greaney is smiling James Doak, standing right behind Chris Suttaby with whom he will team up in a test of their lives the following day. Along the line is Carmichael, Rousseau, the boy they called "Wally" (whose name no one seemed able to remember), and Kevin Black's twin brother, Owen, who has just won the year's award for being the most improved student. Beside Black II is Tim Pryce, who is hoping people will not fall asleep on their paddles on this trip, Dean Bindon, and Andy Hermann, whose singing at chapel and compline services could bring people to tears, it was so clear and pure. Senior boys Amati and Cave finish the line.

And finally, in the back row standing on chairs are all of the biggest, oldest boys who are all on the senior trip with Mr. Felletti, except Mike Mansfield, fifth from the right end of the line, looking tall and handsome, still thick but not nearly as roly-poly as he was when he first arrived at the part-time school the year before. St. John's had been good for Mike; he had slimmed down and developed new confidence. He had never really been part of the Harling/Cunningham fiefdom in the dorm; in fact, he had taken on his own leadership role with some of the other boys. He had developed lasting friendships with guys like Andy Hermann, Rob Patterson, and, down to the left in the line ahead of him, David Greaney. At one time, he was to be with the older boys on the senior trip, but Mr. Felletti had suggested that it would be good to add his size and strength to the Junior Brigade. Mike was pleased to oblige, or so he said to Mr. Felletti at the time.

In the formal awards portion of the ceremony, a prayer is said that could well have been drawn from the text of Romans 5:3–5, reminding everyone of the conviction that "Suffering produces perseverance; perseverance, character; and character, hope. And hope does not disappoint us, because God has poured out His life into our hearts by the Holy Spirit, whom He has given us." In sequence of the service, the four new blue canoes are christened and brigades blessed by the attendant clergyman using a verse attributed to Sir Francis Drake and found in *The Book of Common Prayer* as a blessing for people at sea: "O Lord God, when Thou givest Thy servant to endeavors any great matter, grant us also to know that it is not the beginning but the continuing of the same until it be thoroughly finished, which yieldeth the true glory; through Him that for the finish of Thy work laid down his life, our Redeemer, Jesus Christ. Amen."

Only when attention shifts to the new canoes do some parents notice that the new boats look different from the Manitoba canoes the boys had used the year before. Joan Mansfield remembers thinking that they did not have the same draft as the other canoes, and she was concerned that the food boxes the boys had built with their fathers did not fit under the seats. The boys would have no place for their feet. Their center of gravity would be too high. But these masters knew what they were doing. St. John's had been doing this for years. She puts canoe thoughts out of her mind for now, but they will return.

With the formalities of the day finished, the barbecue supper cleaned up by the mothers, goodbyes are said and parents drift away, leaving their boys to concentrate on last-minute packing. Parents who are going to be driving to Lake Timiskaming on the overnight journey try to find someone who knows who is supposed to go where. The Senior Brigade keep their packs and supplies on one side of the school, the Junior Brigade on the other. They have done much together this year, but now they must part, knowing that there is a big reunion planned for Moosonee in three weeks' time. Thinking about that first day when he and his best friend got everyone to sign the piece of baseboard that issued the

first swats at the new school, Mike Mansfield looks around for
Peter Knight. Something has not been quite right today. Knight
has been different, distant, as if he has somehow detached himself
from the rest of the school. He was there for the awards, but now
he is nowhere to be found. "Where's Knight?" Mansfield finally
asks Frank Felletti. "He left with his parents." "Will he be going on
the trip?" "No. It's time to go, Mike. Get in the van." No goodbye. No Knight. A year ends, just like that.

The Tragedy: In Deep Waters

After much flurry in the days leading up to the final Open House—studying for exams, writing exams, making food boxes, preparing blanket rolls, packing food for the canoe trip, and cleaning the school from top to bottom—there can be little doubt that some of the boys and masters were relieved to see the last parent leave the school parking lot when the festivities ended on Saturday, June 10, 1978. Others might have been a bit homesick, wondering what kind of pain and suffering the pending canoe trip would bring, but there was work to be done. Canoes had to be loaded, personnel had to be assigned to the four vans that were going to transport the Junior Brigade to the start of their trip, and last-minute details had to be looked after so that the two expeditions might depart from Claremont on time. It took until almost midnight for leader Peter Cain, master Neil Thompson, and alumni volunteers Richard Bird and Mark Denny to get the Junior Brigade organized—never really having worked as a team before—but, finally, with Jack Suttaby and Peter Croft among a crew of volunteer drivers, they loaded up and headed north.

David Cunningham and Simon Croft tussled like caged bear cubs in the back of Simon's dad's car for much of the early trip, but eventually drifted off to sleep as they headed north on Highway 11 toward North Bay. Mike Mansfield traveled in a van with six other boys, one on top of each other, among packs, paddles, life jackets, and food boxes, the smell of old canvas and new Keds running shoes mixed with nervous sweat and the damp, fishy essence of dead bugs on the windscreen and night highway. Traffic was thin in the wee hours, but as they would meet transport trucks hauling freight south to Toronto, vague yellow light would highlight the curves of closed eyes on the flawless faces of sleeping boys. Three hundred miles and a couple of roadside coffee stops later, the convoy crossed the Ottawa River into Quebec on the dam in front of a massive pulp and paper plant, and headed through town to the Timiskaming boat launch. It was 7:30 a.m. No one had slept well on the ride. Alumni volunteer Richard Bird later told the inquest that he hadn't slept at all.

June 11 dawned sunny. It was a clear Quebec morning, ideal for getting partners paired up and their bedrolls packed once and for all. This was the moment that Barry Nelson and David Cunningham had been dreading. They had been paired for their own good—the masters knowing full well of the animosity between them. They had to communicate about what was in their packs, and go through the checklist of plastic tarp, rainwear, sleeping bags, ground sheets, extra rope, all of the things they would need for overnight warmth and shelter in the three weeks to come. Mercifully, when expedition leader Peter Cain read the list of who was in which canoe and with which leader, the two of them would at least be paddling in different canoes: Cunningham would be with Richard Bird, and Nelson would be in Cain's canoe. Thank goodness for small mercies, they both thought, that neither of us is with the weakest steersman, Neil Thompson. At least they would be spending days apart. Nights would be a different story, but for now, night was a long way off. The canoes had to be loaded and trimmed and it was a great day for paddling.

These canoes were different from the ones they had borrowed from the Manitoba school and used on the Ear Falls trip the previous summer. The food boxes did not fit under the seats as they had done in the big yellow St. John's Cathedral School "Selkirks" because they were too high, but it was not that important, because they could tie bedroll packs and other supplies under the seats. There would not be much room for feet. And when the four crews got in and went for a little circle away from the wharf on the calm, sheltered water near the Timiskaming boat launch, the new blue canoes seemed higher and tippier than the old yellow canoes. Of that everyone was sure. Fortunately, Mike Maunder had come along to see them off. After assisting Neil Thompson with getting his crew and their gear aboard, Maunder balanced the loads and reassured the boys, especially those in Thompson's canoe, who seemed especially nervous about the new canoe and their green steersman. With everyone in canoes, cursory loops were made near the dock, a short prayer was said, and they were off. "God bless," called Mike Maunder just before they were out of earshot, no doubt thinking that had things been different, had he not been called to help sort things out at the Alberta school in the middle of term, he would have been leading this trip instead of Peter Cain. It was 8:15 a.m. Thompson's canoe wasn't taking the straightest of lines up toward the first narrows at the foot of the lake, but he was making progress, and the water, for now, was calm. If anything, they had a very, very gentle tailwind.

Those first moments inside the four canoes must have been quite unsettling for the boys, especially for those who had not been on the Far Falls trip the previous year. When paddling in a canoe with one or two people, there is a palpable sense of action/reaction as muscle force on a paddle is transferred through one's body into the movement of the canoe. Paddling in big canoes is a totally different experience, like going from a Cessna to a jumbo jet. For example, if the canoe is tipped away from one's paddling side—because of the way people are sitting, or because of the way it is loaded, or both—simply leaning away from the canoe, out over the gunwale, will rarely make enough difference to change the way the canoe is floating in the water. Canoes, large and small, work best when the hull of the boat is free to bob and roll on the water, meaning that to make a canoe move best, there needs to be a fluidity in the hips of everyone in it. Canoeists need to keep their upper bodies more or less stationary as paddles are pulled, but let their bottom halves pitch and roll with the boat.

Unfortunately, rolling hips with the canoe requires balance and experience and, for a team, letting one's hips roll with the boat requires trust—something that takes time and practice to develop. These boys had not paddled together for ten months, and never in these new blue canoes. They had had no canoeing practice or instruction prior to embarking on this trip. The natural inclination of a new paddler, or even an experienced paddler in a new canoe, is to stiffen when the boat starts to move. As soon as fluidity of hips is absent, the paddler's center of gravity rises. And, if a nervous paddler latches onto the gunwales with a stiff arm, the actual center of gravity of the canoe is raised, making it feel much tippier. Even with a load of plywood food boxes and bedroll packs in the bottom of the canoe, it is quite likely that there was some nervous shifting and settling going on as these four brand-new canoes began their journey up Lake Timiskaming that sunny June morning in 1978. Just being in the canoes likely required quite a bit of the boys' energy to keep them balanced, especially these new ones, which seemed higher and tippier than the old canoes.

The decision to cover the seats with a layer of half-inch plywood would have raised the boys that much higher. Add to that height a layer or two of clothing to thwart "voyageur's bottom" from sitting on the hard seats, and the human part of the load is getting dangerously high above the waterline. Photos taken at the time show that all four steersmen chose to follow the St. John's tradition and, instead of sitting on the stern seats of the canoes, thereby putting their mass closer to the rotation point of the canoe, sat perched on the stern decks of the canoes, putting the biggest person in each of the four canoes on a seat that was as much as two feet off the water—a good position for leverage, a bad position for stability of the canoe.

As was St. John's practice, the crews had been hastily put together with no thought to team building beforehand. Toughing it out was the St. John's way, even if it meant a dump or two before the boys learned that working together is better than not. And even though in Neil Thompson's canoe there were boys like Dean Bindon who could have sterned the canoe, at St. John's, boys were to defer to masters. The master's place was at the back, perched high on the deck where he could command his crew. It was always much easier for a master to verbally admonish a recalcitrant paddler when the offender could be seen, and it was always easier to move forward, up the middle of the boat, when it was necessary to quell insurrection with a paddle swat to the side of an unsuspecting boy's head. In this trip, as many boys remembered, Cain and Bird got first choice of crew. "That's the way St. John's worked," recalled one member of the expedition. "You put the strong with the strong and let the rest fend for themselves."

Central among the problems of the Timiskaming trip that morning in June was the fact that all the knowledge of canoeing and canoe expeditioning had been garnered only through experience with St. John's schools. Some of the boys, like Ian Harling and Barry Nelson, who had canoed with their families and at summer camp, had considerable canoe training and experience, but at St. John's this potential resource was never tapped—boy knowledge was never part of the St. John's leadership equation. The norms that Cain, Bird, Denny, and Thompson carried with them that day were defined by St. John's, a learn-by-experience, no-training leadership circumstance that never had the benefit of information from other schools, camps, and organizations that were doing the same thing—knowledge and experience that were published long before 1978 in pamphlets, training manuals, lesson plans, learning progressions, books, and films; knowledge and expertise that would certainly have made a difference in their awareness of the risks they were taking.

St. John's had no organized canoeing, swimming, or lifesaving instruction for the leaders or the boys. Big keyhole life jackets would save the day. Gear was lashed in, a practice discouraged by many canoe manuals and anyone who has ever tried to empty a loaded canoe. There were no bailers in the canoes. No one was aware of techniques like the heat escape–lessening position (HELP) and the huddle technique for keeping warm in cold water, which had been developed in the late 1960s and early 1970s by the Red Cross and the Royal Life Saving Society of Canada. In fact, no one seemed aware of the danger of paddling on a lake in northern Ontario just weeks after spring breakup. By now St. John's had thousands and thousands of trail miles logged. No one had died on a canoe trip. No need to change what had been working since 1962.

The usual St. John's way of research had been employed—situating the trip in its historical context—but nothing beyond that, such as checking other trip logs, or consulting with people along the way about local conditions, research that would have revealed that those who live on Lake Timiskaming are not in the habit of crossing the narrow body of water to escape the wind because of the tunnel quality of the cliffed sides. Locals know that on Timiskaming there is no place to hide, but of this the expedition was unaware, even as wind was building from the south.

The canoes continue up the lake on this beautiful June day. At a "weigh up" (a rest stop in voyageur parlance) David Cunningham removes his T-shirt from under his life jacket and strips down to his Speedo bathing suit—he wants to "catch some rays" so that he will come back from this trip with a tan. Cottager David Radway heads down a rocky trail to get a bucket of water from the lake and sees them riding high and "making good time with a full, following wind" in the sunshine. Moving up the Quebec shore of the lake, the wind pushing them along, they make more than fifteen miles by the time the sun is overhead. Mike Mansfield remembers one of the boys in his canoe declaring that they had paddled exactly five hours and ten minutes as they shipped their paddles and made ready to get out on the shore for lunch near McMartin Point. Cain's and Bird's crews are first in, Denny's next, and, as the lunch of granola and leftover peanut butter and jam sandwiches from breakfast is opened and spread out on the rock, everyone watches Thompson's crew make its way toward shore.

There is no condition more difficult in which to steer a canoe than a tailwind. As the breeze has freshened throughout the morning, Thompson has felt the propensity of the big canoe to rotate on waves and settle broadside in troughs. The curse of extra freeboard is windage; the sides of these modified canoes are like sails sticking up into the wind. Without knowledge of the strokes needed to steer properly, Thompson finds his boat starting to wallow in troughs as the wind spins it off course. The young master has been ordering his crew to back paddle on one side of the boat to bring it around perpendicular to the waves. This has put them well behind the other crews. Thompson is tiring with the exertion. His boys are tiring as well, and some of them are getting scared. The first thing they hear on arrival is one of the boys in Denny's boat announce that he has had enough and wants to go home. Thompson's crew hear, but say nothing. They head for the food, eyes averted. There is nowhere for Parker—some thought it was Parker—to go. Eventually, the master will win. Tears, protests, admonishments, supplementary protests, threats, capitulation—it is a cycle familiar to them all. "Pick up that paddle, get to work, and shut up" is a common refrain. They will go on.

Last in, but eager to prove himself enthusiastic, if not up to the task in terms of skills, Thompson is first back on the water. At the north end of the lake, in the town of Ville-Marie, game warden Simon Levesque's men decide not to go out on the lake because it is looking too windy and rough. But here, the waves have had many more miles to build as they roll north along the rocky corridor that is Timiskaming. Back at McMartin Point, Cain and Bird have looked at the waves and decided to press on. The plan is to cross the mile-wide lake on an oblique angle to see whether there might be shelter on the Ontario side. Although Thompson has a head start, in minutes the other three canoes have passed him. Cain's and Bird's crews have decided to race to the other side of the lake. Handpicked by the two senior leaders on the trip, the boys in these two canoes are among the strongest on the expedition. Andy Hermann, an excellent canoeist himself, has subbed in after lunch and is pulling hard in the bow of Bird's canoe. Another experienced summer camp canoeman, Ian Harling, is digging deep and setting a strong pace in the front of Cain's canoe. David Cunningham is still in his Speedo and new runners, topped with his keyhole life jacket, thinking he is in for an afternoon of tanning. The boys are laughing, talking, and surely pulling away from Denny and Thompson and their crews of smaller, less able boys.

Some boys are surprised that James Gibson, one of the three boys who was not on the Ear Falls trip, has ended up in the bow of Denny's canoe. In the bow of the last canoe in line is athletic Todd Michell, who in spite of his experience on the English River trip, has neither the training nor the skill to compensate for Thompson's struggles in the stern. Behind him, Jody O'Gorman, Dean Bindon, Owen Black, Tim Hopkins, Simon Croft, and little Tom Kenny are pulling their best, but without effective rudder action from Thompson to keep the mounting waves on their port stern quarter, they might as well be paddling in the air half the time.

By 2 p.m., Cain and Bird are nearly across the lake, but all is definitely not well with the other two canoes. Denny's boat does not have the power of the first two canoes, and he too is having trouble steering. Perched up on the stern deck, he is using an extra-long paddle, but to keep on course with a following wind (tailwind), one must anticipate when the boat will surf ahead on a crest and when it will spin and wallow in a trough. An effective steering stroke in a trough, if misapplied on a crest, will put the craft off line instead of keeping the boat straight. When the boat works itself parallel to the waves, the boys stiffen, some grab the gunwales and get out of synch with their paddling, and the canoe starts to rock. Denny knows that forward momentum is the only feature of motion that will keep them on an even keel but, like Thompson, he is having a difficult time making this happen on every stroke. "Come on, you whiners, and put your backs into the stroke, for God's sake. Paddle, you guys! We're falling behind."

At the back of the line, now some distance behind Denny, is Neil Thompson and his flagging crew. "Port side, back paddle," he yells. "Back paddle!" "Forward paddle on the right!" A sense of urgency has crept into his voice because, as strength has waned, as they have slowed down in yet another dark, deep-water trough, fear is starting to take hold of everyone. Not only are they having problems keeping on course in the wind, but they are becoming increasingly isolated on the big lake.

Someone in Denny's canoe catches a wave, and a paddle slips out of hand and into the water. They must stop, turn, and pick it up. In the meantime, the distance between the two last canoes is narrowed to only 100 yards or so. Denny's crew feels powerless as they "lie to" between the waves, trying to retrieve the paddle. Finally, they grab the paddle, turn, and begin picking up speed to get back on course. At this point, they may be about halfway across the lake on their angled trajectory. Suddenly, there is a cry on the wind. Thompson's canoe has upset. Seven tired boys and their frustrated master are in water that was later estimated at 50°F or colder. Denny turns to assist. Boys and volunteer master are so anxious to see what is happening on the water that they do not pay attention to the business of keeping their canoe afloat. In an instant, two canoes, fourteen boys, and two frightened leaders are in the waves. They are 100 yards apart, close enough to hear the cries, but too far to render assistance to one another. "Hang onto the canoe," yell the leaders. In the distance, as they bob up and down in the waves— estimated later to be somewhere between one and three feet high— they can see flashes of light from paddles in the other two canoes, which are out of earshot and almost out of sight. Neil Thompson has lost his glasses in the upset. He is having trouble seeing Denny and the crew who are only 100 yards away, and they are separated by an impenetrable barrier of waves. The house of cards is falling.

From the moment they hit the water, the crews of these two canoes began to suffer the immediate and unavoidable effects of cold. Immediately, there was the shock of entry, from hot sun to ice-cold water. And shortly thereafter, their autonomic nervous systems would have reduced peripheral blood flow to keep blood and precious heat flowing to vital organs. Uncontrolled shivering started. Numbness quickly followed, and, after several minutes in the water, hands that had so nimbly held paddle shafts would have had difficulty grasping the thick gunwales of the canoes. By the time Cain and Bird realized what had happened—it seemed to Thompson like an eternity, but it was more likely minutes—already the most insidious process of hypothermia, core temperature cooling, had begun, especially for the smaller boys, who made up most of Thompson's crew. With core cooling comes even more pronounced effects on movement, speech, and mental acuity.

Neil Thompson himself would have felt these effects and he watched it happen among his crew. After forty minutes in the water, with still no sign of rescue, Thompson decided there was nothing to be done but to swim for the Ontario shore. His plan was to send his boys in pairs, perhaps Todd Michell and Jody O'Gorman, Dean Bindon and Tim Hopkins, Owen Black and Simon Croft, linking with Tom Kenny himself to see if they could float and swim their way to safety on the other side of the lake. But already the boys seemed spent, except O'Gorman, who, as a non-swimmer, was panicking at the prospect of letting go of the canoe. "Try, try—you have to help yourself," Thompson implored the crew. Taking charge of O'Gorman to see if he could quell his fear, Thompson left Todd Michell to help the smaller Kenny. But the cold was in control.

Meanwhile, Cain and Bird rushed to the Ontario shore, dropped off a couple of packs and some of the smaller boys in their canoes—likely Kevin Black, Robin Jensen, Robbie Kerr, Paul Nyberg, and Paul Lockie—and paddled furiously back across the lake. Ian Harling remembers Cain fishing around for what seemed like an inordinate amount of time to find and untie the right packs to put on the shore. Later, Harling would learn that the pack that Cain had wanted was one with an ax, a saw, and some food, to establish an effective drying and rewarming camp on the shore as soon as the rescue was complete.

For whatever reason, likely the size of the gap between Denny's and Thompson's canoes, Cain and Bird both picked up members of Denny's crew to run them to shore, leaving Thompson and his crew—the first ones to hit the water—to continue struggling. With the powerful threesome of Ian Harling, Barry Nelson, and Chris Bourchier pulling hard in the front of his canoe, Peter Cain guided his blue craft into the wind beside Denny and his boys and hefted in Scott Bindon, Andrew Skinner, and David Parker. But with a lightened load, the canoe was riding even higher in the water, and felt even more tippy. He ordered Bindon II, Skinner, and the hefty Parker to sit still on the bottom of the boat, called his voyageurs to the ready, and headed to shore to drop them off with the other boys. Richard Bird did the same, picking up Frazer Bourchier and bowsman-for-a-day, James Gibson.

For the ten boys on the shore, five dry and five wet, a painful drama was unfolding before them. They could hear the cries and see the blue canoes bobbing on the water. They could feel the wind and see it rustling the trees that clung, as they were doing, to the rocks against the high-cliffed Timiskaming shore. They could hear the rush of the whitecaps, and over it an occasional panicky cry. Scott Bindon knew his older brother Dean had drawn a place in Thompson's canoe, and was out there somewhere in the waves. He knew the last place Dean had wanted to be was in Neil Thompson's canoe. They had talked about it in the dorm. Kevin Black knew his twin, Owen, was in the same predicament. Chris Bourchier knew that his twin, Frazer, was okay because he had seen him in Mr. Bird's canoe as it had passed on the rescue runs.

Richard Bird, with his crew of silent Trojans, was first back to complete the rescue of Mark Denny and his remaining two paddlers in the water. Mike Mansfield—the one the boys called "Tank," who, like Parker, had a bit of extra body fat—seemed to be doing better than the others, certainly better than his steersman, the slightly built Denny, who, rather than comforting and encouraging the last of his crew, was becoming totally irrational. Bird, with five boys at the paddles—likely Hermann in the bow with Suttaby, Doak, Cunningham, and Pryce in the "pit"—tried first to tow

Denny's canoe with the crew holding on. With that kind of weight—three tons of water, 300 pounds of canoe, and at least that much gear, to say nothing of the resistance of three tired swimmers hanging onto the side—or the tippiness and wind-buffeting of his own lightened canoe, there was no possible way a tow would work. So the next best thing was to try to bring Denny and his two remaining crew members on board, as they had done with Frazer Bourchier and James Gibson. But in the process of executing this plan, Bird and his crew also dumped. Now three of the four new blue canoes were upset and out of commission. At that spot in the lake, about 300 feet from the Ontario shore—not far at all by rested-swimmer standards—there were now two leaders and seven boys in the water, some of whom had been there since the Denny boat dumped, and some who had been paddling full out for the past two hours, first burning with sweat in the sun and wind and now freezing as their bodies tried to shunt blood to their brains and vital organs. To the south, ostensibly gone and out of reach, was the entire crew of the first boat to upset—Neil Thompson, Todd Michell, Dean Bindon, Jody O'Gorman, Owen Black, Tim Hopkins, Simon Croft, and Tom Kenny—who had been in the water now for more than an hour and whom nobody had really seen or heard from since they dumped.

After dropping his first round of rescuees on the shore, Cain, Harling, Nelson, and Bourchier reached the Denny canoe soon after the Bird canoe dumped. To Cain, the designated leader of the expedition, this sight was particularly devastating because he knew as well as anyone that whatever the school forms might have said about who was leading the expedition, Bird was the most experienced canoeist of them all—he was the *de facto* expedition leader—and now *he* was in the water too. This was getting serious, but Bird was still lucid and in control. Bobbing in the water among Denny, Mansfield, Greaney, Hermann, Doak, Suttaby, Pryce, and Cunningham, advising them to stay calm and not to try climbing onto the canoes, Bird shouted to Cain that if he could see Thompson's boat, he should continue on to rescue them. Cain thought that he could see the fourth canoe. "Okay, I can handle this. We can swim in, you go get them," said Bird.

Bending their heads down to propel their big blue canoe directly into the wind one more time, Ian Harling, Chris Bourchier, and Barry Nelson, with Peter Cain in the stern, paddled south for about thirty minutes, but found no sign of Thompson, his crew, or his boat. They had disappeared from the surface of the lake. Cain turned again in the surf and headed back to the other canoes.

Pulling up close, being careful not to let waves push his canoe against one of the submerged canoes and crush one of the paddlers in the water, Cain threw Bird a line, hoping to use what strength he and his crew had left to tow the rest to shore. The boys in the water were moving toward Cain's canoe. Bird warned him not to take anyone in, fearing that the last canoe would upset as well. But before the towline could be attached, volunteer leader Mark Denny panicked and hauled himself up and over the side of Cain's canoe to get out of the cold water. He was halfway in before Bird could say anything more. Cain heaved him the rest of the way into the canoe, his paddlers doing their best to steady the canoe, which rocked furiously from wind, wave, and shifting weight. No longer in a rational state of mind, Denny stood up in the pitching canoe. "Sit down!" Cain screamed, but it was too late. The house was down. The fourth canoe rolled over, pitching four more swimmers into the deep water, bringing the number in the water to twenty-one: Thompson and his seven boys in their private hell to the south, and here, with the other three canoes, Denny, Mansfield, and Greaney (who had been in the water now almost as long as Thompson and his crew), Suttaby, Hermann, Doak, Cunningham, Pryce, Bird (who had been in the water for at least half an hour), and now Ian Harling, Chris Bourchier, Barry Nelson, and master Peter Cain, who had worn themselves out trying to find and rescue everyone else. Ten on the shore: Five dry, five drying in the sun and wind, watching, waiting, and wondering. Twenty-one in the water: A group of seven still somewhere out in the middle of the lake with their myopic leader and swamped canoe, and a group of thirteen, within 100 yards of the Ontario shore, with two more swamped canoes. A fourth canoe, likely Denny's, drifted away, driven by the wind and curling waves, and would finish up, strangely, with Thompson's canoe on the Quebec side of the lake.

What happened to Thompson and his crew one can only guess by rebuilding evidence after the fact. The only one to survive was Thompson himself, who washed up on the Ontario shore with the others, but had no idea how he got there. Four of his dead crew ended up on the Ontario side, and three were found with the canoe on the Quebec side, though well north of where the dumping first occurred. On the Ontario side were Kenny, O'Gorman, Croft—who were rescued but died on the shore— and one other, who very likely stayed with Thompson as they did their best to swim to safety. On the Quebec side were three boys—who may well have opted to stay with the canoe, as they had been told initially, rather than swim for their lives with Thompson—who were found the following day, floating beside their canoe at the base of a cliff at the water's edge. It is clear that the members of Neil Thompson's crew had no help from the rest of the group until it was too late, until hypothermia had taken its toll. Rescue efforts concentrated, in the main, on the canoe that was closest to the Ontario shore, Mark Denny's crew.

Meanwhile, in the water closer to the Ontario shore, Richard Bird looked at David Cunningham, bobbing there in the water in his Speedo, his slight, bare shoulders looking pale and bony under the orange of a wet keyhole life preserver, semiconscious, saying nothing, hardly moving, and knew that if something was not done soon, they would all succumb to cold. While other boys still had the energy to panic, and still others sang hymns, Bird, in the first of four rescues he would be credited with that day, towed David Cunningham to the shore. Lifting the nearly naked boy out of the water and onto the rocks beneath the dense evergreen underbrush, Bird tried to warm him with his own body, but knew that there were other boys in worse shape who needed his help. He covered Cunningham with his own life jacket, as well as the boy's. "Stay here," Bird said to the groggy boy, and then headed off to search for others.

Bird encountered, in various places along the Ontario shore, the members of his original crew who had been on the shore since the whole thing began, and those whom he had rescued from Mark Denny's canoe. He listened as they spilled out their version of what they had seen, including the fact that there were three boys in a nearby bay calling for help. Bird's rescue efforts continued. Three times he swam back out into the water, and three times he towed another semiconscious boy from Thompson's canoe to the makeshift camp at the base of the cliffs on the Ontario shore. Each time he did so, he took a moment to instruct the boys on the shore on how to do artificial respiration on their incapacitated classmate. When they reeled at the prospect, Bird angrily ordered them to commence resuscitation immediately. The boys did not understand that their friends were suffering from lack of heat as well as lack of oxygen. Still, they worked to resuscitate their fallen friends. At one point, Andrew Skinner thought he saw a flicker of life in the classmate to whom he was ministering aid, but in a moment it was gone. None of the three would survive.

Out on the lake, survivors remembered that Peter Cain started swimming in, like Bird, with one or two of the weaker boys, but partway in, Cain became very distressed about his decision to leave the canoes and turned back out, leaving the boys to go the last distance alone. What happened at the canoes depended very much on the character and temperament of the individual people. Some cried, some panicked, but most, by all accounts, were remarkably brave. Boys remembered the minister's son, Tim Pryce, locking hands across the swamped canoe with another boy, and saying, "May God be with us all."

The powerhouse trio from Cain's canoe—Ian Harling, Barry

Nelson, and Chris Bourchier—last into the water, were determined to act. They had been dumped into the water as a result of
the total mental collapse of volunteer leader Mark Denny. Ten
other people were struggling in the water around them, and there
were no real instructions as to what to do besides "Hang onto the
canoe," so Harling assumed leadership, a role he had perfected in
the dorm with bunk mate Chris Bourchier and friend Barry
Nelson. The three boys decided to attempt a "splash out," a technique of emptying the water from a swamped canoe. They took
turns getting up into the swamped canoe, with the other two
steadying on either side, and sloshed and splashed much of the
water out of one of the canoes. Had the canoe not had packs and
food boxes firmly tied into its bottom, they might have been able
to remove more water than they did, but on the other hand, the
lack of weight would have made the tall-sided vessel more susceptible to wind. Nevertheless, they were successful enough to start
contemplating a paddle back to shore, and were quite pleased with
what they had achieved. But just as they were about to begin that
process, another person in the water panicked, reached for the
gunwale in a last desperate grasp for safety, and rolled the canoe yet
another time.

This time, Ian Harling ended up about twenty-five feet away
from the rest of the crew, on the shore side of the boat. Increasingly devastated by the hopelessness of the situation, he saw that
Bourchier and Nelson were fading fast. Bird and Cain were either
on the shore or somewhere between the canoes and the shore.
The three boys had found the energy they needed to do the splash
out, but their hopes were dashed when the canoe rolled like a
great blue whale and filled again with black lake water. Now they
were facing death.

Harling talked to his two compatriots, knowing in his heart that
the situation was grim. Even Barry Nelson, who was such an
athlete and a good swimmer, was beginning to succumb. Their
voices were slowing. Their teeth had stopped chattering. Harling

was thinking about all they had done together—the initial drop-off, paddling madly to Denny's canoe, picking up Skinner, Parker, and Scott Bindon, taking them to shore, watching Mr. Bird dump, looking in vain for Thompson's canoe, and then dumping themselves. The stress of the experience brought these three together like nothing else they had ever been through, but Harling knew that he had arrived at the point of no return. "I can stay with them or . . . [try to swim to shore]. I still remember the debate I had in my own mind at that time," Harling recalls. "We had been told to stay with the canoe. I was pretty sure the other two couldn't make it to shore in the state they were in. I finally said I'm out of here, and swam toward shore. I told them I was heading in and they both responded. This is so hard, remembering."

At some point in the mêlée, Chris Suttaby and James Doak also decided to go out on their own and swim to shore. Said Suttaby to a *Toronto Sun* reporter immediately following the tragedy: "We had been told to stay with the boat but my friend James Doak saw that that was getting us nowhere so we decided to try and reach the shore a half mile away." By now, having been in the lake for some time, they were swimming to a place on the shore well north of the location where boys were first dropped off. They swam desperately and eventually made it, hauled themselves out on the rocks in the sunshine, and promptly passed out, waves still splashing on their new Ked runners.

Similarly, Mike Mansfield came to the conclusion on his own that the only way to survive was to swim to shore. Of all the boys in the water, Mansfield was the most experienced swimmer. His steersman, Mark Denny, by now was totally exhausted. The cold had rendered Denny almost senseless. One of the last things Denny had done was tie himself and one of the boys, using painter ropes, to the ends of the two canoes. The only other member of his canoe crew left in the water was David Greaney. The others had been rescued by Bird and Cain and were now on the shore, 250 feet away. Greaney was in pretty bad shape, but he had dug deep and found the resolve not to waste energy on panic. He was quiet, but Mansfield could see that there was not much time left for him either.

As Mike Mansfield made his decision, he did not know that the sound of planes he had heard flying over the lake from a distance was significant. His father, Oz, an Air Canada pilot, was flying local routes in the area that day and had passed over Lake Timiskaming that very Sunday afternoon, not once but four times, each time thinking about his son and the rest of the St. John's Junior Brigade and how much fun they must be having down there in the sunshine, paddling their big new canoes on the sparkling blue waters of Timiskaming.

Mike Mansfield had decided to act. He would swim to shore, but he would do what he could to help others do the same. As the boys struggled in the water, buffeted by waves, other people, and the wind, Mike and David Greaney found themselves near Mike's best friend, Andy Hermann, who had been in the bow of Richard Bird's canoe before it dumped trying to rescue theirs. Willing his numbed and heavy legs to do the inverted scissors kick that he had learned in his lifesaving lessons, Mansfield reached under Greaney's life preserver and grabbed the collar of his T-shirt. Meanwhile, Greaney did his best to make his stiff fingers hold onto Hermann, who reached back in the water to get a grip on Greaney's thick orange life preserver. With Mansfield as the motor, finding strength he didn't know he had, and with Greaney and Hermann kicking with what little resources they had left, the three of them started out, moving parallel to the waves, to swim to shore. At some point in the process, Mansfield suggested they try a hymn to keep their spirits up, but the exhausted boys were unable to sing.

Partway in, Andy Hermann could not hang on any longer and let go. As difficult as it was to see his best friend drift away in the waves, Mansfield sensed that now was not the time to turn back. He would come back out and get him later. But by the time he kicked himself and his remaining passenger to shore and clambered out, Greaney was unconscious and Mansfield himself was spent. Backing up onto the slippery black rocks, dragging Greaney as he went, Mansfield got the two of them almost out of the water and sat cradling his canoe mate on his lap. He could hear Andy Hermann calling out in the water. There was the will but not the energy to move, to re-enter the water to rescue his friend. Instead, Mansfield listened to Hermann calling, and did what he could to warm Greaney's wet, cold form with his own chilled body. Greaney felt so still and heavy on his lap. Using another lesson from swimming classes, he probed for a pulse in Greaney's neck with his numb fingers and, in the process, faded from consciousness himself. As he lay in the sunshine, waves rolling up at his feet, Hermann's cries for help drifted in and out on the wind.

Back at the makeshift camp, Richard Bird was trying to get things organized, fighting exhaustion—by now he had been without sleep for thirty-six hours—and the certain knowledge that what had begun as a routine accident at the start of another St. John's canoe trip had turned into a debacle, and it was not over. There were three boys dead on the shore. There were still boys and a master missing. They had some food and gear in the packs that had been dropped off, but this was far from an ideal campsite. They had landed at the base of a very steep, rocky shore. There was almost no flat ground at all among boulders and thick undergrowth at the base of what was basically a cliff at the water's edge, but they would have to make do. The boys would build a fire. Eventually, they would have to make some kind of mark to show others that they were here.

Warmed by the sun, Mike Mansfield eventually regained consciousness. There were no calls. Just the sound of the wind. And Andy Hermann was gone. It all seemed surreal. Greaney was still on his lap, but showing no signs of movement, his skin very pale. Gently getting out from behind his canoe mate and resting Greaney's back against the rock where they had been sitting, Mansfield started back along the shore toward where he thought the others would be. After finding two life jackets among the rocks on his way, he started to call and found Peter Cain, who was also out looking for survivors. He led Cain back to Greaney. Cain started artificial respiration, but quickly realized that the boy was dead, so the two of them headed back toward the camp. Mansfield told him about Andy Hermann. Cain said little.

When they reached camp, Mansfield saw three groups of boys still working on the three lads from Thompson's canoe who had been pulled one by one from the lake by Richard Bird. As one of the bigger boys on the trip, and one who still seemed to have energy, Mansfield joined the team that was cutting a hole in the dense forest at the base of the cliff. Using the ax and Swede saw that Peter Cain had found when they first dropped boys on the shore, Mansfield started to cut trees to open up the site. The saw blade got stuck as a big conifer teetered on its stump. In pulling out the saw, Mansfield skinned his knuckles—the sight of skinned knuckles and the smell of fresh sap was a memory that would flash back for years, triggered by the smell of evergreen. But a hole was made, fresh air and sunshine filtered in, life jackets were hung around the opening to mark the spot. Slowly the enormity of what had happened was starting to register.

When Doak and Suttaby regained consciousness on the shore, it was dark, but while they had slept, the sun had dried their clothes. Their bodies, however, were still ravaged by the cold water and the exhaustion in the aftermath of their dump. Somehow they knew that they were north of the makeshift camp, so they climbed a set of steep pitches because there was no way they could see to get south without going back into the water. Their heads were still muddled and fuzzy. At one point, guided only by starlight, Doak stepped into the darkness and disappeared with a thud and a grunt. Aware that something had happened to his canoe mate, but unable to comprehend the danger of falling, Suttaby stepped off the same ten-foot cliff, fell, and landed partly on his chum, narrowly missing his head. Luckily, there was no permanent damage. They stumbled on. The moon had risen, the wind had fallen. When they finally smelled smoke and reached the others, the first thing they saw was the pale, moonlit skin and face of Tom Kenny and the backs of classmates who were still trying to revive him.

At the end of Sunday, June 11, 1978, the final count on shore was grim: Three dead, ten missing, and eighteen survivors huddled in moss-covered scree at the base of a cliff on the Ontario side of the lake. Fires that had been built near the three fallen boys to warm them had been snuffed out as their deaths had been determined. Near a bigger fire, set at the base of a reflecting gray granite rock face, the three leaders had set up a small plastic tarp shelter for themselves. The boys had done their best to find shelter and warmth as well. David Cunningham, who was nearly naked but still alive, was cradled on the laps of Harling, Mansfield, Skinner, and Parker, who sat in a row with their backs to a rock— "as close to the bodies as to anyone else," one would recall. Cunningham could not stop shivering, but by this time they realized that shivering was a good thing—it was a sign of continuing life. Cunningham had a pulse, and that was more than they could say about Tom Kenny, Jody O'Gorman, and Tim Hopkins lying down near the water, whom Andrew Skinner and the others had tried for so long to resuscitate.

With darkness came the bugs and a sprinkling of rain. The wind eventually subsided. Using what gear they had—two and sometimes three boys to a wet sleeping bag—they prayed and huddled as yellow light from punky firewood licked shadows on the rocks. Some even slept fitfully, exhaustion overtaking any worries about comfort on a cold, wet, and mosquito-infested rock pile of a bed. Had they not been so chilled and exhausted, their minds might have wandered over the events of the day. It started out as such a beautiful day—sunshine, tailwinds, singing. How could things have gone so horribly wrong? Where was the rest of Thompson's crew? Why had the school put Thompson in the stern anyway? Every boy in his boat had been worried. If only someone had listened. The crackle of green boughs on the embers did little to mask the memory of the cries on the water. Mike Mansfield felt the weight and warmth of Cunningham on his lap. He felt him breathing. Hearts beat. Mansfield stared at the fire and thought of Greaney, Hermann, and his bunk mate Bourchier. He knew where Greaney was.

And so ended day one of the Junior Brigade's canoe trip at the end of St. John's School of Ontario's first year. For twelve boys and a young volunteer master, life had come to a tumultuous end. They had faced the challenge, dug deep to find the resources necessary to survive—in the St. John's way—and died. For eighteen others, life would never be the same.

On the morning of Monday, June 12, twenty-eight-year-old Gary Smith was ferrying his Trans Quebec Airlines piston helicopter from Mattagami back to Ottawa for routine maintenance. The strong south wind of the previous day had died, but as warm moist air had settled over the cold waters of Timiskaming during the night, a thick fog had formed, so Smith was flying down close to the water, knowing he could follow the river right to home base, if that turned out to be necessary. There was not much chatter on the radio, partly because he was in the north country where few people were flying, and partly because the weather conditions had fogged reception as well as visibility. Instead of listening to the world in his pilot's headset, he was paying attention to what was below, and wheeled quickly when he spied what looked like two big blue canoes floating in the middle of the lake. Hovering close to the water, he confirmed that these were canoes, but floating beside them, tied to the boats with rope, were two people in orange keyhole life jackets. One looked to be in his early twenties and the other was in his teens. Neither waved.

Unable to raise anyone on the radio, Smith continued south down the Quebec shore of the lake. He spotted a big radio tower behind what looked like some kind of fishing camp at the mouth of the Kipawa River, but there was nowhere to land, so he continued to fly low to keep the ground in sight through the fog.

One mile south of the lodge, he saw two more blue canoes, this time with three more people floating near them. No sign of life there either.

Still unable to make contact with anyone on any of his radio frequencies, Smith turned back to have another look at the fishing camp to see if there might be a place to land. He thought that, with the big tower nearby, there must be a radio phone in the lodge that could be used to summon help.

Inside the lodge, twenty-six-year-old outfitter Scott Sorensen and his family were finishing breakfast. They had heard the helicopter earlier, but now there was the unmistakable Doppler thump of it flying low directly toward their camp, with the intention of landing. Thinking that the pilot must be in some kind of technical trouble, Sorensen raced out. Smith carefully guided the aircraft down onto the lawn and told his story. It seemed a bit difficult to believe. Ten miles up the lake, two bodies tied to two big blue canoes. And one mile below the camp, two more canoes and three more people, up against a cliff that Sorensen had used for rock climbing with some of his clients. The bodies were eleven miles apart. This seemed strange indeed.

Sorensen explained to Smith that the radio telephone that used to send a signal through the big tower no longer worked. There was no road into the lodge. To get help, he should fly north to the village of Ville-Marie where he could report the incident to the Sûreté du Québec (SQ), the Quebec Provincial Police. Smith took off, and Sorensen and one of his guests prepared to rescue whoever was left from this ill-fated expedition. If the four canoes were as big as Smith described—he thought they might be as much as twenty feet long—there must be more than four people. Sorensen was puzzled because the few canoes he saw each year normally traveled on a short, oblique line from north to south, from the mouth of the Matabitchuan River to a portage called "The Indian," which took them up into Kipawa, avoiding the falls and rapids on the lower Kipawa River. The lake had been very rough the day before; even so, he or someone else at the camp would have seen them if they had come down from the north. Sorensen gassed and loaded his big open fishing boat, fired up the outboard motor, grabbed a pneumatic air horn for signaling, and headed south.

Scott Sorensen's first concern was for any survivors. There must be more people than those in the water. As he made his way south to the climbing rock, where Smith had reported sighting two canoes and three bodies, he did so at trolling speed, stopping periodically and turning off the motor to listen. He would sound the air horn, call, and listen. Nothing. Eventually, rounding a slight headland near his rock-climbing cliff, he saw what Smith had described. Two canoes, upright and awash, and three lifeless bodies in completely calm water at the base of the cliff. They were so small, he remembers thinking. Their eyes were open, their hair was dry. One of them was even still wearing a blue baseball cap embroidered with the red and white mark of the Montreal Expos. They were so small, so young, and so devoid of life.

Thinking back to that terrible moment, remembering the calm water and the fog still hanging in the air, Sorensen recounts:

The whole situation was quiet, so unreal. An eerie silence had fallen on the surrounding forest. Even the normal chatter of birds and squirrels had disappeared, and there was no trace of wind to rattle the leaves or stir the surface of the lake. The air felt heavy and stagnant, and I found myself straining for breath as though someone had placed a blanket over my head. Suddenly I felt an instant of panic, an overwhelming urge to cry out and hear a human voice break the silence. I yelled at the top of my lungs, but even my voice echoing from the overhanging cliffs had a hollow and empty ring to it.

Knowing there were two other canoes eleven miles up the lake, Sorensen pushed his big boat away from the boys with a paddle and started his big outboard. He went back to the lodge and then continued north, looking, listening, calling, and blasting his air horn into the fog, hoping that someone would answer. Nothing.

Again, just as Gary Smith had reported, ten miles up the lake, he found a lifeless Mark Denny and one of the boys firmly tied to the ends of two blue canoes. They looked so alive, heads well supported by excellent life jackets on calm water. By now, though, a wind out of the north was rising, the fog was lifting, and the lake was starting to ripple with the promise of another blow. Sorensen had now seen four big blue canoes. They were longer than twenty feet and, without a doubt, contained more than five people each. There had to be more people somewhere on the big lake, but he had searched over eleven miles of shoreline and found nothing, except the two macabre scenes.

Sorensen decided to cross the lake and search the Ontario side. As unlikely as it seemed at the time, it was the only place he could think of that might have survivors. Reaching again to start the motor, he heard the sound of another boat coming south toward him. It carried two SQ policemen and two volunteers who had heard the news from Gary Smith. Having no boat of their own, they had borrowed a splashy red fiberglass twenty-two-foot inboard/outboard tri-hulled cruiser owned by the local hotel owner in Ville-Marie. They spoke French and little English, Sorensen the reverse, but all talk stopped when Sorensen pointed to Denny and the boy tied to the ends of two blue canoes out toward the middle of the lake, the bodies bobbing in building waves.

After the police untied the bodies and loaded them into the cruiser, Sorensen tried to convince them that there must be survivors and that finding them was top priority, but the officers wanted him to take them to the location of the other three bodies. Sorensen complied, worried that if the survivors had been out all night, they would be in bad shape. It had been chilly, and another ripper of a wind seemed to be building, this time out of the north. He learned from the SQ that they had officially enlisted the support of Gary Smith and his helicopter to continue the search.

At the rock-climbing site, Scott Sorensen watched as the three small boys were pulled from the water and laid with the bodies of Mark Denny and their classmate in the front of the tri-hulled cruiser, bringing the total occupancy to nine: four burly men, Mark Denny, and the bodies of four slight schoolboys. As the boat squatted low in the water, Sorensen looked out at the lake, which now had sizable waves rolling down before a freshening north wind, and wondered what the SQ had in mind to do next.

Of all Timiskaming blows, it is the north wind that Scott Sorensen respects the most. He understood that the two officers' intention was to go back to town first with the bodies and the news. Sorensen considered the waves and knew that more trouble was afoot. Five miles up the lake was Point Martel, where the long narrow lake pitched east and straight into the eye of the north wind. Sorensen knew from experience that if the waves in front of his camp were two-and-a-half feet with breaking whitecaps, then around Point Martel there would be ten miles of foaming white water with four-foot troughs to motor through. As the boat was front-loaded and the officers were apparently not too familiar with handling the borrowed craft, Sorensen did what he could to dissuade the SQ from carrying out their plan. Said Sorensen later:

I tried to tell these policemen just how bad I thought it would be, but I'm trying to tell people who lived on this lake all their lives what to do. They're telling me, "Look, kid (I was twenty-six at the time), we're in our fifties, we know this lake. We were born and raised here. We know this lake." That was the impression they were giving. And I just said, "I hope you know that place up by Point Martel, because it is nasty." I couldn't get through to them. Maybe they didn't care enough. Maybe they thought they'd found everybody. It seemed to me they were saying, "This is it. It is over. We've found the victims." Then they took off and headed north.

Later, Sorensen would learn from neighbors who helped rescue the SQ and retrieve the bodies—for a second time—that when the loaded cruiser rounded Point Martel, it ran into heavy seas.

Sorensen's neighbors, Jake and Harley Helm, described watching the red cruiser buck seas as it rounded the point that day. The bow was digging into the troughs, until one particularly big wave rolled over the boat and sheared off the windshield. With that, the driver gunned the cruiser to the rocky shore, right to the clearing where the Helms were coming down to draw water. The boat was awash, and while the inboard/outboard motor was still functioning, the object was to get to dry land as quickly as possible. To the amazement of the Helms, the driver rammed the damaged boat right up onto the shore and four big men scrambled out, just before the cruiser and its remaining occupants were sucked back into the lake by the waves and started to sink. Thinking that the five people in orange keyhole life jackets were passengers in need of rescue, the Helms waded into the water, only to learn from the men on the shore that haste was not required. Denny and the four boys were already dead.

While all that was going on, pilot Gary Smith reconnoitered the lake and saw smoke and survivors on the Ontario side, about a mile north of Grand Encampment Bay. He landed again at the lodge to pass on the news. Sorensen was relieved—finally, word of survivors. The lake was rough and getting rougher by the minute, but his boat was built for rough seas and he had lots of experience on this very route. He headed out anyway, hoping in his heart that he would return with survivors.

Motoring directly to the Ontario shore of the lake, he again slowed, and stopped occasionally to blow his horn and call out in case Smith was mistaken about positioning, or in case survivors were spread out along the west shore of Timiskaming. Two miles south of Nagel Bay, he found two more victims. The heartbreaking scene had become familiar: life jackets secure, faces up, eyes open, hair dry. No canoes this time.

Sorensen continued slowly south, past a rocky point. He quickly shut off the motor. On the shore was another boy, but he was out of the water. He had hauled himself out and now sat or leaned on a log or a rock. Finally, a survivor, thought Sorensen. He called repeatedly. He drifted closer and called again, but there was no answer. Like the others, the boy was dead. He had come so close to life. He had survived the cold water that killed his classmates and dried himself in the wind and the sun, only to die in the end. The utter sadness of the image constricts Scott Sorensen's throat and brings tears to his eyes today as it did then on that windy Monday in June 1978 when he floated on Timiskaming, hoping to find life, not more death. "He was just a child. He had tried so hard. He had succeeded in getting out of the lake. He had done what he was supposed to do and still he died," Sorensen says to me years later as we visit the site, his voice drifting to a whisper.

Just as Gary Smith had said, Sorensen found the survivors' camp about a mile north of Grand Encampment Bay. He saw the smoke and the hole in the thick woods at the base of the cliffed shore, and the orange life jackets hanging listlessly in the trees. When he heard the motor, Richard Bird emerged from the trees and waved from a partially submerged rock. Sorensen asked if he was part of the canoeing expedition with the blue canoes and the little boys. Bird said, "Yeah, that's all part of our group." Bird asked how many others they found. Sorensen said eight, none alive, and watched the news knock the wind out of Bird. Sorensen asked how many people were in the camp. Eighteen, the beleaguered leader replied. After a pause, recovering, Bird asked if Sorensen had found a leader, an adult male. Yes, but he was dead. Again, Bird recoiled but steeled himself. He asked Sorensen not to discuss the deaths, and mentioned that three of the survivors had brothers, two of them twins, who were still missing. He said they had three bodies in camp. Sorensen would have to take the survivors back to the camp in two trips.

Bird ushered Peter Cain and the first round of boys out of the makeshift camp and into Sorensen's big boat. Cain said little. One of the boys spoke to Sorensen as he stepped aboard, and he recognized him as the identical twin of one of the first victims he had seen earlier in the day, floating at the base of the rock-climbing cliff. "Have you seen my brother?" he asked politely. The hair, the eyes, the Expos cap—was too much. "We're still looking" was all Sorensen could think to say before turning away.

By nightfall on Monday, the surviving boys were tucked into warm sleeping bags at Sorensen's camp. Their bug bites were horrendous, but they had eaten, they were dry and warm, and they were together in a safe place. One of Sorensen's daughters lent David Cunningham a pair of faded jeans and a powder-blue sweatshirt to cover his Speedo bathing suit. Guests at the lodge did their best to comfort the boys. Sorensen talked long into the night with Bird, Cain, and Thompson. There was no doubt in his mind that Bird was bearing up, in spite of all odds, but Cain and Thompson were still in shock.

Outside in the darkness, the covered bodies of eight boys rested on Sorensen's dock, their new Ked runners sticking out from under the tarp, as if they were only resting, playing some sort of nighttime game of hide-and-seek. With no direct communication to the outside world, Gary Smith had to ferry to the lodge a variety of medical and police officials, who did their best to determine what happened, who lived, and who died, to get the news out. Reporters started arriving by air, commandeering every floatplane in the north country. The boys snuggled up to the big oil drum stove in Sorensen's main lodge, talking quietly. Some slept, finally, at what they thought was the end of the nightmare. They had no idea that the worst was yet to come.

And with that, the day came to a close. The lake again settled against the rock and the darkness. Whippoorwills called from the safety of nests on the shore. Nighthawks wheeled. Bats dipped silently over deep water reflecting silver wings and stars turning on the arc of a rising moon. Up from the dock, where all was quiet, silhouetted in a cabin window against butter-yellow kerosene light, Scott Sorensen and the leaders talked on.

66

Rivière des Quinze

11

New Liskeard
Devil Rock

101

Lac
des
Quinze

Ottawa River

Haileybury

Ville-Marie

THE
TRAGEDY

N
W — E
S

Two canoes and two victims
found by helicopter

Point Martel (police boat swamps)

Sorensen's camp

Whistler's Point

Lac
Kipawa

Rapelling Rock
(two canoes and three victims)

Survivors' camp

Grand Encampment Bay

First canoe upset

McMartin Point (lunch)

66

Ontario

101

64

Timiskaming Wharf
(start of trip)

Timiskaming

11

63

Quebec

Hudson
Bay

533

Ottawa

17

North Bay

Mattawa

River

Trans-Canada Highway

17

DAWN HUCK

VII

The Aftermath: Waiting for Answers

Like Oz Mansfield who unknowingly flew over tragedy four times in his DC-9 that Sunday in June, other parents went about their business contentedly through the day and most of Monday, thinking their sons were in good hands, paddling hard, and having the time of their lives. Jack Suttaby, who had hauled canoes with his trailer and watched the boys depart on Sunday morning, drove directly home and arrived back in Toronto mid-afternoon. Thelma Cunningham had asked him to check in on his return, so before turning in for much-needed sleep, he called Mrs. Cunningham to report that all was well. It had been a beautiful morning at the Timiskaming landing. The boys seemed fit and fine, a little tired perhaps, but everything seemed in order. "If I eat one more peanut butter sandwich," he said, laughing, "I think I'm going to be sick. Just wanted to let you know that they got away in fine style. I'm off to bed."

While Jack Suttaby slept, news started to filter out, beginning with spotty radio reports that no doubt originated from small stations in the vicinity of Lake Timiskaming. The fact that the incident occurred on the border between a French- and an English-speaking jurisdiction may have slowed and perhaps even confused the outflow of details about what happened. Officials on the scene at Scott Sorensen's lodge at the mouth of the Kipawa River, all of whom were French, were getting information from English-speaking sources, including Sorensen himself, as well as from Richard Bird and Peter Cain. At source, there was ample opportunity for confusion as English information was translated into French for passage up the line, via aircraft or boat, to Ville-Marie. At Ville-Marie, when news was conveyed to the school and to English-speaking news outlets, the same information had to be translated back into English, creating, at least initially, several versions of what happened.

Back at the school in Claremont, Mike Maunder, like Jack Suttaby, went straight to bed when he arrived home on Sunday afternoon, unaware of what was transpiring with the St. John's Junior Brigade. But on Monday, after the first garbled bulletins came to his attention, Maunder tried to call the SQ in Ville-Marie. The early reports did not name St. John's School, but there were clues, such as the phrase "Anglican boys' school from Toronto," that gave him reason to worry. Confirmation that the accident did involve St. John's School of Ontario's Junior Brigade came in a rather surprising way. As Maunder tried to get through to Ville-Marie, an operator broke into his telephone connection saying that NBC News in New York was trying to contact him. With that came unofficial confirmation that it was his school's trip. He would not sleep again for days.

With remarkable presence of mind, Maunder then made several telephone calls in quick succession. He phoned a parent and asked that all the other parents be notified of the accident and to come to the school; he phoned Ted Byfield in Edmonton, who apparently promised to be on the next plane east; and he phoned two other friends of the school with a request that they come to help answer the phones in the hours to come. Already reporters were calling for details, facts in the early hours that Mike Maunder did not have. What he had heard sounded ominous. He would need to concentrate on the boys and the parents.

Like Mike Maunder, some parents got their first inkling of the accident from radio and television. Again, the sketchiness of reports, with no mention of the school by name, left them wondering. But word spread, and the level of detail in the news reports increased, as did the scope of the reporting. Ron and Marion Kenny heard first from Marion's mother in England, who phoned after hearing the story on BBC Radio. Joan Mansfield got a call from her sister in Ottawa, who had heard that there had been an accident involving boys from an Anglican private school near Toronto. Her sister thought that there could not have been too many Anglican boys schools from Toronto on Lake Timiskaming at one time. Later in the day, when the call came from the school to tell Joan about the accident, they were also able to tell her that her son Mike was alive because, during an altercation with the SQ about getting into his duffel bag to fish out extra clothes after arrival at Sorensen's lodge, the officer had written down his name. She was the only who found out early that her son had survived the ordeal.

Norm Bindon was off Monday. Early that evening he was in Square One Mall in Mississauga with his daughter when a request for him to report to the mall office came over the shopping center's public address system. It was a moment that would haunt him forever, wife Ruth with deep fear in her voice relaying the request that they go to the school to await further news of sons Scott and Dean. The drive to Claremont was chaotic. They drove, with sheets of rain falling from a prematurely dark evening sky, windshield wipers flailing to keep up with the downpour, while they flipped from radio station to radio station to get the breaking news.

Thelma Cunningham, who was just getting back to some sense of normalcy three weeks after her husband's death, was back to her volunteer role as chairperson of the Metropolitan Toronto Girl Guides. She was in a church auditorium having supper with a group of Girl Guide leaders. She remembers the call, the rainy night, the blue dress she had on. She remembers one of her friends being called away to the phone during the meal. It was Thelma's pastor from St. Stephen's on the line, asking that they keep Thelma at the meeting until he could come by and pick her up. Something terrible had happened. So instead of getting the news directly, families received it at least once removed. There had been an accident and all parents were to go to the school. She would have to wait until her minister came to pick her up. In the meantime, that was all the information they had. The Girl Guide dinner, the drive, the rain, the school, the crowd of anxious parents, her husband's death, the talk of Timiskaming at the wake— it was all a bit of a blur.

For Joanne Harling, too, it was all so surreal, going from a nice dinner out with the family to imagining the possible death of a son:

> We had been out for dinner. My brother-in-law and sister-in-law heard it on the news and came and waited at our house. They drove us out to the school immediately. I always had it in the back of my mind that Ian was a strong swimmer, and I had two other children, so I never really gave up at that point. I've lost him. I've got two other children. Aren't I lucky? I also kept in the back of my mind that he was a survivor.

At the Michell home, near Uxbridge, that Monday, Todd's mother was doing the laundry. While emptying pockets of her son's old blue jeans, left behind as he packed for his canoe trip, she found a poem that he had written on the last day of school and stuffed into his pocket. The boy who was so hampered by reading and writing because of his dyslexia prior to going to St. John's was writing poetry of his own volition. It was a discovery that with the ringing of a phone would become almost too much to bear. She read:

> St. John's School is a jolly place
> Everyone has a smile on their face
> Kids jump and kids shout
> Even though they got a clout.
> When the canoe trips start in the fall
> The kids seem to climb the wall
> A swat or two never hurt anyone
> Really it is rather fun.

Midway through Monday evening, most of the parents of the Junior Brigade had been contacted and were either at the school or on their way. Also at the school by then were dozens of journalists, two police officers who were friends of one of the families, and nine clergy, including Lewis Garnsworthy, Anglican Bishop of Toronto, who had first given permission for Mike Maunder and Frank Felletti to set up the part-time school in St. Jude's parish hall. Later in the evening, when the names of the living and the dead were read, and parents grieved, Bishop Garnsworthy invited everyone to pray. Someone lashed out in an accusatory tone, as if the hopelessness of prayer for a son already dead were too much to bear. "Who are *you?*" he asked. "I am the Bishop of Toronto, and we will say a prayer!" replied the bishop.

It was a time of uncertainty, a crowd of frightened people, each of them, except Joan Mansfield, confronted with the ultimate agony—the possible death of a child. Time dragged on. The rain continued, and darkness fell, though no one noticed. One parent pulled all the thumbtacks out of a bulletin board, recently cleared in the hurry to make the place shipshape for Open House, and spelled P R A Y with tacks on the cork board. Others just waited in numbed silence. Sheena Suttaby recalls:

I've gone through several painful episodes in my life—sickness, childbirth—but nothing, *nothing*, came near to that pain of imagining your child dead because it had never really come home to me before then. It was the worst physical pain I could even try to describe. I thought I was going to explode. There's no relief for such pain. Now, I got relief several hours later, but those parents who didn't—I don't know how they coped. I think I would have gone insane.

At 9 p.m., having been on the phone repeatedly to Ville-Marie, Mike Maunder was told that the list of survivors and dead would be ready in an hour. Several mothers collapsed from the strain. An ambulance crew was called to treat them for shock. "My God," a distraught parent breathed, "it is like playing roulette."

Sometime after 10 p.m., the call came in. Mike Maunder asked the parents with boys who were on the canoe trip to join him in an office on the second floor, where the list of survivors was read first: Scott Bindon, Kevin Black, Frazer Bourchier—three of whom had lost brothers, two of them twins—Paul Lockie, James Gibson, Mike Mansfield, Robin Jensen, Rob Kerr, Paul Nyberg, David Parker, Andrew Skinner, Chris Suttaby, Ian Harling, David Cunningham, and James Doak. Then was read the list of those presumed dead: Dean Bindon, Owen Black, Chris Bourchier—who had rescued others and with extraordinary bravery shaken out the canoe while his brother waited on shore—Simon Croft, David Greaney, Andy Hermann, Tim Hopkins, Tom Kenny, Todd Michell, Barry Nelson, Jody O'Gorman, and Tim Pryce. The only victim's name not read was Mark Denny's. His mother, Jean, had chosen to await news at home. She called. People heard Maunder say, "Oh Jean! I'm so sorry, I'm so *sorry*."

As if he had been trained for the role, Mike Maunder pulled himself together after awaiting the unofficial verdict from Ville-Marie. He managed to track down Frank Felletti, who was with the Senior Brigade north of Wawa, as well as Frank Wiens, who was leading a trip in northwestern Ontario. He drafted a statement for the media, convened a press conference at the school, and did his best to answer a barrage of probing questions. In the middle of all that, he chartered a school bus to take the parents to Ville-Marie, and sometime after midnight the bus arrived. Parents like the Harlings had had to make hasty arrangements for their departure, or draw on the goodwill of neighbors and friends who had been caring for siblings of the boys. Sheena Suttaby rushed home to change and picked up Chris's school jacket—it smelled like woodsmoke, like all his St. John's clothes, and like him. Thelma Cunningham's older children were living away from home. Her husband was newly dead. Her youngest was alive but sitting in a fishing lodge with no phone on the shores of a godforsaken northern lake, probably scared out of his wits. Still in the blue dress she had worn to the Girl Guides' dinner, but now armed with blankets for the boys, she joined the other stricken parents and boarded the yellow school bus at 2 a.m. on Tuesday morning. On the same road along which their sons journeyed into darkness two nights before, occasional headlights caught glistening cheeks that were streaked with fear.

Many parents were lost in their own reverie of grief, anger, and guilt. Sixty minutes into the six-hour trip, one parent became ill. Another began drinking a big bottle of rum. The alcohol didn't help smooth the ride or calm nerves. Sheena Suttaby remembers a journalist following the bus. At a stop for coffee and something to eat, *Toronto Star* reporter Christie Blatchford approached Sheena's husband, Jack, probing for details for the story she would write for the following day's paper. During the emotional bus ride, she remembers thinking, "I almost hated [Jack]. I resented the press. I wondered, 'Why the hell is he talking to that woman?' We just wanted to be left alone."

Through a sunrise that some thought would never come to relieve the gloom, the bus eventually arrived at the Ville-Marie community center at 7:30 a.m. It had been a long, long night.

The people of Ville-Marie did all they could to make the parents welcome. Food, drink, cots, phones, and cognac were freely offered by the Knights of Columbus, the Red Cross, the Golden Age Club, the Christian Women of Ville-Marie, and a host of private citizens who knew that their lake could kill and who could imagine, some from personal experience, what it was like to lose a child. What might have been a collision of mother tongues turned out not to be an issue at all. Hospitality and welcome, given freely and without expectation of return, overwhelmed already overwhelmed parents.

Thelma Cunningham was called to the phone. It was a reporter from North Bay who wanted to know about her son, David. She had no idea how he got her name. Cameramen were taking photographs through the window of the ladies' washroom in the community center. Someone taped newspaper over the window to protect what little privacy they had left.

In these early moments on Tuesday morning, June 13, 1978, even before the parents were reunited with their surviving sons, news had spread around the world and back again. Headlines eerily reminiscent of Balsam Lake were emblazoned on newspapers near and far. "12 boys, teacher, drown on canoe trip," said the *Globe and Mail.* "12 boys, teacher, die in lake as storm capsizes three canoes," trumpeted the *Toronto Star.* "13 die on survival adventure," said the *Ottawa Citizen* over a picture of bodies on Sorensen's dock. "School canoes swamped; 12 boys, teacher drown," printed the *Winnipeg Free Press.* "12 youngsters drown while on canoe outing in Quebec," reported the *Halifax Chronicle-Herald.* "13 canoeists die in Quebec storm," said the *Washington Post.* "12 children and adult drowned in Quebec lake," was the headline in the *New York Times. The Times,* England, wrote, "16 school group canoeists drown." From the beginning, there was no consensus about what happened at Timiskaming. The *Toronto Star* was most vigilant in getting the full story and quoted Ted Byfield's response to the news: "Perfectly hideous. You're always haunted by the dread that something is going to happen—then whack! You take all the safety precautions you can take and then some more . . . but it's always luck or the grace of God that saves you."

Meanwhile, twenty miles south of Ville-Marie at the fishing lodge, every available floatplane brought news crews, all of them anxious to put a face on human tragedy. Overnight, Mike Mansfield, who had slipped out of his sleeping bag and been accosted by a reporter through the Sorensens' bathroom window, was told he couldn't go back to bed until he gave a comment on what had happened. Now, with the surface of the lake once again stirred by the wind, and with all the planes under hire by news agencies, deals had to be struck between the media and the on-site officials in order to get the boys and the bodies out to Ville-Marie. Gary Smith would ferry the bodies north in his helicopter.

The boys remained together inside the Sorensen family cabin, and watched as their deceased classmates were carried on makeshift stretchers, one by one from the dock to the back lawn, right past the partitioned windows of the cabin. They talked and cried among themselves, seeing only the white treads on the soles of new running shoes under gray woolen blankets as the bodies were carried past them. Later reports in various papers would include quotes that many of the boys would later agree could only have been recorded with parabolic microphones aimed up at the cabin wall or windows during this part of the aftermath. They had been told to be careful about what they said to the media, and were staying indoors to avoid questions that everyone knew the reporters would ask. Scott Sorensen did not know where to turn. Still very upset by what he had seen, he slipped out to a back cabin for respite. The haunting images of the past twenty-four hours would not fade.

On the first plane to arrive in Ville-Marie from the fishing lodge was Junior Brigade leader Peter Cain, David Cunningham (still without shoes), and Ian Harling. Cain was still in a state of total shock, and was ushered into the back of an SQ cruiser where he was photographed looking tearful and exhausted. A reporter from the *Ottawa Citizen* persisted with questioning and reported that "the rugged looking Englishman in charge of Sunday's expedition refused to comment on the accident." Elsewhere, Cain was quoted as saying, soon after landing in Ville-Marie, "My God, what can I say now? We are a Christian school and are just thanking the Almighty that we are not among the dead. I have nothing more to say until I talk to the parents. I still don't know what I'll say to them."

Joanne Harling had a large bottle of Caladryl that she applied liberally to son Ian and to the rest of the boys when they arrived at the Ville-Marie public dock. Parents of two of the deceased asked to be shown their bodies in the Ville-Marie morgue. The Nelsons, from Markham, who had lost their only child, found transportation and disappeared home on their own.

Later, in a story that became headline news the next day, in what could be described as a courageous act, Richard Bird stepped up to the microphones and presented an account of the accident for the press. Described later as a person of poise and breeding, a man who "glitters when he walks," Bird, now into his fourth day without sleep, looked spent. But he squared his shoulders to the task and stopped periodically to regain composure, while the press cameras clicked and the television cameras rolled. He began: "I'm going to tell you a story—it's not going to be easy for me to tell." Eyes sunken, face grizzled, and wearing a once-white T-shirt, Richard Bird fiddled with a tissue, alternately wiping his eyes and wringing the tissue in long, grubby fingers. He described a "chain of small accidents that took away our chances," and assured the press that as far as he was concerned, strong winds and waves were not a factor in upsetting the canoes. "At no time up until the dumping of the first canoe did I think there was any hazard to canoeing," said Bird. He was the only one to speak to the press. Peter Cain was nowhere to be found.

In the aftermath, Bird behaved like a leader. Given his performance at the Ville-Marie press conference and his background, it was not surprising that the media assumed he was the leader of the Junior Brigade. They learned he was a private pilot, that he commanded his own forty-foot ketch on the Great Lakes, that he was by vocation a professor of mathematics and economics at a prestigious Canadian university, that he was an experienced canoeist, and that he was a St. John's old boy from the Manitoba school. When media accounts named Bird as the expedition leader, no one challenged the assumption—not the school, not Cain, not Bird himself. It was a noble and possibly canny gesture on Bird's part that would make a world of difference in how the Timiskaming tragedy would be perceived by parents and the public in the fullness of time. No one seemed to notice that on day one of reporting about Timiskaming, June 13, Peter Cain was listed as the leader of the St. John's Junior Brigade and that, by the next day, June 14, responsibility had apparently shifted from a full-time St. John's master to a willing volunteer. With the arrival of the last survivor, everyone reboarded the bus bound for Claremont, and the media circus pulled up stakes and left the town of Ville-Marie.

The boys, though exhausted and tearful, were quietly talkative when reunited with family, describing the Sorensens' place, their plane rides, fading in and out of reporting on the tragedy itself and what it might mean. Thelma Cunningham remembered son David turning to her in the bus, saying, "I've got to go to the funerals. I've got to go to the funerals." Those who lost sons sat silently in their unspeakable grief as they watched others hold onto the sons they had been reunited with. The Blacks and Bourchiers had both lost and found a twin; the Bindons held Scott, knowing that their stronger and elder son, Dean, had died. Eventually, the knife that Dean had worn so proudly at the Open House would be returned to Norm Bindon, having been removed from his son's body as it was prepared for burial. How difficult it must have been for the unsuspecting Neil Thompson, Dean Bindon's steersman, who had told Maunder and Felletti that he wasn't ready to stern a canoe, to sit among the parents knowing he had lost all seven of his first-time crew. How inspired they had all been by Richard Bird's stoic recounting of the tragedy for the press. How necessary it was to start thinking about the next steps, about funerals, healing, and getting back to some sense of normalcy.

In the days that followed, debate raged in the papers about every aspect of the tragedy. People took strong stands, both pro and con, regarding the responsibility of St. John's School. With so much unfolding, no one thought to analyze the roots of the tragedy, St. John's twenty-five-year history, or the group-paddling canoes built especially for St. John's schools by the Chestnut Canoe Company. A reporter from the *Ottawa Citizen* contacted the general manager of the Chestnut Canoe Company, Mike Mallory, who explained that the canoes were modified to make them less prone to taking on water while providing greater depth to increase carrying capacity. Mallory was quoted in the paper as saying the canoes were "unsinkable, but not immune to capsizing," which had to be one of the great understatements of Timiskaming.

The four new blue canoes were impounded in Ville-Marie. On June 16, it was announced that June 28 and 29 were set for an inquest that would be convened by special coroner Stanislas Dery. Dery was a Quebec Crown prosecutor, defense lawyer, and a former lieutenant-commander in the Royal Canadian Navy in the Second World War. It was expected that the inquest would hear from twenty witnesses in proceedings to be conducted in the Ville-Marie provincial courthouse. That same day, the first of the victims, Owen Black, was buried and a huge memorial service was held at the Church of St.-Martin-in-the-Fields in Toronto.

The sanctuary of St. Martin's was filled beyond capacity with 300 mourners in attendance. The parents of the dead were ushered in with an honor guard of older boys from all three St. John's schools. An overflow crowd of 200 sat on chairs in the damp basement of the hundred-year-old church and listened to the service through crackly public address speakers.

The sanctity of St. Martin's and the solemnity of the biblical texts were comforting for some and utterly incongruous for others who remembered the bubbly cacophony of youth in full stride. There was not a sound in the pews, except for the songs of birds in courtyard trees that drifted in through open windows of the old stone church, as clergy struggled to find meaning in the word of God. Among the readings were portions of Psalm 65:5: "By terrible things in righteousness wilt thou answer us, O God of our salvation, who art the confidence of all the ends of the earth, and of them that are afar off upon the sea." A passage from the Apostle Paul's letter to the Romans (8:31–39) asked "If God be for us, who can be against us?" finishing with the assurance that "neither death, nor life, nor angels . . . nor height, nor depth, nor any other creature, shall be able to separate us from the love of God." Bishop Garnsworthy spoke, as did Frank Felletti, searching for words of solace for all who grieved.

Just as school officials had moved so deftly to shape public opinion in the wake of Markus Jannasch's death nearly thirty years before, in his address at the memorial service, the headmaster did his best to develop the unavoidable accident idea, saying: "My immediate reaction [was] absolute despair combined with sudden anger. What have we done to offend You? Why have You deserted us? Then I heard radio reports, reports of violent storms, of inexperience. Inexperience? We paddled Great Slave Lake, Lake Superior, Lake Athabasca—Lake Winnipeg, the worst lake in the world for suddenness of storms is our home lake. I said so myself, we have paddled lakes far colder than Lake Timiskaming. We were prepared." What he did not say was that they had had nasty dumps on all of them, in similar canoes, in similarly cold water, and it was only through luck and the grace of God, as Ted Byfield pointed out immediately following the tragedy, that the school had not sustained other unfortunate deaths.

The *Toronto Star*, in its coverage of the service, highlighted Felletti's defense of Richard Bird in his eulogy: "Richard Bird—that fine young man, I trust him completely. He has a pilot's license, he is familiar with weather conditions. He would never allow a storm to slip up on him." The *Star* was the only news outlet to notice that there was a slight shift in the school's accounting of who was in charge of the Junior Brigade, referring to Bird in their memorial service article as "the unofficial leader of the trip." Frank Felletti finished his speech with a flourish: "We are a Christian school with Christian values and the outdoor program is such a small part. I was convinced that we were doing the right thing, doing God's work. If there is doubt in anyone's mind, we were prepared."

As a courtesy to the parents who had lost boys on the lake, Frank Felletti linked with Richard Bird, Peter Cain, and Neil Thompson to visit the homes of the deceased to offer their condolences, grieve with families, answer questions, and offer explanations of the circumstances under which their sons died. Neil Thompson, who had lost his entire crew, was a physical and

emotional wreck, but still somehow found the strength to partici-
pate in these visits. Todd Michell's parents, still holding onto the
poem they had found in Todd's trousers, reached out to Thompson without anger. They prayed with him and invited him to join
them for a meal so he could, however haltingly, tell them what
had happened to their son. Thompson's strength of character in
visiting Tom Kenny's parents in Markham—the only leader from
the expedition to do so—moved these parents as well. Ron
Kenny later recalled, "Neil suffered terrible guilt as a result of the
accident, but was one of the few teachers brave enough to come
to our home to share our grief and agony." The consensus was
that Thompson was as much a victim of Timiskaming as anyone
else who was in the lake that life-changing day in June.

With twelve funerals dominating the coverage over the next
week—Barry Nelson and Tom Kenny were interred side by side
in a joint ceremony in Markham—the debate about the whys and
wherefores of Timiskaming moved from headline news to the
editorial pages, but around the school and its version of events was
a cordon of parents whose loyalty was fierce and enduring. The
reporters were persistent, but publicly the parents had nothing but
praise and support for the school. Behind the public mask was a
different story, but most of them had been involved with the
school since day one and felt implicated by association, if not by
their silence, about little things they had noticed throughout the
year, such as unusual canoes on the lawn at the Open House. Oz
Mansfield drove reporters off his front lawn in Angus, Ontario,
asking them to leave his boy in peace. Many of the parents
expressed the conviction that not only would their boys be
returning to St. John's in the fall, but also they would be accompanied by their younger brothers. It was an impressive show of
solidarity and support. The notion that Timiskaming was an accident pervaded the overall impression presented in the media.
People struggled to put away the tragedy, and, for many, the only
explanation that seemed to make sense was that this was the act of
a mysterious, if not benevolent, God.

The press continued to push for answers to the tragedy, so the false assumption by headline writers of a storm on Lake Timiskaming went unchallenged. Reported wind velocity varied widely, and wave height went from a low of two feet to a high of twelve feet, crest to trough. Reports of a storm warning issued by Environment Canada out of North Bay sometime on Sunday afternoon only fueled the storm-cause theory. By the time Frank Felletti attempted to put the idea to rest for good, in his memorial service defense of Richard Bird, it no longer seemed to matter. The lake and the weather had been implicated, vilified even, as unpredictable and capricious. Mistakes had been made, but the weather was something over which no mortal had control.

In fact, the wind and waves on Lake Timiskaming had elicited from boys and staff acts of selflessness and courage. The Mansfields had a family friend who worked for the *Barrie Examiner*, and, as a way of helping his son tell his story with a minimum of trauma (Oz also hoped secretly that this accounting might keep Mike from having to testify at the inquest), they gave the friend and reporter access to their son. The reporter asked if he could name one outstanding hero among the many who emerged as a result of the accident. Mike replied: "It would have to be Mr. Bird. He got everything organized and kept watch the whole first night. He only got about 15 minutes' sleep when another boy and I kept watch until the morning."

Generally, the reportage kept to the high road, more or less supporting the accident line of thinking and the notion that everything was done according to protocol to deal with the victims and survivors in the wake of the tragedy. The story of the red cabin cruiser being driven up on shore at Point Martel and five of the bodies being subjected to the indignity of a second and completely unnecessary dunking in the lake was soft-pedaled. However, someone who was at Point Martel on Monday, June 12, had snapped a picture of the sinking boat and gave or sold the lurid image to the Quebec tabloid *Allo Police*, which ran it in their next edition, mercifully without more than a caption to explain what was going on. Mainstream papers, like the *Ottawa Citizen*, said simply, "The first six bodies [it was really only five] . . . were relayed by boat to a point north and transported by ambulance to the morgue in Ville-Marie."

Working on damage control of their own, the school invited all parents and boys from the Junior Brigade to the school on the weekend following the memorial service, where they offered—in private and away from the press—maps, charts, diagrams, and explanations from Bird, Cain, and Thompson about their version of events. Once again, there was never any effort to look deeper into the historical ethos of St. John's School than absolutely necessary. Parents seemed to accept Richard Bird as the *de facto* leader of the trip and if they *did* ask questions about canoes or why Mike Maunder was not on the trip—thereby leading to the promotion of Cain as the expedition leader and the assignment of neophyte canoeist Neil Thompson to a task for which he had absolutely no skill, aptitude, or training—these questions were never aired publicly. At the end of this briefing, Maunder and Felletti suggested that any boys and parents who would like to could join a group of staff for a "picnic" at Rice Lake, where they could enjoy outdoor fellowship and a St. John's-style camp-out, and where, if they chose to do so, boys and their parents could get back in canoes—not the dubious new canoes at Ville-Marie, but the same four older-style "Selkirk" canoes that had been borrowed from the Manitoba school for the Ear Falls trip.

From a public relations perspective, the Rice Lake outing provided much-needed relief from the funereal images that dominated the news. The outing provided happy, life-as-usual, courage-getting-back-into-canoes reportage about adventuring à *la* St. John's—the ideal media photo op to orchestrate the weekend prior to the opening of the coroner's inquest in Ville Marie. Reports in the papers following the event, which quoted Mike Maunder, said that St. John's had made an effort to keep the outing private, but a *Toronto Star* reporter managed to find their campground, which was scattered with canoes, kayaks, tents, plastic tarps, Mansfield's camper van, and various other vehicles. The reporter was invited to go for a paddle with parents and boys in one of the big canoes. He wrote of "St. John's boys among the paddlers react[ing] to crisp orders from the instructors at the back of each canoe," implying that the situation was somehow analogous to Timiskaming. It was not—as the inquest would soon determine—but the rally of support from parents and opinion about St. John's was as impressive as it was positive. Ron Kenny, who had lost his son, Tom, was quoted as saying, "I don't think there is a parent here who wouldn't have his boy go back to St. John's. It was the best year of my son's life." Andy Hermann's dad, William, talked about the comfort the parents derived from sitting around on Saturday night with the boys and their families, singing songs around the campfire. The school could not have had better post-Timiskaming publicity if they had scripted it themselves.

Even twenty years after the fact, Sheena Suttaby, whose son, Chris, came out of the lake alive, remembers that pivotal weekend with deep fondness:

> That was one of the most wonderful nights of my whole life. We didn't even have tents. We just slept on the ground and we had pieces of plastic put over a blanket to cover us. I remember Chris came over that night and tucked me in, asking if I was okay. He seemed so grown up. No one was forced to canoe. Only one boy—I think it was Robin Jensen—didn't want to canoe. We had a fantastic time. We ended up tipping the canoes and throwing the headmaster into the water. The weekend helped our confidence, otherwise we wouldn't have enrolled our other son, David. We knew that mistakes were made at Timiskaming. It was just one of those things that shouldn't have happened, but it did.

As time passed, the incident continued to haunt people across Canada and around the world who had been affected by

Timiskaming. Columnists like Michele Landsberg addressed the "ultimate nightmare of parents," the death of a child. In his column in the *Toronto Star*, Gary Lautens reacted angrily to reports that the school was thinking about putting the survivors back into canoes and continuing the trip. Other citizens wrote letters in support of the school and what it was trying to achieve, but others asked questions. Paula Feigelsohn of Toronto wrote in the *Star*: "Regarding the canoeing accident at Timiskaming, as a mother of two teenagers, I, too, believe in discipline but am wondering if St. John's School ideology went too far in this case. The idea that these boys should be raised as 'men' is a philosophy I do not adhere to. Childhood is only for a short time." Television news anchor Lloyd Robertson was among those who suggested there was more at play in the situation than God's will, joining, among others, John C. Meagher, director of the Institute of Christian Thought at the University of Toronto, who wrote in the *Globe and Mail*, "it is entirely unacceptable to claim that 'It was God's will and not human error that caused the tragedy.'"

There was also a significant body of comment that raised questions about the canoes. In the June 22 edition of the *Globe and Mail*, a writer from Barrie asked, "Is a 22-foot canoe, for example, whose beam is only two inches wider than many regular 16-foot canoes, as stable and manoeuvrable in adverse conditions as the extra six feet of length might imply?" And, in the same paper, James A. Long, of Winnipeg, also focused on the boats:

I consider such canoes to be unsuitable, especially for boys aged 12 to 16 to be using. The depth of 18 inches makes the canoe somewhat vulnerable to capsizing during gusty wind conditions. The beam should be at least 48 inches or more, particularly when the depth was specified to be 18 inches and a length of 22 feet. A canoe with a beam of 48 inches or more will not ship water as easily for the same load even if the depth is less than 18 inches and will be considerably more stable for a group of boys to paddle sitting two abreast.

By the time Quebec coroner Stanislas Dery began the inquest in the spacious courtroom of the Ville-Marie courthouse, there had been much public comment in the papers, on television, in schools, at outdoor education centers, and around kitchen tables throughout Ontario. In opening the two-day proceedings, Dery went to some lengths to explain that in Quebec, contrary to other jurisdictions, notably Ontario, the position of coroner is usually occupied by a lawyer instead of a doctor because a Quebec coroner has the obligation and the authority to lay criminal charges.

Present at the inquest were selected boys from each of the three canoes from which there were survivors, along with their steersmen and parents. Also with standing were officials involved in the rescue as well as a representative from the Ontario Department of the Attorney-General, an Ontario regional coroner, a detective-inspector from the Ontario Provincial Police, and other experts from the Canadian Recreational Canoeing Association, the Canadian Camping Association, and the Council of Outdoor Educators of Ontario.

Canoeist and outdoor educator Jim Wood, who at the time was the outdoor education consultant for the Muskoka Board of Education, attended the inquest with the blessing of his employer as well as in his capacity as an officer of the Ontario Recreational Canoeing Association. Though without formal standing at the inquest, Wood was among a variety of interested people who drove to Ville-Marie to experience firsthand these historic proceedings. He remembers vividly the pall that pervaded the packed courtroom as the inquest began, and how this solemnity intensified as Dery explained, in French and English, his authority to lay criminal charges in the event that such action was justified on the basis of evidence brought forward in the inquest.

In the dock sat Richard Bird, front and center, looking composed and attentive. To his right were Robin Jensen, James Gibson, and James Doak, all wearing clean white turtlenecks, their hair neatly combed. To Bird's right, also in jackets and ties, were Peter Cain and Neil Thompson. Behind them sat Paul

Lockie and David Cunningham, along with other witnesses from outside the school, all of whom rotated through the witness box.

Halfway back in the room, sitting on rows of pew-like wooden benches, was everyone else, including Jim Wood. To his right sat Donald Fraser from the Chestnut Canoe Company, who was accompanied by a lawyer representing the firm's insurer. And on his left was one of the parents who made it clear, during breaks in the proceedings, that their son was at St. John's because he was not thriving in the public school system and that they were in full support of everything the school stood for. Thinking back, two decades later, Wood remembers the parents more than the boys: "They were all wearing white shirts, like the boys, which I think was a conscious effort to show solidarity with the school. The boys were groomed and well disciplined. So were the masters. They made an excellent impression on everyone there."

Although the coroner spelled out in much more detail how the tragedy occurred, after two days of testimony at the Ville-Marie courthouse, he arrived at more or less the same conclusion as many of the parents and sympathetic members of the public had—Timiskaming was an unfortunate accident. The inquiry heard about the canoes, accepting uncontested proof that each was carrying a load of some 1,200 pounds, a full 800 pounds below the manufacturer's suggested maximum capacity. The burden of testimony about the canoes established that they were, in fact, not overloaded. While this finding may have been accurate, it was also beside the point because added freeboard made the canoes tippy. The discussion of the loads did not touch on the established practice of St. John's steersmen sitting on the rear decks rather than on the seats installed by the manufacturer. In his report, Stanislas Dery called the big blue craft "conventional canvas canoes, made according to the requirements of St. John's School." End of story.

There was testimony about weather, and the lake—how the south wind builds steep, compressed waves against the current, how cliffs on either side funnel the wind and reflect waves back into the body of the lake, and even how high-velocity warm winds over cold water can cause unpredictable downdrafts on the Ontario side. There was testimony about the events of Sunday, June 11, and the rescue the following day. Scott Sorensen arrived late, but had little to add after testimony from other witnesses. Boys representing each of the canoes spoke in turn. David Cunningham remembers Dery asking him if he agreed with what had been said, to which he replied, "I didn't understand the parts that were in French, but the parts that were in English were pretty much what happened." Pictures taken by one of the boys who died had been developed and were shown to the jury. There were different opinions about the strength of the wind and the height of the waves. There were differences of perspective on the loading and suitability of the canoes.

From time to time, Dery would leave his chair and move to an annotated large-scale topographic map on the wall of the courtroom for clarification about location of various steps in the disaster or the sequence of events. Newspaper photographs show him conferring with the boys informally during breaks, and talking with them as they examined together one of the canoes that had been brought to the courthouse as an exhibit. In concluding the inquest, choking back tears, the coroner said, "From the moment I saw those kids, I was filled with emotion, particularly when they asked me if they could see their canoes." In the end, Dery saw no reason to lay criminal charges, finding evidence of mistakes, but nothing to support a charge of criminal responsibility against anyone. As proceedings came to a close, he offered in French the only verbal rebuke to the organizers of the trip. "I have no congratulations to offer to the planners," he said as the jury began its deliberations.

The coroner did, however, highlight in his report, published two weeks after the inquest, a number of criticisms of the outing: Scant preparation for the trip, no radio, dearth of local knowledge, lack of swimming ability, staff learning on the job. He listed a variety of other concerns that he thought those reading the report should keep in mind for future reference. And, surprisingly, given that he did not exercise his option to assign criminal responsibility, he concluded the report with the following condemnation of St. John's School:

> To summarize, it does not seem presumptuous to assert that from all points of view, the long-term and immediate preparations for this trip were insufficient and inadequate.
>
> It does not seem an exaggeration to state that, without some unlikely stroke of luck, this expedition would have struck disaster sooner or later. We repeat the substance of a remark made by [an expert witness] to the effect that if Lake Témiscamingue had not claimed them, the Abitibi River would have.
>
> Certain aspects of the preparations and of the departure strike us as incredible, to say the least.
>
> Why, for instance, the hasty departure from Témiscamingue-Sud? Why was not more time taken, perhaps even the entire morning, to make certain that everything, including the balancing of the canoes and the assignment of paddlers, was properly done?
>
> It should be recalled that during the inquest, one of the steersmen told how, as early as lunch stop at McMartin Point, one of the boys wished to quit and had to be persuaded to change his mind.
>
> We feel that for boys from 12 to 14 years of age, this entire expedition constituted an exaggerated and pointless challenge.

There is no doubt that Dery had hit upon the essence of the St. John's situation, but it is clear from the fifteen recommendations that he had no idea of the extent to which the organizers of St. John's schools had had opportunities to learn from the same mistakes, which had been made more than once. The blessing and, in this case, the curse of the coroner's inquest is that it focused on individual circumstances surrounding premature death. Dery chided the organizers of the expedition for no chain of command, no provision for canoe-to-canoe communication, no advance route planning, no emergency procedures, no pretrip medicals, no paddling practice prior to embarking, driving all night, not eating enough breakfast, Neil Thompson's incompetence, no rescue equipment (a recommendation that big canoes carry life rafts is still being debated in the canoeing community to this day), no swim testing for the boys, and no special training for "bowsmen." But he did *not* say that many of these factors were not only known to St. John's schools, but also actually standard practice. These factors—individually and in combination—had repeatedly led to the same kinds of accidents.

Prior to the Timiskaming tragedy, no one had died on a St. John's canoe trip, but plenty of boys and masters had been put at significant risk by, among other things, cold water immersion and hypothermia. Referring specifically to Neil Thompson's lack of competence, Dery stated that Thompson had mentioned his misgivings about his inexperience to Peter Cain and Richard Bird prior to the trip, but that he had been told that he would learn on the way. That was how St. John's did things. But *that*, as events transpired, turned out to be the error that brought the house of cards tumbling down. What the coroner did not or could not see was that Neil Thompson was as much a victim of the hubris and arrogance of St. John's schools as were those who died. Thompson just happened to survive the tragedy. For all the good intentions of Dery's inquest, it failed in the end to identify the underlying reasons why thirteen people died in Lake Timiskaming in June 1978.

The school's response to the coroner was fast and efficient. Relieved that St. John's administrators had not been held criminally responsible, Mike Maunder announced at a press conference immediately following release of Dery's report that he had been appointed by the Company of the Cross to define standards in academic and outdoor work for each of the three St. John's schools across the country, and that it was his intention to incorporate Dery's recommendations—with Mr. Dery's help—into a safety handbook that would be used by all of the St. John's schools. During the press conference, Maunder said that the school admitted it was at fault in the accident and that the school's former safety standards were inadequate. He went on to indicate that the school's new standards would include extensive training sessions in dumping and rescuing canoe crews as well as proper instruction for all boys and staff.

After a media lull while the coroner was writing his report, headlines such as "Pointless and exaggerated challenge" and "Coroner finds no fault in deaths of 13, weather shift blamed for canoe tragedy" were quickly followed by "St. John's School accepts blame for canoe deaths" (*Toronto Star*), "Prober will help write handbook" (Canadian Press), and "School head promises training for canoeists" (*Globe and Mail*).

As part of the new plan, officials at the western schools decided that they too should institute safety standards because the media spotlight had turned from time to time to the other schools, although less intensely. Manitoba school alumnus Bruce Christie was asked by a canoe instructor friend, another old boy, to help run a safety course for Cathedral School masters that summer. It had been thirteen years since his sojourn at St. John's and images of stern, disciplined masters, quick with a reprimand (backed up with the dreaded "stretcher"), were still fresh. "They surprised me," he said. "Both of us went into the course with the impression that they were these rigorous mental paragons, but they didn't seem to know too much. They sort of goofed around and we had to work to get their attention. It wasn't a contrite, shameful thing for them at all."

But for Mike Maunder, back in Ontario, learning about safety had become a very serious business indeed. It was apparently the first time that anyone from St. John's actually consulted with other people about practices and protocols for safe and informed canoe trips—standard information that, in most cases, had been around since the Second World War, if not before. Maunder began talking to experts and collecting material from other sources that became the basis of his new manual. One of the items in his research was a 1974 pamphlet published by the

Royal Life Saving Society of Canada that had detailed instructions for artificial respiration and cold water survival. He entitled the manual *The Brigade Leader's Handbook to the Large Canoe*, which, he admitted later, assumed that there actually was *a* brigade leader. Supporting Maunder all the way in this effort were two parents he had known now for some time, Norm Bindon and Oz Mansfield, who repeatedly emphasized, as they met to discuss the draft manual, the notion of leadership, standards, and visible structures of accountability.

Conspicuous in the manual's new procedures for St. John's School was a lengthy section on stability—much more than any standard canoeing manual by several pages—specifying the extra freeboard that St. John's had asked Chestnut to add to their standard "Selkirk" model, and Maunder's perception of the safety implications that this feature might entail. Maunder chose to illustrate, with text and diagrams, the effect of center of gravity on canoe stability with what he called the old cork-and-spike experiment: "When the spike is driven through the cork, the cork can support it and remain very stable . . . but if the spike is simply set on top of the cork, the centre of gravity of the entire assembly is now raised considerably. Small waves will suffice to move that higher centre of gravity outside the cork's support. Now unsupported, the spike will fall."

Further on in this section, which gives one the distinct impression that it is written with reference to the Timiskaming canoes, there is a particularly telling bit of text regarding the inspection of the placement of seats in new canoes. Maunder writes:

> Before a brigade uses a new canoe, that new canoe should be inspected, and one should make sure that the seats are a good six inches below the gunwales. Seats running only 1 or 2 inches higher will create a very tippy canoe. . . . The proper position of the seats is probably the most important element in the design of a canoe to ensure stability once the boat is under way.

In fact, there was much discussion among the parents and the boys about the canoes. The inquest had focused on whether or not the canoes were overloaded, but this was not the issue. Everyone agreed that the new canoes were different from the older "Selkirk" canoes made by Chestnut. The new canoes had higher sides, some thought, the seats were placed differently, they had a smaller keel, and, most significantly, they seemed to have a rounder bottom. The sides of the new canoes, unlike the sides of the old canoes, which were straight up and down or slightly flared, had tumblehome or inward curve, meaning that they were narrower in the beam than the old canoes and, when heeled over, had much less resistance in the water. The differences were subtle but noticeable, and everyone thought they made the new canoes tippier than the old ones. Outdoor education consultant Jim Wood remembers seeing the canoes at the inquest and thinking that they were different. "The depth caught me," he said in an interview. "They seemed deep[er] than they should have been. And they had an extra thwart put into the big space behind the bow seat to accommodate two more paddlers. There was definitely something noticeably different about those canoes. But once the coroner established that they weren't overloaded, he just moved on. The canoes were no longer an issue."

Joanne Harling articulated a theory about these differences:

The canoes were ordered through the same company that made the original "Selkirk" canoes. [I think] they had lots of orders for a fast canoe. They used bits and pieces of the old design, but not the majority of it. As a result, the new canoes were nothing like the canoes that went out west [on the English River trip] in sturdiness, in freeboard, in the kind of keel they had. The keel was a very, very slim little thing. The bigger order at the time was for racing canoes. They turned our order into racing canoes—because we only had an order for four canoes, and they had an order for 16 or 18 of the faster canoes, so our four were made with the new design that the other customer had come up with. So we got racing canoes, tippy racing canoes. But we hadn't seen them on the water. All we did was see them. . . . I think that is why the school took one hundred per cent of the blame, because they knew the canoes weren't the kind of canoes they had out west. I'm not talking about length. I'm talking about sturdiness and stability. That's why they didn't put the blame on anybody, because that was their mistake.

It is evident from the introduction to *The Brigade Leader's Handbook* that the boys and parents of Timiskaming are not the only ones who are fighting grief, anger, and guilt about the canoes and much else. Maunder writes:

This handbook comes as a result of the tragedy on Lake Timiskaming. In part, the accident occurred because of weaknesses within the Company of the Cross; weaknesses which this book attempts to correct. . . . I am dedicating this handbook, even in its incomplete form, to the parents whose boys were lost on Lake Timiskaming. Their support throughout has been a source of strength and inspiration to all who have known them. They and their sons came to the school because they believed in the principles it set forth. I hope this book will set forth standards as strong and true as those principles. I hope that someday I will be able to write a better book about their sons, their lives and their devotion to these principles. I would like to reserve the dedication of that book to the boys themselves.

This connection between St John's staff and the parents, a bond secured from the very early days of the part-time school in the expectation of parental involvement in building the school and running its programs, made all the difference between the school imploding after the Timiskaming tragedy or carrying on. When reflecting on the show of parent support and on his role in helping Mike Maunder develop the handbook, Captain Norm Bindon focused on Richard Bird stepping into the breech in Ville-Marie when brigade leader Peter Cain was in a state of emotional collapse:

It was a noble gesture, but it was also to protect the school. Usually after an accident like this, the mob starts to gather to lay blame. Quite often that mob is led by families of the victims. In this case, it became very, very clear, very quickly, that the families of the victims were going to gather around the school. If the families had gone in the other direction, the school would have disappeared quite quickly. I don't think it's a coincidence that the approach was to find the cause and fix it rather than to lay blame, because two of the people involved in finding the cause and fixing it—myself and Oz Mansfield—were parents of two of the boys. We had come up through the military and the airline, fighting the concept of pilot error, looking at human factors, but trying to look at the whole package of factors to determine what you can fix. When the families rallied around, I think it was in part inspired by Richard Bird stepping in to say, "Okay, I was the leader. I'll take responsibility," supporting the concept of let's find the problem and fix it, let's not lay blame. Peter Cain probably didn't have the strength to do that.

Jim Wood was also impressed by Richard Bird, much more so than by the other two leaders at the inquest. "I was in awe of him," commented Wood. "I don't know if I would have stood up as well as he did. I think he was a good leader of those boys. I think he came across very, very well. He was concerned. He was strong and compassionate, and in charge."

Once the inquest was over, the new blue canoes disappeared. The emotional connections they had forged, however, lived on. The Greaneys and the Hermanns asked Mike Mansfield to come and stay with them for a couple of weeks that summer, knowing he had been with their sons at the end. Barry Nelson's parents knew that David Cunningham had been their son's tent and pack partner on the trip and wanted to give him the fancy new bicycle that they had given Barry prior to the trip. It was all David Cunningham could do to tell them, in all honesty, that he had not liked Barry very much and that he didn't feel very good about accepting his bicycle. The Nelsons insisted. They said they understood.

Quietly, other canoes disappeared as well. There were stories in both of the western schools about destruction of other canoes that may have been ordered that same year. Alumni of the Manitoba school talk about a phone call to a mission in northern Manitoba, where canoes had been hastily left (some thought by a brigade that stopped to attend the funerals of the Ontario boys), to ask the Oblate priest to break up the boats with an ax and burn them. Various affiliates of the Alberta school tell a similar story, only this one involved hiring a bush plane pilot to locate another group of cached St. John's canoes and burn them too. These were dramatic, if private, acknowledgments in the minds of at least some St. John's personnel that faulty canoes were a factor in the tragedy on Lake Timiskaming.

Even straight-shooting Captain Bindon had things to say about the old canoes versus the new canoes:

I've used both. Were the new ones less safe? They were certainly less stable. [If you were] sitting up on the stern of one of those [and] somebody shifted, you did a dance on the stern, particularly if you weren't running full. If you had people sitting on the seats and you weren't absolutely full with a low center of gravity, or if you were running with a high center of gravity because you'd loaded it wrong, with stuff sitting up on the gunwales, if somebody shifted, you did a dance. It got to be natural, like riding a bike, after a time. If you had experience, they were not an unsafe canoe for an experienced person. They were definitely more tippy though, like [racing] sculls.

Typical of the extraordinary lengths to which parents went to support the school, Norm Bindon was one of several fathers who accepted an invitation from Felletti and Maunder to join St. John's staff on what became an annual exploratory canoe trip to plot out new canoe routes for future brigades. On the first of these so-called "Beaver Bashers," named because of the inordinate number of beaver dams they encountered en route, Norm Bindon was asked if he would sit behind Neil Thompson in one of the old Manitoba canoes. The reason for the pairing was ostensibly for Captain Bindon to "learn" from Neil Thompson the responsibilities of a bowsman. The real reason for the connection was to attempt to rehabilitate Thompson. "It was the school's way of bringing Neil back in," said Bindon. "It was a conscious decision on their part. In fact, I was asked if I would mind that, because obviously if I could sit behind him and take instruction from him and share a tent with him, and I was the father of one of the boys that died in his canoe, then that would indicate a level of support for him. After that, he kind of drifted away. I think he went back to England."

Ron Kenny, the father of another victim in Neil Thompson's canoe, was absolutely devastated by the death of his son, Tom, but he too found the courage to accept Mike Maunder's offer to be part of the Beaver Basher team. His recollection of an experience on one of these trips is not as positive as Norm Bindon's:

> I remember the guy that started the school, and Cain, and a couple of other people talking around the campfire one night—I forget where it was—about being in the water, in the dark. They had all kinds of difficulties [similar to Timiskaming]. It was cold. They were lucky someone didn't drown. And yet . . . if you had all those kinds of experiences . . . wouldn't you look into doing things better? Boy! Was I angry after that! I used to come home at night and dream about taking some of those people, putting them in frigid cold water with a rope around their neck, and dragging them around until they were frozen solid. But [the dream] goes after a while. It's always easier in hindsight.

In mid-September, four parents traveled to Lake Timiskaming, where they connected with Scott Sorensen. One of these couples was thinking about legal action. Other parents knew that the husband was being assisted by lawyers from the firm where he worked to see what kind of suit might be brought against the school for damages in the death of his son. He was bitter about the St. John's philosophy of pushing boys past their limit. Other parents had gone on record as saying, "Sue for what? The best year of my son's life?" For a time, the couple persisted. There were too many unanswered questions, but going to the lake that autumn, when golden hues of larch and poplar glowed against rich greens in the sunshine over deep water, helped to set their minds at ease. Scott Sorensen remembers one of them saying, "This place is so beautiful and serene. It is more like a cathedral than the scene of a horrible tragedy." It became a time of healing and closure. While the boat idled slowly up the lake, one father turned to his wife and said, "We did our level best in raising our son. I have no regrets. He is in God's hands now."

In the end, the couple did not sue. Nor did anyone else. Boys from the tragedy returned, lessons continued, younger brothers were enrolled. Aspects of the school's operation changed, notably the outdoor program as a result of Mike Maunder's handbook, but much stayed the same. Honey selling continued, only now as the boys went door to door, they met people who had very definite opinions about St. John's School. They were no longer anonymous representatives of a quaint little back-to-basics operation on the periphery of the public and independent school systems. St. John's was infamous. No one was ambivalent. Honey sellers were either invited in as a gesture of support or curiosity, or had doors slammed in their faces. For a few years, it looked as if St. John's School of Ontario would survive almost by parents' support alone.

In the wake of Timiskaming, the Company of the Cross was approaching a state of total disarray. Ted Byfield was now no longer connected with the schools and was running a very successful magazine publishing business. (Years later, commenting on Timiskaming, Byfield noted that he thought the incident might have been caused by flaws in the administrative structure of the school, but not by a failure in its central concept. In 1978, he'd been running a magazine for five years and was out of the St. John's sphere.) Frank Wiens was approaching retirement. Replacement leadership was working best at the Alberta school, but things were definitely far from perfect in the organizational structure of the Company of the Cross. Just as he was transferred from St. John's

School of Ontario to the Alberta school in the winter of 1978 when he should have been helping to run the Ontario operation after the Timiskaming tragedy, now Mike Maunder was asked to help salvage the Company of the Cross, which was self-destructing.

A portrait of this tumultuous time is contained in a 1982 report to the Company of the Cross written by Maunder called *The Second Twenty Five Years*. It contains a terse analysis of the problems encountered in franchising an idea called St. John's School. Addressing his colleagues with what he saw as the plain truth, Maunder wrote:

We started as a cell group at St. John's Cathedral, became a choir, then a Sunday School for choir boys, then a rowboat expedition, then a week-end school, then a religious community called the Dynevor Society, then a full-time boarding school in the country, and finally in 1965, legally became "The Company of the Cross"—a "religious community" whose works were running a boarding school in the country "and other functions." We immediately complicated this by becoming two boarding schools and a "Society" in Alberta. We wrestled for a while with whether we were really one or two, and out of this emerged a group called "directors" and someone called the "coordinator." Then we added a press, then a score of press corporations and holding companies, then a "recruiting centre," then another school in Ontario, this time a "corporation without share capital."

Using the example of another Christian school for illustration, Maunder characterized the Company of the Cross as "a charismatic bunch of undisciplined people, working twenty-four hours a day, floundering in debt, [and] running a sinking school. . . . As long as we're praising God in the Chapel, we figured we were all right. It was unreality—two-hour charismatic services in the Chapel while the place was falling down around our ears. Undisciplined. The school wasn't clean. Each of us was our own little repository of rebellion, jealousy, and envy. Our prayers were great, [but] it was our lives that were rotten." At the end of this indictment of himself and his peers, Maunder observed, "We are a lot better at disciplining the boys than we are at disciplining ourselves."

In the text of this report were clues about what might have happened during the winter of 1978 that led the Company to transfer Maunder from the Ontario school to the Alberta school:

> I know in my own experience of working with Frank Felletti in Ontario that something blocks us. The only reason we survived that first year was because we lived and prayed together, and even then the silences were long. I can remember many communion services where we sat at separate ends of the pew and it was only in the last few seconds before going to the front that I slid toward him or he slid toward me and we said "sorry." It's sometimes very hard.

The upshot of *The Second Twenty Five Years* and its aftermath was that the three interconnected schools were closed on paper and reopened as separate entities. Like any nasty divorce, this process took its toll on everyone. Whether it was related, or whether it was a separate and unconnected event, after a round of carousing on the night of the final snowshoe race at the Ontario school in 1983, a car containing St. John's staff members slid off the road west of Claremont, injuring everyone and nearly killing founding headmaster Frank Felletti. This, many feel, was the beginning of the end for the Ontario school.

As they had done time and time again, St. John's parents rallied, this time outside the intensive-care unit of Sunnybrook Hospital in Toronto where Felletti lay in a coma as the result of a severe head injury sustained in the crash. The parents set up a roster of people to sit at Felletti's bedside around the clock to pray for his recovery. Felletti's body healed and he awakened from the coma, but he had suffered extensive brain damage, leaving him still functional but with much diminished intellectual capacity. Some parents, who were absolutely devastated by this because Felletti had been such a charismatic leader at St. John's from the very beginning, would refer to the car accident as "the death of Frank's memory," and would mark his calamitous change of circumstance as "the result of a stressful life." There was no conceivable way that Felletti could continue as headmaster. After various attempts at rejigging the leadership of the Ontario school, Mike Maunder became headmaster.

On the tenth anniversary of Timiskaming, he led a group of boys on a canoe trip back to deep water. By now, every boy at St. John's had heard the stories, the myths—accurate, apocryphal, speculative, sublime—and Maunder wanted to take the boys who were living with the stigma of the tragedy back to see the lake, to see the place where the boys died, and "know that there's nothing deadly or black magic about Timiskaming," remembers Scott Sorensen. At the site of the makeshift camp on the Ontario side, Maunder and the boys attached a small wooden plaque to the rough, scaly bark of a red pine tree at Whistler's Point within sight of Sorensen's lodge. On a shield-shaped background, the boys affixed a wooden cross made of 1" × 4" pine. On the top of the cross was carved the number 13, and on the crossbar were the initials S J S O, separated by a carved likeness of the school crest. In haltingly rendered letters reading down from the crossbar is the word J E S U S. No names, no details.

That same year, Maunder had what he later described as a "little nervous breakdown." He was headmaster. Enrollment was dropping. Funding and finances were a nightmare. Dealing with the staff, the parents, and the board of directors of the school was more than he could stand. "I tried to remain as close as I could to the staff and the kids," he later explained, "but as headmaster I was in the orbit of the parents and the board, and I just couldn't hold it together."

Maunder left the school in the summer of 1988, with the blessing and encouragement of the board, to go on a six-month sabbatical to India. He did volunteer work at a school in the Himalayas. He hiked to the base of Mount Everest, trying to find and rebuild a context for understanding St. John's. When he returned in January 1989, he found the school in worse shape than it had been when he left. They struggled through to the end of the 1988–1989 school year, but when they started up again in the fall, almost thirteen years to the day since he and Frank Felletti came to Toronto, they "crunched the numbers and it was clear we weren't going to make it through the year without some kind of disaster." St. John's School of Ontario sent their boys home and closed mid-season in October 1989. Having gone on record as saying, "Those boys died building this school . . . it must not fail, or they will have died in vain," this must have been a sad, sad day for Mike Maunder.

VIII

The Legacy: Living with Tragedy

Sometime after the school closed, an auction was held at the Claremont site in an attempt to turn assets into cash. As with the breakup and dissemination of any houseful of worldly goods and chattels, the St. John's auction was a bittersweet affair. What had happened inside the big old house and on its grounds outside had shaped the lives of families who hated to see it go, but who nevertheless may have heaved a sigh of relief when the auctioneer's gavel first hit the table.

The 16" × 20" color class photos that had been framed and hung inside, each year from 1978 to 1988, were among items on the block. "Whadda ya bid, whadda ya bid, whadda ya bid? Whatsa matter, don't ya like it? Whadda ya bid?" The audience comprised alumni parents and old boys—mostly parents. Thelma Cunningham had looked at the photo in its chipped, dark frame, propped up on an old table out on the lawn before the sale began. She remembered that day back in June, eleven years earlier, when that first class had gathered in their white turtlenecks and new blue jackets, on the day before Timiskaming. Son David, in the middle of the second row, Chris Suttaby, four places to his left, Ian Harling, four places to his right. They looked so young, so innocent. All the boys from St. Stephen's, so fresh-faced, so unsuspecting, on the day before the tragedy. And all the little boys sitting cross-legged in the front row: Barry Nelson, Jody O'Gorman, Kevin Black, David Parker, Tom Kenny, Scott

Bindon, Robbie Kerr, and the Bourchier twins—half the front row gone.

The picture that was supposed to hang in the school for all time was now for sale to the highest bidder. "Who'll start the bidding at fifty dollars?" called the auctioneer. "Twenty-five? Twenty? Ten dollars, who'll start the bidding at ten dollars? Thank you, ma'am. Ten, ten, ten, who'll give me twelve-fifty, fifteen . . ." Thelma's hand went up several times in a few rounds of lackluster bidding. Finally the auctioneer said, "Sold! To the lady right over there."

She gave the picture to son David when next she saw him, and David promptly stored it in the back of a closet. Some time later, while between jobs, he lived for four months in an apartment with no heat and the pipes froze. Water damaged many of his things, including the old photo. Anxious to salvage this piece of his past, he opened the back of the frame and attempted to pull out the print, but the emulsion had already dried on the back of the dust-encrusted glass. Try as he might, he could not remove the photo without damaging it. Not to worry. At least you could still see all the faces.

In 1999, when I catch up with David Cunningham, he is living with his new wife in an apartment in the basement of his mother's house about two hours north of Toronto. When we first spoke, it was in a noisy restaurant near the site of the old school. At the time, he was working as a landscaper and horticulturalist for a company that is reintroducing wildflowers into the urban ecosystem. Now, some months later, he has quit the landscaping job and is back "bending tin," installing commercial and residential heating and air-conditioning ductwork. Changing jobs is the story of his life, he tells me with a sigh. Knowing my interest in the school and the whole idea of building character through adventure, he rummages through a box of old St. John's books and papers and pulls out the damaged class photo. He still knows almost all the boys by name. But then with pinpoint accuracy, almost proudly, he indicates each of twelve faces, many in the front row. "He died. He died. He died."

In the twenty-one years that have passed since the accident, David has finished high school, but only after going back as an adult. "There's no doubt about it," he says, "when I left St. John's I was confused and distraught. I wasn't sure where to turn, and I guess my rebellious side started to come out. I wasn't sure what I wanted to do, and ended up doing lots of different things." He tells me he has been to college and earned a diploma to become a dispensing optician, but he has never actually worked as one. He was engaged to be married once before, but when his betrothed took three hours to pick out her china pattern, he had second thoughts and eventually backed out. He has been a laborer in a Toronto steel mill. He has changed tires at a local garage, sold waterbeds, driven a truck, been a baker and a sheet metal worker. He has done shift work at a drug mart distribution center, made shock absorbers, done landscaping, worked in merchandising, and managed a restaurant. And, he tells me, he has been to "hundreds of funerals."

One of the volunteer duties that David undertook as a boy before, during, and after the time he was at St. John's was to accompany his mother in her work with senior citizens. Many of these people died over the years, and David has made a point of attending their funerals. Many of these seniors have had friends who died, and David has driven them to churches and funeral homes to pay their last respects. He has known death from a very young age, he tells them, having lost his father and twelve friends in one month when he was a teen. And through it all, he has frequented neighborhood bars and watering holes and made friends there too, some of whom died—some accidentally, some naturally, some violently and unnecessarily. And now the only place to have a drink on a Saturday night is the Royal Canadian Legion Hall in the little village near his mother's rural house. "When a comrade falls," he tells me, "I'm there for them. Even if I don't know them well, I go to the funerals. A lot of people don't go. That's what I do. It's a sign of respect for the dead." I wonder if each of these visits in respect for the dead is a way back to June 1978, when he helped carry six of his closest friends to their early graves.

"He wears his dad's death and Timiskaming like a medal," says Kathy Gorin, David's wife of twelve months. She continues:

> My dad drowned, fishing with three other guys, when I was eleven. They didn't find his body for three weeks. But you get over it. David has to tell people. After a while it got to be redundant. Either he stopped saying it, or I stopped listening. I call it his demon. I said he's got to face it. One day, I put on an old powder-blue sweatshirt from his drawer. He said, "Be careful with that," because it was the one the girl had given him when he got to that lodge after the accident. He still had it after all those years. All they taught those kids at that school was how to be tough, how to be macho. Character and adventure— it's all bullshit!

Thelma Cunningham speaks openly about what happened to the "twelve-year-old monster" who went to St. John's. There is no doubt that the strict rules and discipline at the school brought her wild son into line, taught him to at least show respect to elders, including his mother and father, but, in retrospect, she questions the deeper implicit messages that came with the superficial courtesy and plastic smiles. From those first snowshoe outings, when she bathed the boys' raw feet and put salve on open sores and blisters, she wondered about the notion of forcing the boys to continue through pain and physical discomfort, about the message that to give in was to fail, no matter what the cost. "Some of his macho-ness is completely misplaced," she says, "He certainly didn't get it from home."

Mrs. Cunningham explains her early work with the Girl Guides and how she and her husband worked hard never to distinguish between male and female jobs in the household. But in David's world, she laments, there are clear distinctions between what men do and what women do. "I can't think that this came from anywhere but St. John's," she adds. "I remember the staff of the school being horrified and telling the boys that the ordination of women in the Anglican Church was wrong. That's just another example of mixed messages that came from the school. I don't know what you can blame St. John's for. I just know that all of this macho stuff is not as positive as it might have been."

She is convinced that the teamwork idea, which is so much a part of canoe trips and snowshoe runs, backfired as well. Looking at David now, she says, "teamwork is not something that he uses here in the family at all. He is very independent, very selfish in some things. He works in other things as well, occasionally, but on his time. He'd like to know what Kathy is doing at all hours of the day and night, but it's not a problem for him to carry on his business or change plans at a moment's notice, without letting anyone know." Lessons in punctuality backfired too, says Thelma Cunningham:

I'm convinced that he learned that there is time and then there is St. John's time. He's never on time for anything, and I love him for it. In our family, punctuality mattered, but not to David. We just know now that if David is coming to lunch at twelve that we shouldn't start setting the table until two. That's the way he is, and I think he is that way because of St. John's. They beat the boys for not being punctual, but the masters were never on time for anything. Generally speaking, I think David has come to the conclusion that rules are for other people. If he can get away with something, he will. He has been like that since he was little, but I don't think St. John's did anything to make it better. They may have made it worse. He has definitely struggled, with all of his jobs, since he left there.

And I know he drinks too much. I wish he wouldn't do that, but he does. It might have something to do with his friends and his father being snatched away. I suspect he drinks because it is easier to do that than to deal with it. He surprised me though, when he went to Ville-Marie this fall. He wouldn't have done this without Kathy.

Just after the twentieth anniversary of the tragedy, spurred by

Scott Sorensen's book about his life on Lake Timiskaming, a volume that included two chapters about St. John's Junior Brigade and his role in the dramatic rescue, David and his new wife drove to Lake Timiskaming. Kathy describes the long journey and how the music in the car got louder the closer they got to Timiskaming. David's tapping of the steering wheel got more and more animated. By the time they crossed over the bridge at the base of Lake Timiskaming, the loud music was hurting her ears. "Had we been going anywhere else," she said, smiling, "I would have flung the tape out the window!"

His mother says that this was, as far as she knew, the first time David had been back in a canoe since the tragedy. Before paddling on the waters near the lodge, David and Kathy went in the big motorboat with Scott Sorensen to the site of the makeshift camp. Along the way, he sat with Scott Sorensen's scrapbook on his knee, flipping through articles and photographs in yellowed plas- tic pages. David settled down for the first time since they started the journey and turned to a page in the binder on which Sorensen had placed a photocopy of eighteen names and comments written in the lodge guest book before departure to Ville-Marie. By now, tears were falling onto the aged plastic cover of the page.

Later in the day, David and Kathy borrowed a canoe from Scott Sorensen and paddled across the mouth of the Kipawa River to Whistler's Point, where they sat beneath the red pines, watching the sun set over the black cliffs of Lake Timiskaming, which rise more than 600 feet straight out of the water on the Ontario shore. The distance across looks deceptively short, less than a mile. They had crossed earlier in the day in Sorensen's motorboat, but not tonight, and not by canoe. David, better than anyone, knows just how far it is from here to there, from one side to the other, from before to after, and now back again. Behind them, affixed to one of the trees, was the memorial plaque placed at Whistler's Point by Mike Maun- der and his last group of boys. Most of the varnish had peeled. Some of the wood was still blond, but around the edges, especially near the top, the wood was gray, weathered, and cracked. "Next time I come here," David said to Kathy, "I'm going to bring some lacquer and sandpaper to fix that up a bit. It's looking kind of old."

Mike Mansfield, like David Cunningham, lives in an apartment in the basement of his parents' house, but in Canmore, Alberta. Oz has retired from Air Canada and is wintering with Joan in the American Southwest. Mike, his wife, and two preschoolers have moved upstairs while they are away. After years of wandering—working as a ranch hand in Alberta, guiding big game hunters in Yukon, being a "tin basher" (his words for installing heating and air-conditioning ductwork), pitching in as a bouncer at a tough bar in Vancouver, where he met his wife—he has gone back to school to study computers at the DeVry Institute of Technology in Calgary:

> Did the school work for me? To hear some people talk, it didn't do anything for me. I've been doing the Peter Pan thing, not growing up, just growing old. For years, I drove around with a saddle in the back of an old pickup. The saddle was worth more than the truck. But I got tired of that. Yeah, I'm thirty-six years old, living in my parents' basement. This isn't where I expected to be. Where did I expect to be? I haven't a clue, but this wasn't it.

Mike continued at St. John's after Timiskaming, but because the school only went to Grade 10, he eventually left and tried to re-enter the public school system. As with David Cunningham and many other St. John's boys, without the structure, the values, and the attitudes he had learned at St. John's, blending into a regular high school was a disaster. Things went poorly at school, and even worse at home in Angus. As they had relatives on a farm near Wainwright, Alberta, Oz and Joan offered the recalcitrant Michael the option of moving there to finish Grade 12, while learning a ranch hand's job.

School in the West was more successful. He finished Grade 12 and went on to college for three years, earning a diploma in agricultural mechanics, but there was a restlessness that Mike could not shake. With his ag-mechanic's papers, he went to work on the rigs in the Alberta oil and gas industry and "watched them kill a man or two doing that." Then he worked as a guide for tourists on packhorse tours in the mountains near Banff, Alberta. Answering the same questions day after day from eager tourists eventually honed a cynical edge that his employer could not tolerate, so Mike tried other types of work with packhorses and fewer people.

Over tea, Mike describes moving from job to job, going back to the family farm, and nearly being killed—again—when he and his uncle hit a power line with a piece of farm machinery, an accident that put him in the burn unit of the University of Alberta Hospital in Edmonton for seventy-five days. "It was a shocking experience," he says, watching for my reaction to his tried and true bad pun, "but I got a real charge out of it—16,000 volts." There is no smile in his face or his voice. "There was a lady in the next bed whose husband had poured gas on her and lit her up. We came in the same day. We both got out a month and a half later." He talks of taking a farrier's course to learn how to shoe horses. "The hottest flame makes the hardest steel . . . but sometimes the hardest steel is the most brittle." In his own way, he is telling me about character and St. John's.

There is no doubt that Timiskaming still haunts Mike Mansfield. It is equally apparent in our conversations that he is struggling to break free. He brings up the story of a Vietnamese girl whose naked flight from an American napalm attack was immortalized in a picture. "That moment defined her life," he says. "I don't want Timiskaming to define my life, but it's always there. Sometimes I think the guys that died are better off. Death simplifies things, right down to nothing. Frank Felletti is lucky in one respect; because of the brain damage as a result of his accident, he isn't troubled by it. They're not carrying around the big burdens that some people are."

It is the emotional side of trauma that chokes him, the recollection of Peter Knight leaving the night before the trip without saying goodbye. He remains baffled about that. All the deaths, being told to stay with the boat, and deciding to go against his master's wishes and swim to shore. And then there is the memory of David Greaney and his best friend, Andy Hermann, drifting off into oblivion. He is bitter and angry:

They didn't touch the emotional side of learning at all. They didn't do the touchy-feely thing at all, which doesn't prepare anybody for anything. You can have all the reasoning power in the world, but if emotionally you can't handle something, you don't have the tools to deal with a given situation. If you let your anger get away from you, then all the tools you're using are gone. They didn't deal with anything like that. I don't think St. John's did us a service [by] ignoring emotion. There has to be a better way to deal with emotions than packing them away, putting them in a little box. You can deal with it twenty years later when you're an adult. That was the St. John's way. Well it's twenty years later, and I'm living in my parents' basement, trying to get on with my life. Basically, these guys were playing God with people's lives and they didn't do a very good job.

Recollections roll in waves. His fist tightens on his mug of tea.

They might have given the impression that St. John's was a well-oiled machine, but it wasn't that at all. God didn't provide. I'll never forget coming to the fishing camp with Scott Sorensen. He had a floating dock and on it was this pile of bodies. All the guys in my class who were dead, and there was a tarp over them, but their feet were sticking out, and you could see all the brand-new Ked runners. We all got new runners for the trip. I can remember that clear as day. I close my eyes and see that. It was a gray dock, and there was water squishing up between the boards. And those guys were there. . . . They were just stacked up there, and the canoes were on shore. I recognized my canoe and I saw my duffel bag. And I was tired of being wet and dirty and I wanted my duffel bag to get changed, but they wouldn't let me have it. I can remember being ambushed by reporters that first night. I had to go to the bathroom by myself. I got up and was coming back. They had cameras. There was this one great big son-of-a-bitch. Him,

I'm mad at. He wouldn't let me go back in with the other guys until I talked to him. I can remember there were too many reporters and not enough police officers. Yeah, God will provide.

Time and time again, Mike returns to the idea of how little foresight there was in everything undertaken by St. John's. Throughout his life, his dad had emphasized the importance of being prepared. Mike had learned to ask "What if?" Everyone had assumed that the leaders of the 1978 St. John's Junior Brigade had asked all the "What if?" questions. Among a host of others, Mike Mansfield was devastated to learn that the leaders had asked no such questions. He, his classmates, and their parents had been set up, victims of blind faith. Toward the end of our conversation, he tells me that one of the things he was asked to do in his intensive computer degree program at DeVry was to write a short story about a pivotal moment in his life. For the DeVry professor, it was a way of ensuring that everyone in the class would have something to write about because, she reckoned, everyone has had some kind of memorable turning point in their lives. In Mike Mansfield's case, she had no idea what kind of vein she was tapping into. He hands me his story, which, by this time, has been published in the DeVry student newsletter. It is called "Etched in Stone":

There is a memory of mine, an impression that stays with me always—helplessness that appears at regular intervals throughout the day. This memory is so ingrained that it is as if it were etched in stone, so that whatever I undertake, I ensure that preparations are made for the worst then come what may, I am ready. The stark impression is of three terrified men sheltered in a makeshift tent. Fifteen leaderless boys surround them on the shore of a lake with thirteen corpses scattered along its shores.

These memories surface and are exceptionally vivid when I sense that my handle on a situation is slipping. It is during these times of perceived inadequacy that the indelible impressions of the rasp of the life jacket on my chin as I swam for shore towing my two best friends comes crashing back. The punishing memory of my inaction as I sat on the hard, slick rocks of the shore cradling one friend and listening to the other call my name as he slowly drifted past is never far from my thoughts, knowing in my soul that if I returned to the water I would never leave it alive, and, ignorant of the implications of not trying, I allowed him to drift off and die. Also etched is the memory of sitting on the shoal searching with numb hands for a pulse on the goose-fleshed skin of my friend's neck, and finding no sign of life under the puckered skin.

After climbing a cliff up to the forest and stumbling along the shoreline for an interminable time, I smelled smoke and heard the rest of the expedition. As I reached the shore and ambled toward the noise, I encountered the bodies of three of my classmates scattered untidily just above the high water mark. This did not prepare me for the sight of the camp; never in my worst nightmares did I envision the three "Masters" hiding away in a makeshift tent, only emerging to hand out food and to pray. The day before, these men had trod the earth secure in the knowledge that God sat on their shoulders and nothing was beyond their powers to repair; now, they could not bear the gazes of fifteen boys searching for direction.

The disturbing sight of these men hiding in a shelter by a fitful fire, surrounded by fifteen boys in need of direction, and afraid to leave the comfort of their huddled groups, is one that I fear will never lose its power over me. These painful memories cascade through my consciousness whenever I perceive my handle on a situation slipping away.

By all accounts, St. John's and Timiskaming helped put Ian Harling, the hyperkinetic who had had such trouble in the public school system, on track to a happy and successful life. His mother, Joanne, who was always a big booster of the school, is convinced that St. John's turned her son around. "He knows who he is. He is able to face things as they come along and make the best of them. He doesn't have to rely on his parents or siblings or grandparents to make him who he is. He is who he is because of what he's done in his life. If that's what character means, then he has character."

Mrs. Harling is also convinced that Timiskaming was a turning point in her son's life: "It had a profound effect on him," she says. "I still remember sitting with him on the bus on the way home from Ville-Marie, right after the accident, when he said, 'Why should they die and not me? I've got to make something of myself for them.'" For years, she remembers, Ian and his classmates were intent on completing the trip that the Junior Brigade had started in 1978, but that reunion trip never happened. Instead, she reckons, Ian took the tragedy as a marker in time, a point in his life from which to look forward, not back, and with vigor and a positive outlook.

A front door in a fashionable new suburb of Toronto opens on a sunny Sunday morning and a stocky man with a smile and a firm handshake invites me in. "I'm Ian. Welcome." In recent months, one of Harling's friends wrote a couple of articles about Timiskaming and its lessons for canoeists. One of the points he mentioned is that Harling is convinced that the tragedy did not dominate his life, that he moved on as soon as the funerals were over. "In fact," he says, "my wife and I didn't ever really discuss it until Scott Sorensen wrote a book, called *Kipawa River Chronicles*, which came out last year. It had a chapter or two about Timiskaming. She knew it had happened and that I was involved, but beyond that there really wasn't much more to say."

Unlike the others, Harling went back into the public school system after St. John's and did well. After that, he attended university—a move some of his earlier teachers would *never* have predicted—and earned a bachelor's degree in psychology, eventually a master's in abnormal psychology. He digresses from the biographical sketch I have asked for, to a story about how much fun he had selling honey. He loved selling honey. Going door to door was a game at which he excelled. For many of the honey-selling weekends, Harling was the top seller. He smiles when recounting how Mike Maunder rewarded the best sellers with a dinner in downtown Toronto.

We did Honest Ed's quite often. That first year, my team won over-all, and they gave up about $500 and said go and have a good time. We went down to the Imperial Room [at the Royal York Hotel in downtown Toronto] and watched Ed Ames, the guy who played Tonto on the Lone Ranger. He had a vaudeville-style show, and we thought it was great. We had a big meal, watched the show, went to a movie, then we went to one of the guys' houses for a sleep-over and ate all the junk food we could possibly eat. Another year, we went go-carting and then went out to dinner. It was fantastic.

Ian Harling's early success in honey sales with St. John's School later led to sales in the publishing industry. When we spoke, he was regional sales manager for a family of automotive weeklies. He credits his success in the business world in part to his experiences at St. John's as a student, as a honey seller, and as unofficial leader of his dorm for most of the time he was at the school.

Unlike many of his classmates, Ian Harling continued canoeing. In the summers, while at St. John's, he attended a number of boys' camps in northern Ontario, finishing up at Y M C A's Camp PineCrest in the Muskoka region, where he continued the canoe-ing instruction that had given him the presence of mind to attempt a splash out—with his pals Chris Bourchier and Barry Nelson—of the big blue canoe. He also continued with canoe trips, eventually becoming a guide for the younger boys. Although PineCrest used only two- and three-person canoes, Harling was still inclined, much more so than any of his camp contemporaries, to push the kids on his trips a bit. He knew from experience that boys would do a lot more work than they often thought they could, that just because something hurt was no real reason to stop, unless something was drastically wrong. He knew that there were rewards to be gained, qualities of perseverance and tenacity that can be learned only through adversity. But he had also learned when enough was enough, and also when "almost" is sufficient. There is a big difference between providing boys with an opportunity to stretch themselves and pushing them over the line, a distinction that appears to live on in Ian Harling's memory beside images of other boys.

As a guide at Camp PineCrest, Ian Harling fitted right in and developed something of a reputation for being a tough yet fair leader. He was always up for few a more days on the trail, a leader who would never ask his boys to do any task that he could not or would not do himself. As we talked of his camp trips, he pointed at the map of Ontario and mentioned blithely that he had been back to Lake Timiskaming several times since 1978. By the end of our conversation, he has effectively conveyed the impression that it really was no big deal. He halted momentarily as he remembered the splash out, and the gripping sadness he still felt that neither Bourchier nor Nelson survived the ordeal, but he appears by all indications to have moved on. His wife, Lisa, whom he met at camp, concurs. The tragedy is part of his life—she knows that—but it by no means defines who he is. Ian explains:

> I can't honestly say that Timiskaming changed my life in any significant way. I was already the person that I was heading out there. I wouldn't have been at that school, I wouldn't have been on that trip, I wouldn't have been the risk-taker that I was already. It was significant to the extent that I lost a lot of friends and learned quickly about death. When you're a pall bearer at six funerals in Grade 7, you learn about death pretty quickly, sitting there listening to it day after day. Dealing with parents, dealing with siblings— things along that line— everyone pulled together. That's what I remember well.

I connected first with Chris Suttaby by phone, having made the link through his enduring best friend, David Cunningham. We played phone tag for a time, as Chris does shift work —twelve hours on, twelve hours off, seven days out of fourteen, not including overtime. Eventually, a cheery voice called to say that he would be free on the weekend and that I could come to his house in Toronto. "The same house you grew up in?" I inquired. "The very one."

Life after Timiskaming for Chris Suttaby has not been easy. "Encouraged" to stay at St. John's until Grade 10, his re-entry into the public high school system was anything but smooth. Without the structure and iron discipline of St. John's to keep at least part of him on the straight and narrow, his scholastic life after St. John's suffered. The system within a system, the combination of boy rule and master rule, of deception and deceit, had left him with a somewhat twisted view of authority. Life was what you could get away with, and those were the principles Chris took into public high school. Drugs and alcohol crept into his life. He started missing the odd class, then whole days and groups of days in a row. It was the truancy that caught his parents' attention and eventually led to an ultimatum: "Either you go to school or you work. Take your pick. Do one or the other, but you're not living in this house if you intend staying on the path you're on right now."

The Suttabys' younger son, David, had gone to St. John's as well. They made the decision to send him there during the drive to Claremont on the rainy night in June 1978 when they had no idea if their firstborn was alive or dead. They felt that strongly about the school. In hindsight, it appeared, at least to Sheena Suttaby, that David took to the teachings of St. John's better than his older brother. It was either that or the school and its staff had mellowed after Timiskaming. In any case, when the ultimatum was given to Chris—get a job or go back to school—he opted for work. He found a job at a huge printing plant north of town, where he has been ever since.

It was a sunny Saturday spring morning as I made my way through a warren of sidewalks interconnecting blocks of two- and three-story town houses that were likely built after the war. The cracked sidewalks, pale brick, and two-pane sliding windows showed their age, but the grounds were clean and tidy, ornamental trees in the courtyards were leafing out, and songbirds filled the air as they picked at crumbs left behind by children playing the day before. Walking along, I wonder whether I would recognize the face from the picture, remembering the hazel-brown, deep, guarded eyes.

The curtains at the number Chris had given me were drawn. There was a gap in the storm door where a screen or window might have been, and it took a long time for him to answer. I could hear the cat prowling inside long before a tall, lanky lad in T-shirt and jeans opened the door.

"Come on in. You'll have to excuse the mess. It's my day off, and I'd rather talk to you than clean the place. I'd rather do almost anything than clean the place." The smell of hemp is noticeable. The welcome, however, is genuine. The hair is much longer, there is now stubble on the chin, but the eyes are the same, filled with light, until he closes the front door. "I was just talking to Dave Cunningham. He said you've had a couple of great chats. Can I get you something to drink. Coffee? Beer? I'm going to have a beer."

Chris clears away newspapers, mail, and miscellaneous plates and empties from a large wooden dining table opposite a galley kitchen, to accommodate my notes and tape recorder. It takes a few minutes for my eyes to become accustomed to the dim light. I become aware of a presence over my right shoulder, which, as I rotate slightly in my seat, turns out to be a sizable trophy-mounted deer's head, with an impressive rack of antlers that loom over the table. Against a wrought-iron railing separating the dining area from a living room three steps down is an ax and beside it what looks like a rolled sleeping bag and a partially filled backpack.

"I love the outdoors," he says, as he catches me looking at the camping gear. "I spend as much time as I can up at the French River. I've been going there for years. Any chance I get between shifts, I head straight up north. That's what I love to do."

"Do you go with anyone, or by yourself?" I ask.

"Nah, usually on my own. I have a friend up there who owns a lodge. I've had a couple of flings here and there, but I'm not looking for anything serious. Right now, I'm having too much fun. I call the shots. I can do what I want."

Chris has just been promoted to pressman at the printing plant where he was worked for nearly twenty years, since the day his parents, Jack and Sheena, issued their ultimatum at this very table. They have since divorced and gone their separate ways, as has his younger brother, David, who has followed Jack into a career in the correctional service, leaving Chris in the old homestead. The place seems to fit him like an old slipper. He rocks back in his chair, takes a long pull on his beer, and tells me he is proud that he has worked his way up from odd-job boy to running what he calls an "eight-press" as head operator. He has not missed a day at the plant in ten years. "I take my lieu days—we get three of them a year—and I might party hard sometimes, but if it is time to work, I'm there."

He shares the house with another employee at the printing plant, who works the same long hours as Chris does, often on opposite shifts. "The lucky bugger is working overtime right now. I'd like to get as much overtime as he's been getting lately." They keep the shift schedule taped to the front of the refrigerator so they know who is doing what at work.

Chris rambles as he talks. He opens another beer. He tells me how fat and lazy he was before he went to St. John's, how much of a shock the part-time school was to his system. He talked about Mike Maunder's and Frank Felletti's presentations at St. Stephen's Church and how, like David Cunningham and the Bourchier twins, he was captivated by the photographs and stories of dogsled trips in the mountains. "Yeah," he adds laconically and with a wry grin, "they lure you in with all that shit, and then they kick you in the teeth. Discipline? What's this with discipline? Latin? What's this with Latin?" He describes the part-time school homework and how it was much more than anything he ever got from regular school. "I knew I had to do the work before I went back. I had to learn the goddamn Latin, or Walter Deller was going to beat on my ass! As soon as I showed up, I knew I was in for a rough ride. I tried to bail, but to no avail."

Chris described conversations with his parents about St. John's

—the ups, the downs, how he wanted to drop out. "It was the weirdest thing. Right here at this table my parents would always ask if I wanted to go back. I'd always think no, but always say yes. I'd *know* I didn't want to go back, but I'd always say yes. That was what they wanted to hear."

Things got better when he went to the full-time school. He was given responsibility for the kitchen crew. "We had to pass Ministry of Health inspections, and that was pretty hairy, but the Ministry inspections were nothing compared to Felletti's inspections. He'd make us clean under counters, scrub the floors, even if we'd just scrubbed them, shine the pots, organize the cutlery. Felletti's inspections were hell to pass."

Even though he hated many aspects of St. John's when he was there, when he left it to return to the public school system, he "screwed up totally with too much freedom." Looking back, he realizes that the school helped him become the person he is today. "I'm not saying it was for everyone, but for a guy like me, the school was perfect. The school was tailor-made. I can't imagine where I'd be without the discipline and structure of St. John's, which someone like me needs. I had to be a good boy, that's all."

Like Maunder and Felletti, Chris leads his crew at the printing plant by example. He has no idea how many other pressmen lifted a broom in the past ten years but, he tells me, if there is a lull in the work schedule and the floor around his eight-unit is dirty, he's not beyond picking up a broom and giving it a quick sweep. He learned initiative, he says, at St. John's. "Without St. John's," he says over his shoulder on the way to the fridge, "I wouldn't be the go-getter that I am."

He says little about the school or the accidental fire in the dorm during painting detail in the summer before the full-time school opened, except that his early days in St. John's were not the happiest of his life. About Timiskaming, he remembers swimming to the shore with James Doak, their clothes drying in the sun while they slept, exhausted on the side of the lake, then waking up in darkness and staggering like drunken sailors on cliffed terrain. He recalls their fall over a cliff, the moon and the stars, stumbling into camp, and the ghastly blue pallor of Tom Kenny's skin as classmates tried in vain to revive him. He remembers turning thirteen at Sorensen's lodge and writing in the guest book that their deliverance from the lake was the best birthday present he could have imagined.

As Chris talks, the cat jumps up on the table and lolls over my journal, wanting a scratch. He is talking about the notion of character that St. John's masters impressed upon the boys as they confronted them with challenges. By now, my eyes are fully adapted to the darkness. I think of Chris's mother, who worries about him sometimes:

> I don't know how much of Chris's character came from the school. He likes his beer and he likes his funny cigarettes. He does this almost all the time when he's not working, yet he hasn't missed a day of work in years. He has a work ethic that you wouldn't believe. . . . He's stuck at what I think is a miserable job, miserable in that it's physically hard, and noisy and smelly. And he's been there since we gave him the ultimatum. He got that job, and he's still there and doing very well. To me, that's character. I'll never know if [it was] the Timiskaming experience or St. John's that started this. We really have no way of knowing.

For his holidays this year, Chris plans to go back up to French River. He goes ice fishing in the winter, walking long distances between sets. In summer he camps in different places. In recent years, he has been giving his mom a week at his friend's lodge as a birthday gift, so she will join him there later in the season. And in the fall, he takes a week to go up and help put the lodge away for winter. "I don't know what it is about raking leaves," he tells me, "but I love to rake leaves, [clean] up the lawns, [and get] everything lined up in rows and bundled. . . ." Today, though, he is thinking about checking out a couple of apple orchards near where he works. He loves fresh apples, and is always interested in seeing how the trees are doing. Would he like to join me for lunch, somewhere nearby? No, he'll have another beer, maybe a quick snooze, and then head up to the apple place. Has he seen anything of his St. John's classmates since he left the school? Not Doak. Not really, except Cunningham. "He keeps talking about doing another trip together some day. I don't know. Say hi to him next time you see him," he says with a firm handshake and a wave, and I step back outside, thinking about Timiskaming as a possible cause of battle fatigue.

The other boys of the 1978 St. John's Junior Brigade have spread like seeds in the wind, each with his own story, each with his own memories of Timiskaming. Studious Rob Kerr, from Markham, moved very quickly into the head office of the Toronto Dominion Bank to work, ironically, with his classmate Tom Kenny's dad, Ron, but was killed in a car crash in his early twenties. Frazer Bourchier became a mining engineer, worked in various places around Canada, and got married. James Gibson and Robin Jensen entered the business world. Scott Bindon became a commercial pilot, like his dad, Norm. In the spring of 2001, he and his wife, who was expecting their first child, were living in her parents' house in Kitchener, Ontario. He had been flying freight around the world for International Cargo Charter, a firm under hire to Emery Inc. ICC was about to lose its contract with Emery, so Scott was contacting other charter operators around the world, hoping to find new jobs for forty-five pilots, including himself, who would soon be out of work. It was a team obligation that Scott willingly accepted. It is part of his character. Is it something he learned at St. John's? Is it something he has done, remembering his brother, Dean? Absolutely, says his dad.

After Timiskaming, some parents stayed together, others separated or divorced. The Nelsons moved to British Columbia. The O'Gormans, who cut themselves off from St. John's immediately following Timiskaming, separated, as did the Bindons and the Suttabys. Ruth and Norm Bindon tried to have another child after Dean died, but to no avail. They eventually adopted a lit girl and drifted apart. Sheena Suttaby's relationship with her husband, Jack, was rocky when Chris went to St. John's. It worsened the year following Timiskaming when son David was at the school as well. They told the boys, on one of their weekends home, that they were separating. She remembers how they had to phone the school to say that the boys would be back on Tuesday instead of Monday, to give their sons a chance to absorb the news. She remembers how shocked everyone in the St. John's community was to learn of their separation. Was it because of Timiskaming? "Who knows?" she says. "I was at a stage when I wasn't happy in my marriage, and Timiskaming certainly didn't help."

The Bourchier twins' father died in 1998. Andy Hermann's parents both died, one soon after the other. For all parents who lost boys, and even for those who did not, the stress and strain of Timiskaming was a force that shaped their lives. Thelma Cunningham wonders why they trusted so much and did not ask any tough questions about what was going on at St. John's. Joan Mansfield said simply, "In my opinion, the responsibility for that particular accident lies solely on the people who organized it. Having gone through a tragic accident with a bunch of students and staff, my final word would be that we trusted the school too much. We didn't question enough. We trusted them. Everything isn't God's will." But she and husband Oz are getting on with their lives, doing what they can to support Mike and his young family as he valiantly tries to put his anger behind him and start again.

For Captain Norm Bindon, Timiskaming was a jolt that left a nagging guilt. Driven by what he knew as a pilot—the need to identify and correct the systematic flaws and errors that led to the death of his son, Dean—he worked directly with Mike Maunder to draft and polish *The Brigade Leader's Handbook to the Large Canoe*. He continued on the school's board of directors in the years following the tragedy, and was eventually nominated by then-chair Richard Bird to take his turn as chair, knowing by then of the problems in the Company of the Cross. After his "training" with Neil Thompson to become a bowsman on a

St. John's trip, he continued with the Beaver Bashers and eventually earned his steersman's and brigade leader's qualifications and
began leading trips for the school. He became district chairman
for the Rotary Youth Exchange in the Toronto area; trekked
with young people in the Himalayas; canoed in the Amazon; led
brigades across northern Canada; and led snowshoe trips and
camped out at −36.4°F. "[I was] extremely busy at the time of the
accident, and [felt guilty] that maybe I should have paid more
attention to what was happening. My life has changed. Maybe [I
should] spend more time dealing with what's important and not
what is urgent."

I ask Captain Bindon if risk builds character. "No," he replies
without a moment's hesitation.

Risk for risk's sake is a wasted exercise. My answer would be that
challenge builds character, and the obligation of the people [who] are
running it . . . is to manage and reduce the risk while still not dimin-
ishing the challenge. But to take kids beyond their breaking point, to
the point where you know they will fail, I guess I disagree one
hundred percent with that. I've always believed that challenge should
exceed what a person thinks [he or she is] capable of. They can be
pushed—I mean really encouraged and challenged—to achieve
something that exceeds what you expected them to achieve, and
that's where you get satisfaction from the exercise.

I remember one assistant headmaster who asked, when we were
having difficulties with enrollment in the school after the accident,
that we pray to God to send us more students. I said, no, no, we
haven't got time for that. Let's go out and beat the bushes and get
more students and then, when we've got our enrollment, we'll get
down on our knees and thank God for giving us the strength to do it.
But we're not going to ask God to do our work for us. That's one area
where Ted Byfield and I would go in different directions.

It was clear to Norm Bindon, who played a major role in finding the causes of and solutions for the Timiskaming tragedy, that a

substantial factor in the chain of dumpings was lack of organized leadership for the brigade. Prior to the trip, the parents knew that Peter Cain had been designated to lead the Junior Brigade, but they also knew that Cain was not as experienced as volunteer leader Richard Bird. Like the others, Bindon tacitly acknowledged that Bird would keep an eye on Cain and help him with decisions that were beyond his skill level or expertise. As an interested parent, Norm Bindon knew that Cain was learning the ropes as a master in a Canadian school, he knew that his boys quite liked Mr. Cain, and he even knew that while Cain had had his disciplinary ups and downs at the school, no one expected him to collapse in the face of disaster. Norm Bindon remains bitter about Cain's performance during and after Timiskaming:

> I know he went into the priesthood. I know he's had his troubles. But while a lot of people attribute his difficulties to Timiskaming and to other things, the fact that he could not handle responsibilities immediately following the accident is more reflective of the man himself. Peter's response to the accident and his problems in later life weren't caused by Timiskaming. He probably should have gone to St. John's School and developed some character before he became a master.

Peter Cain stayed within the orbit of St. John's for some years after the tragedy, and struggled to come to terms with what had happened at Lake Timiskaming. He married the sister of one of the St. John's boys, but the union failed. He entered the Anglican priesthood and remains affiliated with a Winnipeg area diocese, but, by all accounts, life has been an ongoing struggle for the young man who came to Canada fresh out of the British military, hoping to seek his fortune with peers in the Company of the Cross. Whether he was unprepared for the challenge of Timiskaming, whether he was placed in a position of responsibility without the necessary skills and experience, the fact remains that Peter Cain was the designated leader of the 1978 St. John's Brigade, which lost nearly half of its members on the first day of the expedition.

This is also what continues to trouble parents like Ron Kenny. After twenty years of being haunted by the tragedy and wishing he could subject the staff to the same torment they put his son through, Ron Kenny reflects on the attitude of some of the St. John's leaders, in particular "the arrogance that they were 'experts' in the use of large canoes." In a long letter in response to questions about the legacy of Timiskaming, the retired banker writes:

> Parents had raised some concerns regarding the trips, specifically with respect to safety and leadership. The school's response referred to the fact that they had not had a fatal accident in almost 25 years. The steersman in Tom's canoe, Neil Thompson, was a quiet, sensitive 24-year-old who challenged the leadership regarding his lack of experience in steering these canoes. Unfortunately, it was his canoe that "dumped" and started the whole terrible sequence of events. . . . The two leaders of the expedition, Bird and Cain, did not speak to my wife or myself and did not offer their condolences or share their feelings about the disaster with us. Another serious shortcoming of the school administration was the religious affiliation of some teachers to an organization "Company of the Cross." Conflicts within this religious group concerning salaries, who should be Headmaster, and other concerns led to the eventual demise of the school and may well have played a role in their attitude towards the school's outdoor educational activities.

In Winnipeg, where Mike Maunder and Frank Felletti now live, Felletti does what he can to supplement his wife's income by doing janitorial work. They share Pat's mother's house. The Company of the Cross had no pension system, nor any kind of long-term disability insurance, but there is a mysterious anonymous donor who contributes in some way to the Fellettis' living expenses. Since the car accident, life has been a struggle for Frank Felletti and his family, even if he has no real recollection of Timiskaming. Mike Maunder, on the other hand, remembers

Timiskaming all too well. Since his promise to write a book about the tragedy and dedicate it to the thirteen who died, and since the closure of the school, he has been drifting in and out of the world of journalism. He has been back to India a couple of times. He stays in touch with some of the parents and the boys, and he wrestles every day with the grief, anger, and guilt that linger in his life.

St. John's School was his life. When his father died, Mike floundered, then found structure, discipline—and love—in St. John's. He left the school on graduation, but kept coming back, becoming a volunteer member, then a full-fledged member of the Company of the Cross, a master in Alberta, and finally the cofounder of the school in Ontario. Having left the Company of the Cross and the Anglican church, he is trying to pick up and move on. Sitting in the freshly painted kitchen of a group housing project that he is trying to establish in Winnipeg's core, Maunder is quietly composed, but memories of Timiskaming and St. John's seem to preoccupy him.

There are these incredible forces that maybe as males we shove aside. Grief, anger, guilt. Everybody felt personally responsible for what happened on that lake. I felt personally responsible for what happened on that lake. Kids that came off that lake felt personally responsible too. If you survive a tragedy and your friends [didn't], you feel a real guilt. . . . I could certainly see that in the kids and feel it myself. If only I could die [to] bring them back, . . . I would gladly do that, but it doesn't bring them back. This emotional stuff—grief and guilt and anger—that doesn't go away. . . . I feel that again and again and again.

In June 1990, eight months after the closure of the Ontario school and almost twelve years to the day after Timiskaming, the original St. John's School in Selkirk, Manitoba, closed its doors for good. Lack of enrollment, staffing problems, and bickering about funds and leadership within the Company of the Cross were all factors that led to this closure as they did to the closure of the Ontario school. In addition to all this, there had been rumors for some time that there was a history of sexual abuse at the school. The Timiskaming tragedy and other accidents, physical punishment, and other unsavory characteristics now associated with St. John's, did nothing to swell enrollment. It did not help matters that Robert Enright and a crew from CBC Television in Winnipeg aired a graphic documentary about the school in February 1990 that began with Frank Wiens saying, "We used to put it all into one word—character. Building character. That's what character means—a person who can feel good about himself, can work, has willpower, is a gentleman, has a good sense of morals," and ended with former boys lambasting the school with unprecedented public hostility. "For me," said Winnipeg art teacher Pat Treacy, "it was a place of fear. And it was a place of anger. . . . They would order you in a really loud tone to get the instrument of punishment. It was kind of sadistic." News of senior St. John's boys being charged with assault, after masters had given them the authority to swat the younger boys, only added to the mounting problems that resulted in the inevitable demise of the Manitoba school.

This left the twenty-two-year-old Alberta operation, the last of the three St. John's schools, which also had its share of problems. These, too, were crucial years for it. An anonymous tip to the Alberta Department of Social Services had triggered a protracted investigation with charges and countercharges of physical abuse and governmental meddling. In 1991, during the annual overnight canoe race down the North Saskatchewan River, Cheryl Escott, a young woman who was an occasional helper in the school office, drowned in a dumping accident. The following year, a disillusioned boy—reminiscent of early days at the Ontario school—set fire to one of the dorms and caused extensive damage to the Alberta school. For then-headmaster Peter Jackson, an old boy from the Manitoba school who had joined the Company of the Cross the same year as Frank Felletti, those were tumultuous years. Writing in a 1992 yearbook, he said: "Personally, the last three years have been very difficult for me as Headmaster. Our battle with Social Services, the tragedy at Drayton Valley, and our recent fire have brought me to the point of questioning the vocation I have chosen." Soon after that, Jackson stepped away from frontline school leadership and into a bookkeeping function for the school. He moved off the property with his wife and family, and distanced himself from the day-to-day operation of the school.

There was another unfortunate turn of events just prior to the turning point in Peter Jackson's tenure as headmaster. In 1987, a graduate student from the University of Alberta was given unusually free access to the Alberta school as a venue to conduct a study into whether or not the character-building idea was being realized at St. John's. Gregory Wood took seriously St. John's concern about the plight of boys in the postwar era, and linked the idea of character to the notion of self-concept in the academic literature. If St. John's curriculum was working, he hypothesized, one might expect an increase in self-concept for boys experiencing a year at the school.

Wood used a variety of numerical tests and observations, and spent 600 hours over an entire school year following a group of new boys. He concluded, based on his findings, that the SJSA program did *not* significantly effect self-concept change. "Life of the new boy at St. John's," writes Wood, "is one of powerlessness." In fact, Wood discovered that in some cases, self-concept dropped over the course of the year. He further concluded that "the hierarchical, highly-structured nature of the school program may play a role in negating some of the positive self-concept effects of various portions of the academic, work, and outdoor programs," and that "the perceived powerlessness of new boys to make decisions about their own life, except within a tightly controlled environment, may be a primary factor in the neutral/negative change in student self-concept."

But much has changed at St. John's School of Alberta since those dark days of the 1970s and 1980s. With infusions of new staff, new money from willing donors, serious rethinking of all the lessons that history has offered, and careful reconsideration of curriculum and operating procedures, they found ways to hold onto the original ideal of St. John's—to build character, to teach boys to think, to offer an educational alternative to the public school system. They have moved away from charismatic edict and visionary leadership, and all of the attendant hazards of the old ways, and toward a more democratic and enlightened style of school management. Corporal punishment continues, as does the forced isolation at the beginning of term. New boys are put through their paces by masters and the returning students. When alumni from the Alberta school, or from the now-defunct Manitoba or Ontario schools' visit, they invariably remark on how soft things have become. Through this process of continual evolution, St. John's School of Alberta has found ways to maintain or increase the *perception* of risk by the boys in all of the adventure activities they undertake—especially in the canoeing and snowshoeing—while simultaneously reducing the actual risks of harm in these activities.

On a visit to the Alberta school in May 1999, forty-eight-year-old headmaster (and Manitoba school alumnus) Keith McKay invites me to join a group of boys for dumping practice on the North Saskatchewan River, a few minutes from the school. On the way out to the truck, we pass a poster on the wall outside one of the dorms entitled "Peaceful Conflict Resolution." It is a message of very different tone from that of the early days of St. John's and part of the new way of thinking that has emerged at the Alberta school. I suspect it is there for boys and staff to see. The poster, attributed to Robert E. Valett, reads:

Peaceful Conflict Resolution

- Respect the right to disagree
- Express your real concerns
- Share common goals and interests
- Open yourself to different points of view

- Listen carefully to all proposals
- Understand the major issues involved
- Think about possible consequences
- Imagine several possible alternative solutions
- Offer reasonable compromises
- Negotiate mutually fair cooperative agreements

A panel on an anniversary quilt hung inside the main foyer remembers *The Battle of Maldon*: "Courage has got to be harder; Heart the stouter; Spirit the sterner; As our strength weakens."

We jump into the school pickup and drive to the bank of the river where dozens of boys are boarding big red fiberglass canoes. It is starting to snow. The boys are decked out in running shoes with polypropylene underwear and various other garments under well-secured life vests. They have learned the dumping protocols in theory and today it is time to put them into practice. The milky blue waters of the North Saskatchewan look icy cold, but with only a moment's hesitation, the first crew of eight purposely upsets their canoe. Behind them, the rolling north slope of the valley is greening for spring. A master in the designated rescue canoe shouts, "Kneel!" And with that, the rescue proceeds.

On the shore, as subsequent crews take turns dumping and being rescued, wet boys cluster around a roaring driftwood fire. Two galvanized buckets full of hot chocolate are ladled out to bedraggled customers, who clutch the cups in two hands and pour the steaming liquid past chattering teeth. No doubt about it, this is not an ideal day for swimming, but this is not recreation. This is serious training for June canoe trips. The command to kneel is only one of the safety protocols from Mike Maunder's original *Brigade Leader's Handbook to the Large Canoe*. After many editions, it is a now much more sophisticated and up-to-date *Outdoor Manual* published by the Alberta school.

It is cold in spite of the fire, and I am getting wet standing around watching this practice. Surprisingly, the boys are more or less oblivious to the weather. They are cold too, but they are watching and listening to the masters, chatting among themselves about what they have just experienced. The cagey among them whisper about the location of a sandbar in the river where the water was only chest deep and, with a little care in choosing the location for their purposeful upset, they managed to keep their heads dry through the entire drill. Keith McKay and the other masters have noticed and laugh it off, but not before bellowing across the water to order the remaining canoe crews to dump in deep water.

"Are you having fun?" I ask a bespectacled young lad who looks more miserable than the rest. "No, sir, but this is part of the program. If you don't do dumping practice you can't go on the canoe trip." As he speaks, I remember one of the boys from St. John's School of Ontario in similarly tough conditions and with equal resolve in his voice. A reporter from a Toronto television station caught up with him stomping along on his snowshoes on a wide open lake somewhere north of the city. She asked, "Young man, why are you out here doing this when everyone else in your family is indoors where it is warm and dry?" In his frosted toque and long scarf, he turned to face the camera and said, "Character. We're out here to build character." Today, on the banks of the North Saskatchewan River west of Edmonton, with boys from across Alberta and as far away as the Middle East, their masters having learned the lessons of Timiskaming, that is exactly what is going on.

Epilogue

After spending more than two years exploring the concept of building character with risk in the context of Timiskaming, and trying to wrest meaning from those events of June 11, 1978, I wanted to end this book by writing about how we respond to profound grief and learn from our mistakes, and about the need to put tragedy, if not to rest, then in a place in which generative memories prevail. There is much unfinished business with Timiskaming, but at some point, one must let go. So when I discovered, just days before the book was going to press, the whereabouts of Peter Knight, the young man who left the trip abruptly just as it was starting, I wondered if I should even contact him, fearing more loose threads. In the end, it was a fortuitous connection.

In response to a letter asking about his experience at St. John's, its effect on his character, and why—if I could be so bold—he had left the school so suddenly just prior to the trip, Peter wrote:

Dear James:

St. John's has indeed had a lingering effect on my life as I am certain it did on the other boys who were part of the whole "St. John's experience." I wouldn't classify it as a negative lingering effect, but more like a shadow that crosses over in some way every path onto which you turn. And yet, like most tragedies, it is at once a horrific memory of youth and at another a source of courage and inspiration. Yes, I left just prior to the canoe trip. In fact, it was mere hours before the busses

(I use this term loosely—it was generally a caravan of vans and cars) departed for Lake Timiskaming.

The reason behind this you [may] never believe. . . . You see I didn't go on the canoe trip because my father had dreams that if I did I would die. Seriously. My father is . . . not one given to irrational flights of fancy or spiritualistic nonsense. But thirty or so days before we were set to leave on this trip, my father began having vivid dreams of me drowning. Not mild dreams but the kind where you wake in a total panic. . . . He would wake up in the night bolt upright and say: "Peter is going to die!" To which my rather rational mother would reply: "It's just a dream." He would then relay the contents of the dream to her and she would say it was just nerves and that they could take me out at any time but that I would learn a better lesson if I finished what I had started.

On the day of the trip that was still the plan. They came up. They watched the play and the singing and other performances. And then came the time when the parents were to help us load our "home" stuff into their cars and our "trip" stuff into the caravan set for the trip. As the caravan was to the other side of the parking lot we carried everything—presumably first to the car and then to the caravan. But a strange thing happened. When we arrived at the old station wagon my father opened the back door. He first threw in my home clothes, and then some other baggage, and then he reached over and took my paddle and popped it into the back too. I remember it vividly and would call it a defining moment of my life.

I looked at my father in absolute disbelief and shock. He looked at me and said: "What? You don't *want* to go? Do you?" The absolute truth was that I didn't and I jumped into the back of the car faster than grease goes across a hot pan. When the car was full and the doors were closed he pulled the big station wagon around to the front of the school. I remember him stopping the car at the front of the path. I wanted him to just leave because I was afraid that they would grab me or something. But he insisted that he had to let them know and so he walked up the walkway and into the building in search of Mr. Felletti. When he came out he was striding powerfully towards the car.

Mr. Felletti (aka Tricky Phil) was chasing him like a yippy little dog moving from his one side to the other and mad as hell. He threatened my school, my grades, and everything about my character.

This was when my father, in whose footsteps he had been closely following, abruptly stopped dead in his tracks. He whirled around in one of those military 180 degree turns which left him face to face with Tricky Phil (to be honest it was face-to-chest as my father stood a good deal taller than Mr. Felletti ever did) and he raised his hand with his index and middle finger extended and poked Mr. Felletti in the chest over and over with it while repeating the words that I will never forget should I live to be a thousand years old. He said: "Someone is going to die and it's *not* going to be *my son!*" And with that he whirled back onto his course and marched up to our car and climbed in and we sped off. I was completely in awe. . . .

St. John's is still so vivid. It is like the people who got out of the World Trade Center towers in New York before they collapsed on September 11th. They will always wonder why them. Me too. And yet you move on.

With Peter's words in the back of my mind—the intermingled horror, courage, and inspiration—I thought of the weathered wooden plaque at Whistler's Point on Lake Timiskaming and the distinctive signatures of all the survivors in Scott Sorensen's guest book at the lodge. And then I recalled a visit to Toronto, toward the end of the research, that took me to the original site of the school at St. Jude's parish hall and to the Church of St Martin-in-the-Fields. Looking back, that visit to St. Martin's helped immeasurably in finding closure.

On Roncesvalles Avenue in the heart of western Toronto, St. Jude's Anglican Church and parish hall were still there, but a developer was in the process of transforming the place into studio condominiums. The cast of the musical *The Lion King* had been rehearsing in the building. There were masks, posters, and various props and notes scattered among old wires and new drywall. St. Jude's is moving on. There was no evidence of anybody sleeping on the floor or learning Latin—not even a whisper of St. John's.

Continuing west on Dundas Street, I got lost a couple of times, but eventually found the corner of Indian Grove and Glenlake Avenue where St. Martin's has been since 1890. Both streets have been substantially raised since the church was first built, leaving a splendid walled courtyard tucked out of sight from the corner. I walked down the steps next to the church vestibule and entered the secret garden.

Flagstones curve through verdant shadows toward a herbaceous border along the Glenlake Avenue wall. My reverie was broken by an agitated middle-aged sexton in jeans, white T-shirt, and runners, who burst out of the main door and tipped his head back to look up at the bell tower. He said a distracted hello, and then ducked back inside. Full of questions about St. John's, I followed him in and found him explaining his problem to the minister.

The queen of an errant hive of honey bees had entered the belfry in search of a new home. She led her followers down the tube through which the bell rope slides, and then flew out into the main sanctuary of the church with the swarm. As they flew from window to arched window, from one side of the church to the other, frenzied buzzing pervaded the silence of St. Martin's. The sexton was beside himself until he realized that while they were high up along the windows of the church the hive was unlikely to harm visiting parishioners. Maybe the bees would find their way out or die without incident.

The sexton disappeared. The minister, Canon Philip Hobson, introduced himself and assured me that this was where St. John's boys usually worshipped. In fact, parents would often attend service on Sunday evenings, after having their sons home for the weekend, he told me, and would hand over their children to a master for the ride back to Claremont. He showed me a collage of photos on the wall of one of the church meeting rooms. It read, "These are some of the faces of St. John's School of Ontario. Boys, staff, parents, and supporters made up the St. John's family,

whose home church was St. Martin's from 1977 to 1990." Many
of the black-and-white photos were familiar. In the top left, a
black boy was running. Below that, a smallish blond boy, who
looked like Scott Bindon, mugged for the camera. Front and
center was master Peter Cain serving food in the dining hall.
Below him, to the right, was a shot of Frank Felletti teaching,
hand outstretched to make a point. And below him, in the
bottom right corner, was Chris Suttaby on snowshoes, likely curs-
ing under his breath. Canon Hobson then asked if I had seen the
monument in the garden. I had not.

Back outside, I followed the gently curving path to an imposing
chunk of rock, not unlike the walls of Timiskaming itself, on
which was affixed the memorial that I had expected to find at
Whistler's Point. This one is more forthcoming, more complete.
It has the names and explains what happened in simple text with
crosses in the top corners:

† IN LOVING MEMORIES †

OF THE 13 YOUNG LIVES FROM

ST. JOHN'S SCHOOL OF ONTARIO

WHO DIED ON LAKE TIMISKAMING

ON JUNE 11 — 1978.

MARK DENNY

DEAN BINDON	TIMOTHY HOPKINS
OWEN BLACK	THOMAS KENNY
CHRISTOPHER BOURCHIER	SIMON CROFT
DAVID GREANEY	BARRY NELSON
JODY O'GORMAN	TIMOTHY PRYCE
ANDREW HERMANN	TODD MICHELL

MAY THEY LIVE ALWAYS IN

OUR HEARTS AS SURELY AS THEY

LIVE IN HIS MERCY

I sat on a plain wooden bench that faced the memorial and turned in my journal to the photocopy of the survivors' signatures from Sorensen's guest book. There was the list cast in bronze on the rock and another on the page in my book. The St. John's Junior Brigade of 1978, united again. Some were to live. Some were to die. Choices were made that in retrospect were wrong. But, as Peter Knight's letter illustrates, there are aspects of this particular tragedy that we will never understand. All we can do is take to heart the lessons of history. If we can do this, perhaps we can let go and move on.

I went back inside to the sanctuary of St. Martin's and sat for a long time in the back pew, admiring the simple lines of the altar arch and wondering what the boys of Timiskaming thought about when they were in this holy place. All the while, I was surrounded by the sound of bees.

I stood to go, feeling somehow more settled about things than I had been since the beginning. Some questions will never have answers, but there are lessons to be learned. And accidents do have causes.

I stopped by the door and lit a candle. As the flame came to life, I remembered the survivors of Timiskaming, their families, and the families of those who died, especially their parents—many of whom still struggle every day. And I thought about all the others affected by this and similar tragedies, those whose suffering we can never truly know, but whose strength, courage and spirit can inspire us. Though by accident rather than design, and certainly not in the way St. John's school foresaw, the individuals affected by the Timiskaming tragedy came to share a certain quality. Adversity can beget beauty. Some call it character.

DATE	NAME	RESIDENCE
June 13, '78	Mike Mansfield	Barrie Ont.	God Bless Psalm 1073
"	Kevin BLACK II LOST BROTHER	Toronto, Ont.	God Bless this house for ever.
"	Ian Harley	Toronto Ont.	May the Lord be with you
"	Paul Nyberg	Scarborough Ont.	God bless you + Thankyou
"	Robin Jensen, OAKVILLE, ONTARIO		Thank-you for your loving hospitality. God Bless you all-ways.
"	Scott — LOST BROTHER Burdon MISSISSAUGA ONTARIO TORONTO ONT.		God Bless you all ways THE BEST PRESENT THE LORD COULD GIVE
"	Christopher Noel Tattersby		We all thank you
"	Andy Skinner	OAKVILLE Ont.	God Bless you.
"	David Parker	Mississauga ont.	God Bless this house for saving us from that terror
"	James Doak, R R #5 Orangeville, Ont.		Thanks alot for your hospitality.
"	Francois Bourachier, RR # 1, King City Ont LOST BROTHER		May God bless you and your lovely house. Thanks

HE WERE dead, YE SHALL HE LIVE, AND WHOSOEVER LIVETH AND BELIEVETH IN HE SHALL NEVER die"

DATE	NAME	RESIDENCE
June 13, 1978	Richard Bird	Kingston, Ontario	Thank God you were here.
"	Peter Cain	ST JOHN'S SCHOOL CLAREMONT ONTARIO	God Bless You All !
"	M Gearon	"	God bless you for all you have done
"		93 Markham, Ont.	God Bless for all your friendly hospitality
"	Rob Kerr	Barrie Ont.	Thank you. you've been super.
"	Ed Perkin		
"	Jones Sibson	Tor. ONT	God Bless this house John 11: 23 - 26
"	David Cunningham Tor Ont.		John (3: 16)

"I AM THE RESURRECTION AND THE LIFE, SAITH THE LORD: HE THAT BELIEVETH IN ME, THOUGH

Select Bibliography

Brand, Johanna. "Boy 'Died' on School Trek, Wants to Return to Classes." *Winnipeg Tribune*, Number 42, February 19, 1976.

Byfield, Ted. *The Book of Ted: Epistles from an Unrepentant Redneck.* Edmonton: Keystone Press, 1998.

Canadian Broadcasting Corporation (Manitoba). *The Old Boys.* A 30-minute documentary about St. John's Cathedral Boys' School. Reporter: Robert Enright. Producer: Stephen Riley. Aired February 1990.

Collins, Robert. "God Can Bring Good Out of It." *Reader's Digest*, Volume 114 (682), February 1979.

Company of the Cross. *St. John's Cathedral Boys' School: A Report.* Selkirk, Manitoba, June 1964

———. *99 Boys and a Year: The Annual Report of St. John's Cathedral Boys' School.* Selkirk, Manitoba, June 1965.

———. *St. John's '66: The Year, the Faith and the Gamble—Annual Report of St. John's Cathedral Boys' School and the Company of the Cross.* Selkirk, Manitoba, June 1966.

———. *The End of the Beginning: The Annual Report of the Company of the Cross.* Selkirk, Manitoba, June 1970.

———. *Men Wanted: A Recruiting Booklet for the Company of the Cross.* Selkirk, Manitoba, 1968.

———. *The St. John's Report: A Review of the Activities of St. John's Cathedral Boys' School for the Year 1969–1970 and Other Related Events.* Selkirk, Manitoba, June 1970.

————. *The St. John's Report: The Annual Report of St. John's Schools of the Prairies, 1970–1971.* Selkirk, Manitoba, June 1971.

————. *The St. John's Bulletin* (Spring). Selkirk, Manitoba, June 1973.

————. *A St. John's Scrapbook, 1957–1982* (25th Anniversary). Selkirk, Manitoba, June 1982.

————. *St. John's School, 25 Years, 1967–1992: Student Yearbook, 1992–1993.* Stony Plain, Alberta: St. John's School of Alberta, 1992.

————. *Outdoor Manual.* Stony Plain, Alberta: St. John's School of Alberta, 1998.

Cunningham, Craig A. *"A Certain and Reasoned Art": The Rise and Fall of Character Education in America.* Unpublished master's thesis, University of Chicago, 1992. Available: http://cuip.uchicago.edu/~cac/chared/riseandfall.htm

Dery, Stanislas. Coroner's Report to the Attorney-General Following an Inquest into the Circumstances Surrounding the Death of Thirteen Persons Found Drowned in Lake Témiscamingue on June 12, 1978. Ville de Québec: Ministère de la Justice, Bureau du Coroner, dated July 11, 1978, reference number J/A/352.

Gathorne-Hardy, Jonathan. *The Old School Tie: The Phenomenon of the English Public School.* New York: Viking, 1978.

Giesbrecht, Gordon G. *et al.* "Effect of Task Complexity on Mental Performance During Immersion Hypothermia." *Aviation, Space, and Environmental Medicine,* March 1993.

Globe and Mail. Various stories on the tragedy ran daily from June 13 to July 14, 1978. Detailed reportage contained in issues of the *Toronto Star,* the *Ottawa Citizen,* the *North Bay Nugget,* the *Oshawa Times.* Wire stories of headline news of the tragedy ran in most Canadian daily newspapers as well as the *Washington Post,* the *New York Times,* the *Times of London.* The *Globe and Mail* and the *Toronto Star* also ran detailed coverage of the Balsam Lake disaster beginning with breaking news on July 22, 1926, and continuing until early August of that year.

Hall, E.M., and L.A. Dennis. *Living and Learning: The Report of the Provincial Committee on Aims and Objectives of Education in the Schools of Ontario.* Toronto: Ontario Department of Education, 1968.

Hodgson, E.A. "The Timiskaming Earthquake of November 1st, 1935."

Royal Astronomical Society of Canada Journal, Volume 30 (4), 1936.

James, Thomas. "Sketch of a Moving Spirit: Kurt Hahn." *Journal of Experiential Education,* Volume 3 (1), Spring 1980.

James, William. "The Moral Equivalent of War." An essay based on a speech delivered at Stanford University in 1906. Available: http://www.emory.edu/education/mfp/moral.html

Jeynes, Simon, and Laura C. Hargrave, eds. *Challenge and Achievement: The First 25 Years.* Edmonton: Company of the Cross, 1992.

Johnston, Carl, and David Smart. *Devil Rock: The Anti-Guide.* Ajax, Ontario: Climbmax, 1997.

Katz, Sidney. "The Boy Who Came Back to Life." *Reader's Digest,* Volume 109 (655), November 1976.

Leiss, William, and Christina Chocioloko. *Risk and Responsibility.* Kingston/Montreal: McGill/Queen's University Press, 1994.

Loehrer, Michael C. *How to Change a Rotten Attitude: A Manual for Building Virtue and Character in Middle and High School Students.* Thousand Oaks, California: Corwin Press, 1998.

MacDonald, David. "St. John's: New School for Old Values." Reprinted from *Reader's Digest,* Volume 97 (581), September 1970.

Mansfield, Mike. "Etched in Stone." *The Source.* Calgary, Alberta: DeVry Institute of Technology, July 1999.

Maunder, Mike. *The Second Twenty Five Years.* Toronto/Selkirk, Manitoba: Company of the Cross, 1982.

————. "Hooked and Moulded: St. John's Cathedral Boys' School Reunion Brings Mixed Memories of Early 'Boot Camp.'" *Winnipeg Free Press,* September 5, 1999, B1.

McCallum, Peggy. "The Fun Was Proving It Could Be Done." *The Globe and Mail,* September 7, 1997, B1.

Moodie, Jim. "The Timiskaming Canoe Disaster: Looking Back at Lake Tragedy." *Highgrader Magazine,* Volume 1, January/February 1999.

————. "Back to Timiskaming." *Canoe & Kayak,* Volume 27 (1), March 1999.

National Film Board of Canada. *The New Boys.* A 30-minute documentary about St. John's Cathedral Boys' School. Producer: John N. Smith. NFB Catalogue Number 106C 0174 021. 1974.

Raffan, James. "Images for Crisis Management." *Journal of Experiential Education*, Volume 7 (3), 1984.

————. *Wilderness Crisis Management*. Toronto: Canoe Ontario, 1987.

Royal Life Saving Society Canada. *Alert: Aquatic Supervision in Action*. Toronto: Royal Life Saving Society Canada, 1974.

Ryan, Kevin, and Karen E. Bohlin. *Building Character in Schools: Practical Ways to Bring Moral Instruction to Life*. San Francisco, California: Jossey-Bass Publishers, 1999.

Sayers, Dorothy. "The Lost Tools of Learning." An essay written from a lecture presented at Oxford University in 1947. Available: http://www.brccs.org/sayers_tools.html

Sha-Ka-Nash. "Canoe Trip to Fort Timiscamingue in '79." 1879. Reprinted in *The Journal of the North West Company*, Volume 2 (1), Spring 1973.

St. John's School of Ontario. "Wanted: 40 Boys to Build a School." Original recruitment pamphlet, published in Toronto, circa early 1976.

————. "These Boys Are Building Their Own School." Recruitment pamphlet, published in Toronto, circa 1976.

————. "St. John's School of Ontario." Recruitment pamphlet, published in Toronto, circa 1977.

Sorensen, Scott. *Kipawa River Chronicles: Adventures in the North Woods*. Self-published, 1999. Mail: Box 69, Fabre, Quebec, J0Z 1Z0 or e-mail: Mountman@burgoyne.com

Unrau, Edward. "No Brain Damage Seen in Boy 'Dead' 2 Hours." *Medical Post*, Volume 12 (5), 1976.

Walbridge, Charles C. "Tragedy on Lake Timiskaming." In *The Best of the River Safety Task Force Newsletter*. Lorton, Virginia: The American Canoe Association, 1983.

Wiens, Rick. "Ex-Student Recalls Pain Not Joy: St. John's Was About Cruelty For Some Pupils." *Winnipeg Free Press*, September 18, 1999, B1.

————. "The Secret of Lemons." Unpublished memoir of snowshoe runs at St. John's Cathedral Boys' School, 1995.

Wood, Gregory Albert. *Exploring Self-Concept Change in a Private School: St. John's School of Alberta*. Edmonton: Master's thesis, Department of Physical Education and Sport Studies, University of Alberta, 1998.